SRA Standards and Regulations

JULY 2021 EDITION

D1513360

Other titles available from Law Society Publishing:

Anti-Money Laundering Toolkit (3rd edn)
Alison Matthews

Compliance and Ethics in Law Firms: A Guide for Support Staff and Paralegals (2nd edn)
Tracey Calvert

Regulation and In-house Lawyers (2nd edn)
Tracey Calvert and Bronwen Still

The Solicitor's Handbook 2022
Gregory Treverton-Jones QC, Nigel West, Susanna Heley and Robert Forman

Titles from Law Society Publishing can be ordered from all good bookshops or direct (telephone 0370 850 1422 or visit our online shop at **www.lawsociety.org.uk/bookshop**).

SRA STANDARDS AND REGULATIONS

JULY 2021 EDITION

Solicitors Regulation Authority

This print edition © Law Society 2021

To ensure you are relying upon the correct version and most up-to-date version of the SRA Standards and Regulations, please refer to **www.sra.org.uk/solicitors/standards-regulations**.

This work is owned by and published under licence from the Solicitors Regulation Authority of The Cube, 199 Wharfside Street, Birmingham, B1 1RN which asserts its right to be identified as the author of this work in accordance with the Copyright, Designs and Patents Act 1988 Sections 77 and 78.

ISBN: 978-1-78446-196-6

Published in 2021 by the Law Society
113 Chancery Lane, London WC2A 1PL

Typeset by Columns Design XML Ltd, Reading
Printed by TJ Books Limited, Padstow, Cornwall

FSC
www.fsc.org
MIX
Paper from
responsible sources
FSC® C013056

The paper used for the text pages of this book is FSC certified. FSC (the Forest Stewardship Council) is an international network to promote responsible management of the world's forests.

Contents

Index of SRA Standards and Regulations

[A]   Standards and Regulations

[1]   **SRA Principles**

INTRODUCTION

The SRA Principles comprise the fundamental tenets of ethical behaviour that we expect all those that we regulate to uphold. This includes all individuals we authorise to provide legal services (solicitors, RELs and RFLs), as well as authorised firms and their managers and employees. For licensed bodies, these apply to those individuals, and the part of the body (where applicable), involved in delivering the services we regulate in accordance with the terms of your licence.

Should the Principles come into conflict, those which safeguard the wider public interest (such as the rule of law, and public confidence in a trustworthy solicitors' profession and a safe and effective market for regulated legal services) take precedence over an individual client's interests. You should, where relevant, inform your client of the circumstances in which your duty to the Court and other professional obligations will outweigh your duty to them.

The Principles and Codes are underpinned by our Enforcement Strategy, which explains in more detail our approach to taking regulatory action in the public interest.

This introduction does not form part of the SRA Principles.

Principles

The principles are as follows:

You act:

1. in a way that upholds the constitutional principle of the rule of law, and the proper administration of justice.

2. in a way that upholds public trust and confidence in the *solicitors'* profession and in legal services provided by *authorised persons*.

3. with independence.

4. with honesty.

5. with integrity.

6. in a way that encourages equality, diversity and inclusion.

7. in the best interests of each *client*.

Supplemental notes

Made by the SRA Board on 30 May 2018.

Made under section 31 of the Solicitors Act 1974, section 9 of the Administration of Justice Act 1985 and section 83 of the Legal Services Act 2007.

[Last updated: 25 November 2019]

SRA Code of Conduct for Solicitors, RELs and RFLs

INTRODUCTION

The Code of Conduct describes the standards of professionalism that we, the SRA, and the public expect of individuals (solicitors, registered European lawyers and registered foreign lawyers) authorised by us to provide legal services.

They apply to conduct and behaviour relating to your practice, and comprise a framework for ethical and competent practice which applies irrespective of your role or the environment or organisation in which you work (subject to the Overseas Rules which apply to your practice overseas); although paragraphs 8.1 to 8.11 apply only when you are providing your services to the public or a section of the public.

You must exercise your judgement in applying these standards to the situations you are in and deciding on a course of action, bearing in mind your role and responsibilities, areas of practice, and the nature of your clients (which in an in house context will generally include your employer and may include other persons or groups within or outside your employer organisation).

You are personally accountable for compliance with this Code – and our other regulatory requirements that apply to you – and must always be prepared to justify your decisions and actions.

A serious failure to meet our standards or a serious breach of our regulatory requirements may result in our taking regulatory action against you. A failure or breach may be serious either in isolation or because it comprises a persistent or concerning pattern of behaviour. In addition to the regulatory requirements set by us in our Codes, Principles and our rules and regulations, we directly monitor and enforce the requirements relating to referral fees set out in section 56 of the Legal Aid, Sentencing and Punishment of Offenders Act 2012, and provisions relating to anti money laundering and counter terrorist financing, as set out in regulations made by the Treasury as in force from time to time.

All these requirements are underpinned by our Enforcement Strategy. That strategy explains in more detail our views about the issues we consider to be serious, and our approach to taking regulatory action in the public interest.

This introduction does not form part of the SRA Code of Conduct for Solicitors, RELs and RFLs.

Maintaining trust and acting fairly

1.1   You do not unfairly discriminate by allowing your personal views to affect your professional relationships and the way in which you provide your services.

1.2   You do not abuse your position by taking unfair advantage of *clients* or others.

1.3   You perform all *undertakings* given by you, and do so within an agreed timescale or if no timescale has been agreed then within a reasonable amount of time.

1.4   You do not mislead or attempt to mislead your *clients*, the *court* or others, either by your own acts or omissions or allowing or being complicit in the acts or omissions of others (including your *client*).

Dispute resolution and proceedings before courts, tribunals and inquiries

2.1   You do not misuse or tamper with evidence or attempt to do so.

2.2   You do not seek to influence the substance of evidence, including generating false evidence or persuading witnesses to change their evidence.

2.3   You do not provide or offer to provide any benefit to witnesses dependent upon the nature of their evidence or the outcome of the case.

2.4   You only make assertions or put forward statements, representations or submissions to the *court* or others which are properly arguable.

2.5   You do not place yourself in contempt of *court*, and you comply with *court* orders which place obligations on you.

2.6   You do not waste the *court's* time.

2.7   You draw the *court's* attention to relevant cases and statutory provisions, or procedural irregularities of which you are aware, and which are likely to have a material effect on the outcome of the proceedings.

Service and competence

3.1   You only act for *clients* on instructions from the *client*, or from someone properly authorised to provide instructions on their behalf. If you have reason to suspect that the instructions do not represent your *client's* wishes, you do not act unless you have satisfied yourself that they do. However, in circumstances where you have legal authority to act notwithstanding that it is not possible to obtain or ascertain the instructions of your *client*, then you are subject to the overriding obligation to protect your *client's* best interests.

3.2   You ensure that the service you provide to *clients* is competent and delivered in a timely manner.

3.3   You maintain your competence to carry out your role and keep your professional knowledge and skills up to date.

3.4   You consider and take account of your *client's* attributes, needs and circumstances.

3.5   Where you supervise or manage others providing legal services:

(a) you remain accountable for the work carried out through them; and

(b) you effectively supervise work being done for *clients*.

3.6   You ensure that the individuals you manage are competent to carry out their role, and keep their professional knowledge and skills, as well as understanding of their legal, ethical and regulatory obligations, up to date.

Client money and assets

4.1   You properly account to *clients* for any *financial benefit* you receive as a result of their instructions, except where they have agreed otherwise.

4.2   You safeguard money and *assets* entrusted to you by *clients* and others.

4.3   You do not personally hold *client money* save as permitted under regulation 10.2(b)(vii) of the Authorisation of Individuals Regulations, unless you work in an *authorised body*, or in an organisation of a kind *prescribed* under this rule on any terms that may be *prescribed* accordingly.

BUSINESS REQUIREMENTS

Referrals, introductions and separate businesses

5.1   In respect of any referral of a *client* by you to another *person*, or of any third party who introduces business to you or with whom you share your *fees*, you ensure that:

(a) *clients* are informed of any financial or other interest which you or your business or employer has in referring the *client* to another *person* or which an *introducer* has in referring the *client* to you;

(b) *clients* are informed of any fee sharing arrangement that is relevant to their matter;

(c) the fee sharing agreement is in writing;

(d) you do not receive payments relating to a referral or make payments to an *introducer* in respect of *clients* who are the subject of criminal proceedings; and

(e) any *client* referred by an *introducer* has not been acquired in a way which would breach the *SRA's regulatory arrangements* if the *person* acquiring the *client* were regulated by the *SRA*.

5.2   Where it appears to the *SRA* that you have made or received a *referral fee*, the payment will be treated as a *referral fee* unless you show that the payment was not made as such.

5.3   You only:

(a) refer, recommend or introduce a *client* to a *separate business*; or

(b) divide, or allow to be divided, a *client's* matter between you and a *separate business*;

where the *client* has given informed consent to your doing so.

Other business requirements

5.4 You must not be a *manager, employee, member* or *interest holder* of a business that:

(a) has a name which includes the word "solicitors"; or

(b) describes its work in a way that suggests it is a *solicitors'* firm; unless it is an *authorised body*.

5.5 If you are a *solicitor* who holds a practising certificate, an *REL* or *RFL*, you must complete and deliver to the *SRA* an annual return in the *prescribed* form.

5.6 If you are a *solicitor* or an *REL* carrying on *reserved legal activities* in a *non-commercial body*, you must ensure that:

(a) the body takes out and maintains indemnity insurance; and

(b) this insurance provides adequate and appropriate cover in respect of the services that you provide or have provided, whether or not they comprise *reserved legal activities*, taking into account any alternative arrangements the body or its *clients* may make.

CONFLICT, CONFIDENTIALITY AND DISCLOSURE

Conflict of interests

6.1 You do not act if there is an *own interest conflict* or a significant risk of such a conflict.

6.2 You do not act in relation to a matter or particular aspect of it if you have a *conflict of interest* or a significant risk of such a conflict in relation to that matter or aspect of it, unless:

(a) the *clients* have a *substantially common interest* in relation to the matter or the aspect of it, as appropriate; or

(b) the *clients* are *competing for the same objective,*

and the conditions below are met, namely that:

(i) all the *clients* have given informed consent, given or evidenced in writing, to you acting;

(ii) where appropriate, you put in place effective safeguards to protect your *clients'* confidential information; and

(iii) you are satisfied it is reasonable for you to act for all the *clients*.

Confidentiality and disclosure

6.3   You keep the affairs of current and former *clients* confidential unless disclosure is required or permitted by law or the *client* consents.

6.4   Where you are acting for a *client* on a matter, you make the *client* aware of all information material to the matter of which you have knowledge, except when:

(a)   the disclosure of the information is prohibited by legal restrictions imposed in the interests of national security or the prevention of crime;

(b)   your *client* gives informed consent, given or evidenced in writing, to the information not being disclosed to them;

(c)   you have reason to believe that serious physical or mental injury will be caused to your *client* or another if the information is disclosed; or

(d)   the information is contained in a privileged document that you have knowledge of only because it has been mistakenly disclosed.

6.5   You do not act for a *client* in a matter where that *client* has an interest adverse to the interest of another current or former *client* of you or your business or employer, for whom you or your business or employer holds confidential information which is material to that matter, unless:

(a)   effective measures have been taken which result in there being no real risk of disclosure of the confidential information; or

(b)   the current or former *client* whose information you or your business or employer holds has given informed consent, given or evidenced in writing, to you acting, including to any measures taken to protect their information.

Cooperation and accountability

7.1   You keep up to date with and follow the law and regulation governing the way you work.

7.2   You are able to justify your decisions and actions in order to demonstrate compliance with your obligations under the *SRA's regulatory arrangements*.

7.3   You cooperate with the *SRA*, other regulators, ombudsmen, and those bodies with a role overseeing and supervising the delivery of, or investigating concerns in relation to, legal services.

7.4   You respond promptly to the *SRA* and:

(a)   provide full and accurate explanations, information and documents in response to any request or requirement; and

(b)   ensure that relevant information which is held by you, or by third parties carrying out functions on your behalf which are critical to the delivery of your legal services, is available for inspection by the *SRA*.

7.5   You do not attempt to prevent anyone from providing information to the *SRA* or any other body exercising regulatory, supervisory, investigatory or prosecutory functions in the public interest.

7.6   You notify the *SRA* promptly if:

(a)   you are subject to any criminal charge, conviction or caution, subject to the Rehabilitation of Offenders Act 1974;

(b)   a *relevant insolvency event* occurs in relation to you; or

(c)   if you become aware:

(i)   of any material changes to information previously provided to the *SRA*, by you or on your behalf, about you or your practice, including any change to information recorded in the *register*; and

(ii)   that information provided to the *SRA*, by you or on your behalf, about you or your practice is or may be false, misleading, incomplete or inaccurate.

7.7   You report promptly to the *SRA*, or another *approved regulator*, as appropriate, any facts or matters that you reasonably believe are capable of amounting to a serious breach of their *regulatory arrangements* by any *person* regulated by them (including you).

7.8   Notwithstanding paragraph 7.7, you inform the *SRA* promptly of any facts or matters that you reasonably believe should be brought to its attention in order that it may investigate whether a serious breach of its *regulatory arrangements* has occurred or otherwise exercise its regulatory powers.

7.9   You do not subject any *person* to detrimental treatment for making or proposing to make a report or providing or proposing to provide information based on a reasonably held belief under paragraph 7.7 or 7.8 above, or paragraph 3.9, 3.10, 9.1(d) or (e) or 9.2(b) or (c) of the SRA Code of Conduct for Firms, irrespective of whether the *SRA* or another approved regulator subsequently investigates or takes any action in relation to the facts or matters in question.

7.10   You act promptly to take any remedial action requested by the *SRA*. If requested to do so by the *SRA* you investigate whether there have been any serious breaches that should be reported to the *SRA*.

7.11   You are honest and open with *clients* if things go wrong, and if a *client* suffers loss or harm as a result you put matters right (if possible) and explain fully and promptly what has happened and the likely impact. If requested to do so by the *SRA* you investigate whether anyone may have a claim against you, provide the *SRA* with a report on the outcome of your investigation, and notify relevant persons that they may have such a claim, accordingly.

7.12   Any obligation under this section or otherwise to notify, or provide information to, the *SRA* will be satisfied if you provide information to your firm's *COLP* or *COFA*, as and where appropriate, on the understanding that they will do so.

WHEN YOU ARE PROVIDING SERVICES TO THE PUBLIC OR A SECTION OF THE PUBLIC

Client identification

8.1   You identify who you are acting for in relation to any matter.

Complaints handling

8.2   You ensure that, as appropriate in the circumstances, you either establish and maintain, or participate in, a procedure for handling complaints in relation to the legal services you provide.

8.3   You ensure that *clients* are informed in writing at the time of engagement about:

(a)   their right to complain to you about your services and your charges;

(b)   how a complaint can be made and to whom; and

(c)   any right they have to make a complaint to the *Legal Ombudsman* and when they can make any such complaint.

8.4   You ensure that when *clients* have made a complaint to you, if this has not been resolved to the *client's* satisfaction within 8 weeks following the making of a complaint they are informed, in writing:

(a)   of any right they have to complain to the *Legal Ombudsman*, the time frame for doing so and full details of how to contact the *Legal Ombudsman*; and

(b)   if a complaint has been brought and your complaints procedure has been exhausted:

(i)   that you cannot settle the complaint;

(ii)   of the name and website address of an alternative dispute resolution (ADR) approved body which would be competent to deal with the complaint; and

(iii)   whether you agree to use the scheme operated by that body.

8.5   You ensure that complaints are dealt with promptly, fairly, and free of charge.

Client information and publicity

8.6   You give *clients* information in a way they can understand. You ensure they are in a position to make informed decisions about the services they need, how their matter will be handled and the options available to them.

8.7   You ensure that *clients* receive the best possible information about how their matter will be priced and, both at the time of engagement and when appropriate as their matter progresses, about the likely overall cost of the matter and any *costs* incurred.

8.8 You ensure that any *publicity* in relation to your practice is accurate and not misleading, including that relating to your charges and the circumstances in which *interest* is payable by or to *clients*.

8.9 You do not make unsolicited approaches to members of the public, with the exception of current or former *clients*, in order to advertise legal services provided by you, or your business or employer.

8.10 You ensure that *clients* understand whether and how the services you provide are regulated. This includes:

(a) explaining which activities will be carried out by you, as an *authorised person*;

(b) explaining which services provided by you, your business or employer, and any *separate business* are regulated by an *approved regulator*; and

(c) ensuring that you do not represent any business or employer which is not authorised by the *SRA*, including any *separate business*, as being regulated by the *SRA*.

8.11 You ensure that *clients* understand the regulatory protections available to them.

Supplemental notes

Made by the SRA Board on 30 May 2018.

Made under sections 31 and 32 of the Solicitors Act 1974, section 89 of, and paragraphs 2 and 3 of Schedule 14 to, the Courts and Legal Services Act 1990 and section 57(2) and (8) of the Legal Aid, Sentencing and Punishment of Offenders Act 2012.

[Last updated: 25 November 2019]

SRA Code of Conduct for Firms

INTRODUCTION

This Code of Conduct describes the standards and business controls that we, the SRA, and the public expect of firms (including sole practices) authorised by us to provide legal services. These aim to create and maintain the right culture and environment for the delivery of competent and ethical legal services to clients. These apply in the context of your practice: the way you run your business and all your professional activities (subject, if you are a licensed body, to any terms of your licence).

Paragraphs 8.1 and 9.1 to 9.2 set out the requirements of managers and compliance officers in those firms, respectively.

A serious failure to meet our standards or a serious breach of our regulatory requirements may lead to our taking regulatory action against the firm itself as an entity, or its managers or compliance officers, who each have responsibilities for ensuring that the standards and requirements are met. We may also take action against employees working within the firm for any breaches for which they are responsible. A failure or breach may be serious either in isolation or because it comprises a persistent or concerning pattern of behaviour.

In addition to the regulatory requirements set by us in our Codes, Principles and our rules and regulations, we directly monitor and enforce the requirements relating to referral fees set out in section 56 of the Legal Aid, Sentencing and Punishment of Offenders Act 2012, and provisions relating to anti money laundering and counter terrorist financing, as set out in regulations made by the Treasury as in force from time to time.

All of these requirements are underpinned by our Enforcement Strategy, which explains in more detail our views about the issues we consider to be serious, and our approach to taking regulatory action in the public interest.

This introduction does not form part of the SRA Code of Conduct for Firms.

Maintaining trust and acting fairly

1.1 You do not unfairly discriminate by allowing your personal views to affect your professional relationships and the way in which you provide your services.

1.2 You do not abuse your position by taking unfair advantage of *clients* or others.

1.3 You perform all *undertakings* given by you and do so within an agreed timescale or if no timescale has been agreed then within a reasonable amount of time.

1.4 You do not mislead or attempt to mislead your *clients*, the *court* or others, either by your own acts or omissions or allowing or being complicit in the acts or omissions of others (including your *client*).

1.5   You monitor, report and publish workforce diversity data, as *prescribed*.

Compliance and business systems

2.1   You have effective governance structures, arrangements, systems and controls in place that ensure:

(a)   you comply with all the *SRA's regulatory arrangements*, as well as with other regulatory and legislative requirements, which apply to you;

(b)   your *managers* and employees comply with the *SRA's regulatory arrangements* which apply to them;

(c)   your *managers* and *interest holders* and those you employ or contract with do not cause or substantially contribute to a breach of the *SRA's regulatory arrangements* by you or your *managers* or employees;

(d)   your *compliance officers* are able to discharge their duties under paragraphs 9.1 and 9.2 below.

2.2   You keep and maintain records to demonstrate compliance with your obligations under the *SRA's regulatory arrangements*.

2.3   You remain accountable for compliance with the *SRA's regulatory arrangements* where your work is carried out through others, including your *managers* and those you employ or contract with.

2.4   You actively monitor your financial stability and business viability. Once you are aware that you will cease to operate, you effect the orderly wind-down of your activities.

2.5   You identify, monitor and manage all material risks to your business, including those which may arise from your *connected practices*.

Cooperation and accountability

3.1   You keep up to date with and follow the law and regulation governing the way you work.

3.2   You cooperate with the *SRA*, other regulators, ombudsmen and those bodies with a role overseeing and supervising the delivery of, or investigating concerns in relation to, legal services.

3.3   You respond promptly to the *SRA* and:

(a)   provide full and accurate explanations, information and documentation in response to any requests or requirements;

(b)   ensure that relevant information which is held by you, or by third parties carrying out functions on your behalf which are critical to the delivery of your legal services, is available for inspection by the *SRA*.

3.4   You act promptly to take any remedial action requested by the *SRA*.

3.5   You are honest and open with *clients* if things go wrong, and if a *client* suffers loss or harm as a result you put matters right (if possible) and explain fully and promptly what has happened and the likely impact. If requested to do so by the *SRA* you investigate whether anyone may have a claim against you, provide the *SRA* with a report on the outcome of your investigation, and notify relevant persons that they may have such a claim, accordingly.

3.6   You notify the *SRA* promptly:

   (a)   of any indicators of serious financial difficulty relating to you;

   (b)   if a *relevant insolvency event* occurs in relation to you;

   (c)   if you intend to, or become aware that you will, cease operating as a legal business;

   (d)   of any change to information recorded in the *register*.

3.7   You provide to the *SRA* an information report on an annual basis or such other period as specified by the *SRA* in the *prescribed* form and by the *prescribed* date.

3.8   You notify the *SRA* promptly if you become aware:

   (a)   of any material changes to information previously provided to the *SRA*, by you or on your behalf, about you or your *managers, owners* or *compliance officers*; and

   (b)   that information provided to the *SRA*, by you or on your behalf, about you or your *managers, owners* or *compliance officers* is or may be false, misleading, incomplete or inaccurate.

3.9   You report promptly to the *SRA*, or another *approved regulator*, as appropriate, any facts or matters that you reasonably believe are capable of amounting to a serious breach of their *regulatory arrangements* by any *person* regulated by them (including you) of which you are aware. If requested to do so by the *SRA*, you investigate whether there have been any serious breaches that should be reported to the *SRA*.

3.10 Notwithstanding paragraph 3.9, you inform the *SRA* promptly of any facts or matters that you reasonably believe should be brought to its attention in order that it may investigate whether a serious breach of its *regulatory arrangements* has occurred or otherwise exercise its regulatory powers.

3.11 You do not attempt to prevent anyone from providing information to the *SRA* or any other body exercising regulatory, supervisory, investigatory or prosecutory functions in the public interest.

3.12 You do not subject any *person* to detrimental treatment for making or proposing to make a report or providing, or proposing to provide, information based on a reasonably held belief under paragraph 3.9 or 3.10 above or 9.1(d) or (e) or 9.2(b) or (c) below, or under paragraph 7.7 or 7.8 of the SRA Code of Conduct for Solicitors, RELs and RFLs, irrespective of whether the *SRA* or another approved regulator subsequently investigates or takes any action in relation to the facts or matters in question.

Service and competence

4.1   You only act for *clients* on instructions from the *client*, or from someone properly authorised to provide instructions on their behalf. If you have reason to suspect that the instructions do not represent your *client's* wishes, you do not act unless you have satisfied yourself that they do. However, in circumstances where you have legal authority to act notwithstanding that it is not possible to obtain or ascertain the instructions of your *client*, then you are subject to the overriding obligation to protect your *client's* best interests.

4.2   You ensure that the service you provide to *clients* is competent and delivered in a timely manner, and takes account of your *client's* attributes, needs and circumstances.

4.3   You ensure that your *managers* and employees are competent to carry out their role, and keep their professional knowledge and skills, as well as understanding of their legal, ethical and regulatory obligations, up to date.

4.4   You have an effective system for supervising *clients'* matters.

Client money and assets

5.1   You properly account to *clients* for any *financial benefit* you receive as a result of their instructions, except where they have agreed otherwise.

5.2   You safeguard money and *assets* entrusted to you by *clients* and others.

Conflict of interests

6.1   You do not act if there is an *own interest conflict* or a significant risk of such a conflict.

6.2   You do not act in relation to a matter or a particular aspect of it if you have a *conflict of interest* or a significant risk of such a conflict in relation to that matter or aspect of it, unless:

  (a) the *clients* have a *substantially common interest* in relation to the matter or the aspect of it, as appropriate; or

  (b) the *clients* are *competing for the same objective*,

and the conditions below are met, namely that:

  (i)   all the *clients* have given informed consent, given or evidenced in writing, to you acting;

(ii) where appropriate, you put in place effective safeguards to protect your *clients'* confidential information; and

(iii) you are satisfied it is reasonable for you to act for all the *clients*.

Confidentiality and disclosure

6.3 You keep the affairs of current and former *clients* confidential unless disclosure is required or permitted by law or the *client* consents.

6.4 Any individual who is acting for a *client* on a matter makes the *client* aware of all information material to the matter of which the individual has knowledge except when:

(a) the disclosure of the information is prohibited by legal restrictions imposed in the interests of national security or the prevention of crime;

(b) the *client* gives informed consent, given or evidenced in writing, to the information not being disclosed to them;

(c) the individual has reason to believe that serious physical or mental injury will be caused to the *client* or another if the information is disclosed; or

(d) the information is contained in a privileged document that the individual has knowledge of only because it has been mistakenly disclosed.

6.5 You do not act for a *client* in a matter where that *client* has an interest adverse to the interest of another current or former *client* for whom you hold confidential information which is material to that matter, unless:

(a) effective measures have been taken which result in there being no real risk of disclosure of the confidential information; or

(b) the current or former *client* whose information you hold has given informed consent, given or evidenced in writing, to you acting, including to any measures taken to protect their information.

Applicable standards in the SRA Code of Conduct for Solicitors, RELs and RFLs

7.1 The following paragraphs in the SRA Code of Conduct for Solicitors, RELs and RFLs apply to you in their entirety as though references to "you" were references to you as a firm:

(a) dispute resolution and proceedings before courts, tribunals and inquiries (2.1 to 2.7);

(b) referrals, introductions and *separate businesses* (5.1 to 5.3); and

(c) standards which apply when providing services to the public or a section of the public, namely client identification (8.1), complaints handling (8.2 to 8.5), and client information and publicity (8.6 to 8.11).

Managers in SRA authorised firms

8.1   If you are a *manager*, you are responsible for compliance by your firm with this Code. This responsibility is joint and several if you share management responsibility with other *managers* of the firm.

Compliance officers

9.1   If you are a *COLP* you must take all reasonable steps to:

(a)   ensure compliance with the terms and conditions of your firm's authorisation;

(b)   ensure compliance by your firm and its *managers*, employees or *interest holders* with the *SRA's regulatory arrangements* which apply to them;

(c)   ensure that your firm's *managers* and *interest holders* and those they employ or contract with do not cause or substantially contribute to a breach of the *SRA's regulatory arrangements*;

(d)   ensure that a prompt report is made to the *SRA* of any facts or matters that you reasonably believe are capable of amounting to a serious breach of the terms and conditions of your firm's authorisation, or the *SRA's regulatory arrangements* which apply to your firm, *managers* or employees;

(e)   notwithstanding sub-paragraph (d), you ensure that the *SRA* is informed promptly of any facts or matters that you reasonably believe should be brought to its attention in order that it may investigate whether a serious breach of its *regulatory arrangements* has occurred or otherwise exercise its regulatory powers,

save in relation to the matters which are the responsibility of the *COFA* as set out in paragraph 9.2 below.

9.2   If you are a *COFA* you must take all reasonable steps to:

(a)   ensure that your firm and its *managers* and employees comply with any obligations imposed upon them under the SRA Accounts Rules;

(b)   ensure that a prompt report is made to the *SRA* of any facts or matters that you reasonably believe are capable of amounting to a serious breach of the SRA Accounts Rules which apply to them;

(c)   notwithstanding sub-paragraph (b), you ensure that the *SRA* is informed promptly of any facts or matters that you reasonably believe should be brought to its attention in order that it may investigate whether a serious breach of its *regulatory arrangements* has occurred or otherwise exercise its regulatory powers.

Supplemental notes

Made by the SRA Board on 30 May 2018.

Made under section 31 of the Solicitors Act 1974, section 9 of the Administration of Justice Act 1985, section 83 of the Legal Services Act 2007, and section 57(2) and (8) of the Legal Aid, Sentencing and Punishment of Offenders Act 2012.

[Last updated: 25 November 2019]

[4]   **SRA Accounts Rules**

INTRODUCTION

These rules set out our requirements for when firms (including sole practices) authorised by us receive or deal with money belonging to clients, including trust money or money held on behalf of third parties. The rules apply to all firms we regulate, including all those who manage or work within such firms.

Firms will need to have systems and controls in place to ensure compliance with these rules and the nature of those systems must be appropriate to the nature and volumes of client transactions dealt with and the amount of client money held or received.

This introduction does not form part of the SRA Accounts Rules.

PART 1: GENERAL

Rule 1: Application section

1.1   These rules apply to *authorised bodies*, their *managers* and employees and references to "you" in these rules should be read accordingly.

1.2   The *authorised body's managers* are jointly and severally responsible for compliance by the *authorised body*, its *managers* and employees with these rules.

1.3   In relation to a *licensed body*, the rules apply only in respect of activities regulated by the *SRA* in accordance with the terms of its licence.

PART 2: CLIENT MONEY AND CLIENT ACCOUNTS

Rule 2: Client money

2.1   "*Client money*" is money held or received by you:

    (a)   relating to *regulated services* delivered by you to a *client*;

    (b)   on behalf of a third party in relation to *regulated services* delivered by you (such as money held as agent, stakeholder or held to the sender's order);

    (c)   as a trustee or as the holder of a specified office or appointment, such as donee of a power of attorney, Court of Protection deputy or trustee of an occupational pension scheme;

    (d)   in respect of your *fees* and any unpaid *disbursements* if held or received prior to delivery of a bill for the same.

2.2   In circumstances where the only *client money* you hold or receive falls within rule 2.1(d) above, and:

(a) any money held for *disbursements* relates to costs or expenses incurred by you on behalf of your *client* and for which you are liable; and

(b) you do not for any other reason maintain a *client account*;

you are not required to hold this money in a *client account* if you have informed your *client* in advance of where and how the money will be held. Rules 2.3, 2.4, 4.1, 7, 8.1(b) and (c) and 12 do not apply to *client money* held outside of a *client account* in accordance with this rule.

2.3   You ensure that *client money* is paid promptly into a *client account* unless:

(a) in relation to money falling within 2.1(c), to do so would conflict with your obligations under rules or regulations relating to your specified office or appointment;

(b) the *client money* represents payments received from the Legal Aid Agency for your *costs*; or

(c) you agree in the individual circumstances an alternative arrangement in writing with the *client*, or the third party, for whom the money is held.

2.4   You ensure that *client money* is available on demand unless you agree an alternative arrangement in writing with the *client*, or the third party for whom the money is held.

2.5   You ensure that *client money* is returned promptly to the *client*, or the third party for whom the money is held, as soon as there is no longer any proper reason to hold those funds.

Rule 3: Client account

3.1   You only maintain a *client account* at a branch (or the head office) of a *bank* or a *building society* in England and Wales.

3.2   You ensure that the name of any *client account* includes:

(a) the name of the *authorised body*; and

(b) the word "client" to distinguish it from any other type of account held or operated by the *authorised body*.

3.3   You must not use a *client account* to provide banking facilities to *clients* or third parties. Payments into, and transfers or withdrawals from a *client account* must be in respect of the delivery by you of *regulated services*.

Rule 4: Client money must be kept separate

4.1   You keep *client money* separate from money belonging to the *authorised body*.

4.2   You ensure that you allocate promptly any funds from *mixed payments* you receive to the correct *client account* or business account.

4.3   Where you are holding *client money* and some or all of that money will be used to pay your *costs*:

   (a) you must give a bill of *costs*, or other written notification of the *costs* incurred, to the *client* or the paying party;

   (b) this must be done before you transfer any *client money* from a *client account* to make the payment; and

   (c) any such payment must be for the specific sum identified in the bill of *costs*, or other written notification of the *costs* incurred, and covered by the amount held for the particular *client* or third party.

Rule 5: Withdrawals from client account

5.1   You only withdraw *client money* from a *client account*:

   (a) for the purpose for which it is being held;

   (b) following receipt of instructions from the *client*, or the third party for whom the money is held; or

   (c) on the *SRA's* prior written authorisation or in *prescribed* circumstances.

5.2   You appropriately authorise and supervise all withdrawals made from a *client account*.

5.3   You only withdraw *client money* from a *client account* if sufficient funds are held on behalf of that specific *client* or third party to make the payment.

Rule 6: Duty to correct breaches upon discovery

6.1   You correct any breaches of these rules promptly upon discovery. Any money improperly withheld or withdrawn from a *client account* must be immediately paid into the account or replaced as appropriate.

Rule 7: Payment of interest

7.1   You account to *clients* or third parties for a fair sum of *interest* on any *client money* held by you on their behalf.

7.2   You may by a written agreement come to a different arrangement with the *client* or the third party for whom the money is held as to the payment of *interest*, but you must provide sufficient information to enable them to give informed consent.

Rule 8: Client accounting systems and controls

8.1   You keep and maintain accurate, contemporaneous, and chronological records to:

   (a) record in client ledgers identified by the *client's* name and an appropriate description of the matter to which they relate:

     (i)   all receipts and payments which are *client money* on the client side of the client ledger account;

     (ii) all receipts and payments which are not *client money* and bills of costs including transactions through the *authorised body's* accounts on the business side of the client ledger account;

  (b) maintain a list of all the balances shown by the client ledger accounts of the liabilities to *clients* (and third parties), with a running total of the balances; and

  (c) provide a cash book showing a running total of all transactions through *client accounts* held or operated by you.

8.2   You obtain, at least every five weeks, statements from *banks, building societies* and other financial institutions for all *client accounts* and business accounts held or operated by you.

8.3   You complete at least every five weeks, for all *client accounts* held or operated by you, a reconciliation of the *bank* or *building society* statement balance with the cash book balance and the client ledger total, a record of which must be signed off by the *COFA* or a *manager* of the firm. You should promptly investigate and resolve any differences shown by the reconciliation.

8.4   You keep readily accessible a central record of all bills or other written notifications of *costs* given by you.

PART 3: DEALING WITH OTHER MONEY BELONGING TO CLIENTS OR THIRD PARTIES

Rule 9: Operation of joint accounts

9.1   If, when acting in a *client's* matter, you hold or receive money jointly with the *client* or a third party, Part 2 of these rules does not apply save for:

  (a) rule 8.2 – statements from *banks, building societies* and other financial institutions;

  (b) rule 8.4 – bills and notifications of *costs*.

Rule 10: Operation of a client's own account

10.1 If, in the course of practice, you operate a *client's* own account as signatory, Part 2 of these rules does not apply save for:

  (a) rule 8.2 – statements from *banks, building societies* and other financial institutions;

  (b) rule 8.3 – reconciliations;

  (c) rule 8.4 – bills and notifications of *costs*.

Rule 11: Third party managed accounts

11.1 You may enter into arrangements with a *client* to use a *third party managed account* for the purpose of receiving payments from or on behalf of, or making payments to or on behalf of, the *client* in respect of *regulated services* delivered by you to the *client*, only if:

(a) use of the account does not result in you receiving or holding the *client's* money; and

(b) you take reasonable steps to ensure, before accepting instructions, that the *client* is informed of and understands:

   (i) the terms of the contractual arrangements relating to the use of the *third party managed account*, and in particular how any *fees* for use of the *third party managed account* will be paid and who will bear them; and

   (ii) the *client's* right to terminate the agreement and dispute payment requests made by you.

11.2 You obtain regular statements from the provider of the *third party managed account* and ensure that these accurately reflect all transactions on the account.

PART 4: ACCOUNTANTS' REPORTS AND STORAGE AND RETENTION OF ACCOUNTING RECORDS

Rule 12: Obtaining and delivery of accountants' reports

12.1 If you have, at any time during an *accounting period*, held or received *client money*, or operated a joint account or a *client's* own account as signatory, you must:

(a) obtain an accountant's report for that *accounting period* within six months of the end of the period; and

(b) deliver it to the *SRA* within six months of the end of the *accounting period* if the accountant's report is qualified to show a failure to comply with these rules, such that money belonging to *clients* or third parties is, or has been, or is likely to be placed, at risk.

12.2 You are not required to obtain an accountant's report if:

(a) all of the *client money* held or received during an *accounting period* is money received from the Legal Aid Agency; or

(b) in the *accounting period*, the statement or passbook balance of *client money* you have held or received does not exceed:

   (i) an average of £10,000; and

   (ii) a maximum of £250,000,

   or the equivalent in foreign currency.

12.3 In rule 12.2 above a "statement or passbook balance" is the total balance of:

(a) all *client accounts* held or operated by you; and

(b) any joint accounts and *clients'* own accounts operated by you, as shown by the statements obtained under rule 8.2.

12.4 The *SRA* may require you to obtain or deliver an accountant's report to the *SRA* on reasonable notice if you cease to operate as an *authorised body* and to hold or operate a *client account*, or the *SRA* considers that it is otherwise in the public interest to do so.

12.5 You ensure that any report obtained under this rule is prepared and signed by an accountant who is a member of one of the *chartered accountancy bodies* and who is, or works for, a registered auditor.

12.6 The *SRA* may disqualify an accountant from preparing a report for the purposes of this rule if:

(a) the accountant has been found guilty by their professional body of professional misconduct or equivalent; or

(b) the *SRA* is satisfied that the accountant has failed to exercise due care and skill in the preparation of a report under these rules.

12.7 The *SRA* may specify from time to time matters that you must ensure are incorporated into the terms on which an accountant is engaged.

12.8 You must provide to an accountant preparing a report under these rules:

(a) details of all accounts held or operated by you in connection with your practice at any *bank*, *building society* or other financial institution at any time during the *accounting period* to which the report relates; and

(b) all other information and documentation that the accountant requires to enable completion of their report.

12.9 The accountant must complete and sign their report in the *prescribed* form.

Rule 13: Storage and retention of accounting records

13.1 You must store all *accounting records* securely and retain these for at least six years.

Supplemental notes

Made by the SRA Board on 30 May 2018.

Made under sections 32, 33A, 34, 37 of the Solicitors Act 1974, section 9 of the Administration of Justice Act 1985, and section 83(5)(h) of, and paragraph 20 of Schedule 11 to, the Legal Services Act 2007.

[Last updated: 25 November 2019]

SRA Application, Notice, Review and Appeal Rules

INTRODUCTION

These rules make provision for all notices given by the SRA and applications made to it under the SRA's rules and regulatory arrangements. They also make provision for internal reviews and external appeals against our disciplinary and regulatory decisions.

This introduction does not form part of the SRA Application, Notice, Review and Appeal Rules.

PART 1: APPLICATIONS AND NOTICES

Rule 1: Applications

1.1 An application made under the *SRA's regulatory arrangements* must be made in writing, where appropriate, in the *prescribed* form correctly completed, and be accompanied by:

(a) any *prescribed* fee or charge; and

(b) any information and documents which may be *prescribed*, or reasonably requested by the *SRA*.

1.2 If you make an application to the *SRA*, you do not need to submit all payments, information, and documents simultaneously, but the application will only be made once the *SRA* has received all of the payments, information and documents relating to it.

1.3 You must ensure that all details provided in connection with any application you make to the *SRA* are correct and complete. You must notify the *SRA* as soon as you become aware of any changes to any information supplied.

1.4 As soon as reasonably practicable, the *SRA* shall give notice to the applicant of the decision made in respect of their application, and shall give notice of the decision to any other person to whom the application relates. If the application is refused, the *SRA* will provide reasons for the decision and will inform the applicant and any other person to whom the application relates, of any right they may have to apply for a review or appeal of the decision.

1.5 The *SRA* shall give notice to an applicant for authorisation under the SRA Authorisation of Firms Rules, of the decision in respect of their application before the end of the decision period, which is the period of 6 months beginning with the day on which the application is made.

1.6 The *SRA* may, on one occasion, give the applicant a notice (an "extension notice") extending the decision period in rule 1.5 by such period as may be specified in the notice but:

   (a) an extension notice must only be given before the time when the decision period in rule 1.5 would end, but for the extension notice;

   (b) the total decision period must not exceed 9 months; and

   (c) the extension notice must set out the reasons for the extension.

1.7 If the *SRA* has not notified the applicant of its decision within the decision period in rule 1.5 or as extended by rule 1.6, then for the purpose of any rights of review or appeal under Part 2 of these rules, the application is deemed to have been refused under rule 2.2 of the SRA Authorisation of Firms Rules and that decision to have been notified to the applicant on the last day of the decision period in rule 1.5 or as extended in rule 1.6. This does not prevent the *SRA* subsequently granting or refusing the application.

Rule 2: Notices

2.1 Any notice under the *SRA's regulatory arrangements* must be given in writing by delivering it, or sending it by post or by electronic mail, to the recipient's last notified postal or electronic mail address, as appropriate.

2.2 If the intended recipient of a notice is represented, the notice may instead be given by sending or delivering it to the representative's practising or business address, or electronic mail address.

2.3 The giving of notice will be deemed to have been effected:

   (a) if sent by electronic mail or delivered or left at an address before 4.30pm on a working day, on that day, or in any other case on the next working day after the day on which it was sent, delivered or left;

   (b) if sent by ordinary post:

      (i) in the case of first class post, on the second working day after the day on which it was posted, and

      (ii) in the case of second class post, on the fourth working day after the day on which it was posted.

PART 2: REVIEWS AND APPEALS OF DECISIONS

Rule 3: Power to conduct a review

3.1 The *SRA* may:

   (a) where an administrative error in, or in relation to any decision comes to the *SRA's* attention, correct the error without the need to undergo a review under this Part;

(b) review all or part of any regulatory decision reached by it, of its own initiative, under this Part.

3.2 Subject to rule 3.3, the *SRA* may review all or part of any of the regulatory decisions set out in annex 1 on the application of the *person* who is the subject of the decision.

3.3 An application cannot be made for a review of:

(a) a decision reached following a review or appeal;

(b) a decision which has been made by agreement under rule 8.2 of the SRA Regulatory and Disciplinary Procedure Rules.

3.4 The *SRA* shall not, save in exceptional circumstances, review a decision more than one year after it was made.

3.5 An application for a review of a decision must be made within 28 days of:

(a) notice being given of the decision, or reasons for the decision (if later); or

(b) any deemed refusal under rule 1.7 or regulation 19 of the European Communities (Lawyer's Practice) Regulations 2000,

and must explain the grounds of review and provide reasons and any evidence in support.

3.6 If the *SRA* decides to review a decision on its own initiative, it must give any *person* who is the subject of the decision, notice of its decision to conduct a review and an opportunity to provide written representations on the appropriate outcome under rule 4.2.

Rule 4: Decisions on review

4.1 A review will be determined by an *authorised decision maker* on consideration of written evidence alone.

4.2 On a review, the *authorised decision maker*, as appropriate may, where they consider the original decision was materially flawed or there is new information which would have had a material influence on the decision:

(a) uphold the original decision;

(b) overturn the decision in whole or in part;

(c) make any other decision which could have been made by the original decision maker; or

(d) remit the decision for further investigation or consideration.

Rule 5: Appeals to the High Court or Tribunal

5.1 Unless otherwise provided in the relevant statute, or rules of the *Tribunal, court* or of the Legal Services Board, any appeal to the High Court or *Tribunal* against a decision set out in annex 2 or 3, as appropriate, must be commenced within the period of 28 days from the date of notification of the decision that is subject to appeal.

Rule 6: Taking effect of decisions subject to review or appeal

6.1   Unless specified otherwise, subject to rule 6.2, a decision takes effect:

(a) if no application for a review or appeal is made, on the expiry of the date for bringing such an application under these rules; and

(b) if an application for a review or an appeal is made, on the date any review or appeal has been determined or discontinued.

6.2   The *SRA* may direct a decision to take immediate effect, where it considers that it is necessary in the public interest to do so.

ANNEX 1: DECISIONS MADE BY THE SRA WHICH ARE SUBJECT TO REVIEW

Individual authorisation

As set out in the SRA Authorisation of Individuals Regulations:

1.   A decision made under regulation 3A.2 not to be satisfied that an individual has completed all or any part of the *academic stage of training* or the *vocational stage of training* by equivalent means.

2.   A decision made under regulation 3B.2(a) to refuse to recognise all or any part of an apprenticeship.

3.   A decision under regulation 3B.2(b) to require further steps or training to be undertaken including imposing conditions.

4.   A decision made under regulation 3E.2(a) to refuse to recognise all or part of a *period of recognised training*.

5.   A decision made under regulation 3E.2(b) to require further steps or training to be undertaken including imposing conditions.

6.   A decision made under regulation 5.1 to refuse to issue a certificate of satisfaction.

7.   A decision made under regulation 5.2 not be satisfied as to an individual's *character and suitability* to be a *solicitor*.

8.   A decision made under regulation 5.3 to refuse to admit an individual as a *solicitor* after a certificate of satisfaction has been issued.

9.   A decision made under regulation 5.6(a)(ii) to remove a *solicitor's* name from the roll.

10. A decision made under regulation 5.6(b) to refuse to remove a *solicitor's* name from the roll.

11. A decision made under regulation 5.9 to refuse to restore a *solicitor's* name to the roll.

12. A decision made under regulation 7.1(a) to refuse an application for a practising certificate, or registration or renewal of registration in the *register of European lawyers* or the *register of foreign lawyers*.

13. A failure to make a decision under regulation 6.1 within four months in respect of an application for initial registration in the *register of European lawyers*.

14. A decision made under regulation 7.1(b) to impose conditions on a practising certificate or the registration of a European *lawyer* or *foreign lawyer*.

15. A decision to refuse approval for the taking of steps specified in conditions under regulation 7.1(b).

16. A decision made under regulation 8.4 to revoke a practising certificate or withdraw registration in the *register of European lawyers* or the *register of foreign lawyers* save for where 8.4(b) applies.

17. A decision made under regulation 9.10 not to be satisfied in respect of a *higher courts advocacy qualification*.

Education, Training and Assessment providers

As set out in the SRA Education, Training and Assessment Provider Regulations:

1. A decision made under regulation 1.4(b) or 2.3(b) to refuse to grant *approved education provider, authorised education provider* or *authorised training provider* status.

2. A decision made under regulation 1.4(a) or 2.3(a) to grant the application for approval or authorisation subject to such conditions and for such period as the *SRA* considers appropriate.

3. A decision made under regulation 1.5(a) or 2.4(a) to revoke *approved education provider, authorised education provider* or *authorised training provider* status.

4. A decision made under regulation 1.5(b) or 2.4(b) to make approval or authorisation subject to such conditions as the *SRA* considers appropriate.

5. A decision made under regulation 2.4(c) to require an *authorised training provider* to appoint a new *training principal*.

6. A decision made under regulation 6.3(b) to refuse to approve an organisation to provide higher rights of audience assessments.

7. A decision made under regulation 6.3(a) to grant the application of approval subject to such conditions as the *SRA* considers appropriate.

8. A decision made under regulation 6.5(a) to revoke the approval.

9. A decision made under regulation 6.5(b) to make the approval subject to such conditions as the *SRA* considers appropriate.

Firm authorisation

As set out in the SRA Authorisation of Firms Rules:

1. A decision made under rule 2.2 to refuse authorisation.

2. A decision made under rule 3.1 to impose conditions on authorisation.

3. A decision to refuse approval for the taking of steps specified in conditions under rule 3.3(c).

4. A decision under rule 4.3 or 4.4 to revoke or suspend a body's authorisation.

5. A decision made under rule 12.1 to extend, revoke or vary any terms or conditions on a body's authorisation or to refuse an application to do so.

6. A decision made under rule 13.1 to refuse approval of a *person's* designation as a *manager*, *owner*, or *compliance officer*.

7. A decision made under rule 13.8 to grant conditional approval of a *person's* designation or the holding of a *material interest* in a *licensed body*.

8. A decision made under rule 13.9 to withdraw approval of a *person's* designation as a *manager*, *owner*, or *compliance officer*.

9. A failure to decide an application for authorisation of a *licensed body* or approval of a *manager*, *owner*, or *compliance officer* within the decision period.

Regulatory and Disciplinary

As set out in the SRA Regulatory and Disciplinary Procedure Rules:

1. A decision made under rule 3.1, save for a decision to make an application to the *Tribunal* under rule 3.1(g).

2. A decision made under rule 3.2(a) to impose interim conditions.

2A. A decision made under rule 7.2 that a disqualification should remain in force.

3. A decision made under rule 9.2 to publish a decision.

Miscellaneous

1. A decision made under rule 19.1 of the SRA Compensation Fund Rules not to make a grant of the whole or part of the amount applied for from the Fund.

2. Any decisions in respect of which there is a right of external appeal as set out in annex 2 or 3, that are not covered above.

ANNEX 2: DECISIONS MADE BY THE SRA WITH A RIGHT OF APPEAL TO THE TRIBUNAL

Firm authorisation

As set out in the SRA Authorisation of Firms Rules:

1. A decision made under rule 2.2 to refuse authorisation as a *licensed body*.

2. A decision made under rule 3.1 to impose conditions on the authorisation of a *licensed body*.

3. A decision in respect of a *licensed body* to refuse approval for the taking of steps specified in conditions under rule 3.3(c).

4. A decision made under rule 4.4 to revoke or suspend a *licensed body's* authorisation.

5. A decision made under rule 12.1 to extend, revoke or vary any terms or conditions on a *licensed body's* authorisation or to refuse an application to do so.

6. A decision made under rule 13.1 to refuse approval of a *person's* designation as a *manager*, *owner*, or *compliance officer* of a *licensed body*.

7. A decision made under rule 13.8 to grant approval or conditional approval of the holding of a *material interest* in a *licensed body*.

8. A decision made under rule 13.9 to withdraw approval of a *person's* designation as a *manager*, *owner*, or *compliance officer* of a *licensed body*.

Regulatory and Disciplinary

As set out in the SRA Regulatory and Disciplinary Procedure Rules:

1. A decision made under rule 3.1(a) to give a written rebuke.

2. A decision made under rule 3.1 (b) to direct the payment of a financial penalty together with the amount of that penalty.

3. A decision made under rule 3.1(c) to disqualify a *person* from acting as a *HOLP*, *HOFA*, *manager* or *employee* of a *licensed body*.

4. A decision made under rule 3.1(d) to make an order to control a *person's* activities in connection with legal practice.

4A. A decision made under rule 7.2 that a disqualification should remain in force.

5. A decision made under 9.2 to publish a decision.

ANNEX 3: DECISIONS MADE BY THE SRA WITH A RIGHT OF APPEAL TO THE HIGH COURT

Individual Authorisation

As set out in the SRA Authorisation of Individuals Regulations:

1. A decision made under regulation 3E.2(a) to refuse to recognise all or part of a *period of recognised training*.

2. A decision made under regulation 4.1 to refuse an application for admission as a *solicitor* made under Part V of the European Communities (Lawyer's Practice) Regulations 2000).

3. A decision made under regulation 5.1 to refuse to issue a certificate of satisfaction.

4. A decision made under regulation 5.3 to refuse to admit an individual as a *solicitor* after a certificate of satisfaction has been issued.

5. A decision made under regulation 5.6(a)(ii) to remove a *solicitor's* name from the roll.

6. A decision made under regulation 5.6(b) to refuse to remove a *solicitor's* name from the roll.

7. A decision made under regulation 5.9 to refuse to restore a *solicitor's* name to the roll.

8. A decision made under regulation 7.1(a) to refuse an application for a practising certificate, or registration or renewal of registration in the *register of European lawyers* or the *register of foreign lawyers*.

9. A decision made under regulation 7.1(b) to impose conditions on a practising certificate or the registration of a European *lawyer* or *foreign lawyer*.

10. A decision made under regulation 8.4 to revoke a practising certificate or withdraw registration in the *register of European lawyers* or the *register of foreign lawyers*.

11. A failure to determine within 4 months an application for initial registration or revocation of registration in the *register of European lawyers*.

Firm authorisation

As set out in the SRA Authorisation of Firms Rules:

1. A decision made under rule 2.2 to refuse authorisation of a *recognised body* or *recognised sole practice*.

2. A decision made under rule 4.3 to revoke or suspend authorisation of a *recognised body* or *recognised sole practice*.

3. A decision made under 3.1 to impose conditions on authorisation of a *recognised body* or *recognised sole practice*.

4. A decision made under rule 13.9 to withdraw approval of a *person's* designation as a *COLP, COFA, manager* or *owner* of a *recognised body* or *recognised sole practice*.

Miscellaneous

1. A refusal to grant permission to a *solicitor* to employ or remunerate in connection with their practice any individual who to their knowledge has been disqualified from practising as a *solicitor* as a result of being struck off the roll; or who is suspended from practice as a *solicitor*; or whose practising certificate is suspended as a result of being an undischarged bankrupt.

Supplemental notes

Made by the SRA Board on 30 May 2018.

Made under sections 2, 13, 28 and 31 of the Solicitors Act 1974, section 9 of the Administration of Justice Act 1985, section 89 of, and paragraphs 2 and 3 of Schedule 14 to, the Courts and Legal Services Act 1990, and section 83 of, and Schedule 11 to, the Legal Services Act 2007.

[Last updated: 31 December 2020]

[6] SRA Assessment of Character and Suitability Rules

INTRODUCTION

All individuals applying for admission or restoration to the roll of solicitors or those applying for or renewing their registration to be an REL or an RFL must be of satisfactory character and suitability. Those applying to become an authorised role holder, must be fit and proper to hold the role, and for ease we use the term "character and suitability" in this context also.

These provisions set out the kind of factors we will take into account when considering your character and suitability, and the obligations you have, both at the outset and on an ongoing basis, to provide relevant information to inform the decisions we make.

These requirements are underpinned by our role to act in the public interest. For more information about the issues we consider to present a risk to the public interest, and our approach to taking regulatory action, see our Enforcement Strategy.

This introduction does not form part of the SRA Assessment of Character and Suitability Rules.

PART 1: CHARACTER AND SUITABILITY REQUIREMENTS

Rule 1: Application

1.1   These rules apply where the *SRA* is making a decision as to whether it is satisfied regarding your *character and suitability*:

   (a)   on early assessment under regulation 5.2 of the SRA Authorisation of Individuals Regulations;

   (b)   at admission or restoration to the roll under regulations 1.1, 3.1, 3A.1, 3F.1, 4.1 and 5.9 of the SRA Authorisation of Individuals Regulations;

   (c)   on approval as an authorised role holder under rule 13.1 of the SRA Authorisation of Firms Rules;

   (d)   on registration or renewal of registration as an *REL* or *RFL* under regulations 6.3 or 6.4 of the SRA Authorisation of Individuals Regulations.

Rule 2: Assessment

2.1   When considering your *character and suitability*, the *SRA* will take into account the overriding need to:

   (a)   protect the public and the public interest; and

   (b)   maintain public trust and confidence in the *solicitors'* profession and in legal services provided by *authorised persons*.

In doing so, the *SRA* will take into account the nature of your role, and your individual circumstances, on a case by case basis.

2.2 The *SRA* will therefore consider any information available to it and take into account all relevant matters. These will include but are not limited to the criminal and other conduct or behaviour set out in rules 3 and 4 below.

2.3 If you are applying for approval as a *compliance officer*, in assessing your suitability the *SRA* will consider whether you are of sufficient seniority and in a position of sufficient responsibility to fulfil the requirements of the role.

2.4 If on the information available, the *SRA* cannot be satisfied you are of good character and suitable for the role, and it considers that any risk to the public or the public interest can be addressed by the imposition of conditions on your authorisation or approval under regulation 7.1(b) of the SRA Authorisation of Individuals Regulations, or rule 3.1 or 13.8 of the SRA Authorisation of Firms Rules, as appropriate, the *SRA* must impose such conditions accordingly.

2.5 Following any decision by the *SRA* that it is not satisfied as to your *character and suitability*, you may only seek a further assessment of your *character and suitability*, where there has been a material change in your circumstances relevant to the *SRA's* assessment under these rules.

PART 2: CONDUCT AND BEHAVIOUR

Rule 3: Criminal conduct

3.1 The *SRA* will consider criminal conduct when assessing your *character and suitability*, in accordance with Table 1 below, subject to the Rehabilitation of Offenders Act 1974 and the Rehabilitation of Offenders Act 1974 (Exceptions Order) 1975 and bearing in mind the public interest in supporting the rehabilitation of offenders. For the avoidance of doubt, Table 1 is a non-exhaustive list.

Table 1: Criminal conduct

Most serious (A finding in this category is likely to result in refusal)	Serious (A finding in this category may result in refusal)
You have been convicted by a *court* of a criminal offence: • for which you received a custodial or suspended sentence; • involving dishonesty, fraud, perjury, and/or bribery; • of a violent or sexual nature; • associated with obstructing the course of justice; • which demonstrated behaviour showing signs of *discrimination* towards others; or • associated with terrorism. You have been convicted by a *court* of more than one criminal offence (these could be less serious offences when considered in isolation but taken more seriously because of frequency and/or repetition). You have shown a pattern of criminal offences or criminal behaviours (eg starting from a caution but moving through to convictions). You have accepted a caution from the police for an offence involving dishonesty, violence or discrimination, or a sexual offence. You have been included on the Violent and Sex Offenders register.	You have accepted a caution for, or been convicted by a *court* of, a criminal offence not falling within the most serious category (which is likely to result in refusal). You are currently subject to a conditional discharge or bind over by a *court*.

Rule 4: Other conduct and behaviour

4.1   Table 2 sets out non-exhaustive examples of the types of conduct or behaviour that the *SRA* will take into account when assessing your *character and suitability*.

Table 2: Other conduct and behaviour

Type of behaviour	Examples
Integrity and independence	You have behaved in a way: • which is dishonest; • which is violent; • which is threatening or harassing; • where there is evidence of *discrimination* towards others. You have misused your position to obtain pecuniary advantage. You have misused your position of trust in relation to vulnerable people. The *SRA* has evidence reflecting on the honesty and integrity of a *person* you are related to, affiliated with, or act together with where the *SRA* has reason to believe that the *person* may have an influence over the way in which you will exercise your authorised role.
Assessment offences	You have committed and/or have been adjudged by an education establishment to have committed a deliberate assessment offence, which amounts to plagiarism or cheating, in order to gain an advantage for you or others.
Financial conduct/events	There is evidence: • that you have deliberately sought to avoid responsibility for your debts; • of dishonesty in relation to the management of your finances; • that you have been declared bankrupt, entered into any individual voluntary arrangements, have a current County Court Judgment issued against you or have been made subject to a Debt Relief Order; • that any *company*, *LLP* or *partnership* of which you are/were a *manager* or *owner* has been the subject of a winding up order, an administrative order or an administrative receivership, or has otherwise been wound up or put into administration in circumstances of insolvency;

Type of behaviour	Examples
	• that you cannot satisfactorily manage your finances (eg you have fallen behind with six or more consecutive payments and/or have been registered with a credit reference agency);
	• that you are subject to possession proceedings (eg for falling behind on mortgage payments) and/or are subject to a Liability Order (eg for non-payment of council tax).
Regulatory or disciplinary findings	You have been made the subject of a serious disciplinary or regulatory finding, sanction or action by a regulatory body and/or any *court* or other body hearing appeals in relation to disciplinary or regulatory findings.
	You have failed to disclose information to a regulatory body (including the *SRA*) when required to do so or have provided false or misleading information.
	You have significantly breached the requirements of a regulatory body.
	You have failed to comply with the reasonable requests of a regulatory body resulting in a finding against you.
	You have been rebuked, reprimanded, or received a warning about your conduct by a regulatory body.
	You are disqualified from being a *charity* trustee or a trustee for a *charity* under section 178(1) of the Charities Act 2011.
	You have been removed and/or disqualified as a *company director*.
	You are a corporate person and other matters that call into question your fitness and propriety are disclosed or come to light.
	You have committed an offence under the *Companies Acts*.

PART 3: AGGRAVATING AND MITIGATING FACTORS

Rule 5: Aggravating and mitigating factors

5.1   Table 3 sets out a non-exhaustive list of the types of aggravating and mitigating factors the *SRA* will take into account where you have disclosed, or it has received, information which raises a question as to your *character and suitability*.

Table 3: *Aggravating and mitigating factors*

Aggravating Factors	Mitigating Factors
• No evidence of successful rehabilitation. • No evidence of steps taken to remedy conduct. • No (or little) evidence of remorse. • Repeated behaviour, or a pattern of behaviour, or event occurred very recently. • You were in a position of trust. • You held a senior position. • Vulnerability of those impacted by the behaviour. • Behaviour likely to harm public confidence in the profession.	• Evidence of successful rehabilitation. • Evidence of steps taken to remedy conduct. • Evidence of remorse. • One off event, or event occurred some time ago. • You were in a junior or non-legal role. • No evidence of harm being caused to individuals. • Behaviour unlikely to harm public confidence in the profession. • Credible and cogent supporting references.

PART 4: DISCLOSURE AND EVIDENTIAL REQUIREMENTS

Rule 6: Disclosure and evidential requirements

6.1   Subject to rule 6.3 below, on making an application under any of the provisions set out in rule 1.1, you must disclose all matters, wherever they have taken place (including *overseas*), which are relevant to the *SRA's* assessment of your *character and suitability*, including, where practicable, any information set out in Table 4 which is relevant to the matter in question.

6.2   On making an application under any of the provisions set out in rules 1.1(a) to (c), you must also provide a certificate from the Disclosure and Barring Service, or equivalent, which is no more than three months old.

6.3   If you are making an application for:

(a)   registration as an *REL* or *RFL*; or

(b)   approval as a *manager* or *owner* of an *authorised body*, in circumstances where if approval is granted you will fall within rule 13.2(b) of the Authorisation of Firms Rules,

you must, and need only, provide a certificate of good standing which is no more than three months old from any regulatory body with which you are registered or authorised.

6.4   If the *SRA* requests any further information in order to assess your *character and suitability*, including a certificate from the Disclosure and Barring Service, or equivalent, you must provide it by the date specified (which will be no less than 14 days from the date of the request).

6.5 You have an ongoing obligation to tell the *SRA* promptly about anything that raises a question as to your *character and suitability*, or any change to information previously disclosed to the *SRA* in support of your application, after it has been made. This obligation continues once you have been admitted as a *solicitor*, registered as an *REL* or an *RFL*, or approved as a role holder.

6.6 The onus is on you to provide any evidence relevant to the *SRA's* consideration of your *character and suitability*. However, the *SRA* may undertake any investigation as it considers appropriate to determine your *character and suitability* and may verify any evidence you provide with a third party.

6.7 If you fail to disclose any information relevant to the *SRA's* assessment of your *character and suitability*, the *SRA* will take this into account when making a determination as to your *character and suitability*.

Table 4: Information and evidence relevant to matters disclosed

GENERAL EVIDENCE

- Credible references, where possible written in the knowledge of the matters reported. Credible references will generally be written in the knowledge of the matters reported by an independent person who knows you and your work well, such as a current or former employer or an academic tutor.

- Evidence of any rehabilitation that shows you have learnt from an experience or event, such as probation reports, references from employers or tutors.

- Documentary evidence in support of your case and, where possible, an independent corroboration of your account of the event.

- A statement from you including details of the event leading up to the matter disclosed and which reflects your attitude towards the event.

- Proof that you have also disclosed the matter to any professional or other body to which you have an obligation to do so.

EVIDENCE RELATING TO CRIMINAL OFFENCES

- At least one independent report relating to the event such as a report from the police, a *court*, or a *solicitor*.

- Any sentencing remarks for your case.

- Any Memorandum of an Entry on the Court Register.

- Proof you have paid any penalty or fine imposed or costs ordered for you to pay as a result of the matter you disclosed.

- In relation to any motoring offence, your online driving licence.

EVIDENCE RELATING TO ASSESSMENT OFFENCES

- Any minutes from any meeting and any transcripts from any hearing relating to the offence.

- Outcome of any investigation, any decision, sanction or appeal relating to the offence.

- Details which describe the extent to which you could reasonably have been expected to realise that the offence did not constitute legitimate academic practice.

EVIDENCE RELATING TO FINANCIAL CONDUCT/EVENTS

- In relation to county court judgments or Individual Voluntary Arrangements, proof that you have met the creditor's agreement in full or that it continues to be met; a copy of any judgment; a certificate of satisfaction from the court or a Registry Trust Limited report; and a credit report of no more than one month old.

- In relation to bankruptcy, a copy of the bankruptcy petition; or if you have been discharged from bankruptcy, a copy of the Certificate of Discharge; and a credit report no more than one month old.

Details of any actions you have taken to clear any debts, satisfy any judgments and manage your finances.

Supplemental notes

Made by the SRA Board on 30 May 2018.

Made under sections 28 and 31, of the Solicitors Act 1974, section 9 of the Administration of Justice Act 1985, section 89 of, and paragraphs 2 and 3 of Schedule 14 to, the Courts and Legal Services Act 1990 and section 83 of, and Schedule 11 to, the Legal Services Act 2007.

[Last updated: 25 November 2019]

SRA Authorisation of Firms Rules

INTRODUCTION

These provisions set out the *SRA*'s arrangements for the authorisation of firms. This includes recognised bodies, licensed bodies and recognised sole practices.

The rules set out our authorisation and application requirements, the effect of authorisation by the *SRA* on the legal activities such bodies may provide, and how and when we may restrict or limit a firm's authorisation or bring it to an end.

If you are unsure whether you are eligible for authorisation, or need to be authorised, please see our guidance.

This introduction does not form part of the SRA Authorisation of Firms Rules.

PART 1: ELIGIBILITY

Rule 1: Eligibility

1.1 You will be eligible to apply for authorisation:

 (a) as a *licensed body*, if you are a *licensable body* and have at least one *manager* that is an *authorised person* (other than a *licensed body*);

 (b) as a *recognised body*, if you are a *legal services body* in which all of the *managers* and *interest holders* are *legally qualified*; or

 (c) as a *recognised sole practice*, if you are a *solicitor* or an *REL* who is the sole principal in a practice,

and you intend to deliver legal services, or (if you fall within (b)) the *SRA* is satisfied that it is in the public interest for you to be eligible to apply for authorisation notwithstanding that you do not intend to deliver legal services.

1.2 The eligibility requirements in rule 1.1 are subject to the transitional arrangements set out in annex 1.

1.3 An *authorised body* must:

 (a) if you are a company, be incorporated and registered in England and Wales, Scotland or Northern Ireland under Parts 1 and 2 of the Companies Act 2006; and

 (b) have at least one practising address in the *UK* or, if you are a *licensed body*, in England or Wales.

PART 2: DETERMINATION OF AUTHORISATION APPLICATIONS, DURATION AND VALIDITY

Rule 2: Authorisation decision

2.1　The *SRA* may grant an application for authorisation in relation to one or more *reserved legal activity*.

2.2　The *SRA* will refuse an application for authorisation if it is not satisfied that, if authorisation is granted:

(a)　the applicant's *managers*, *interest holders* or management and governance arrangements are suitable to operate or control a business providing regulated legal services;

(b)　the applicant will comply with the *SRA*'s requirements and *regulatory arrangements*,

or, if the *SRA* considers that it would be otherwise against the public interest or incompatible with the *regulatory objectives* to grant the application.

2.3　In reaching a decision on the application, the *SRA* may take into account any *person* that the applicant, *manager*, *employee* or *interest holder* is related to, affiliated with, or acts together with that it has reason to believe may have an influence over the way in which the applicant, *manager*, *employee* or *interest holder* will exercise their role.

Rule 3: Conditions

3.1　The *SRA* may at any time, whether on grant of an application for authorisation or otherwise, impose such conditions on a body's authorisation (whether indefinite or for a specified period), where it considers it appropriate in the public interest to do so and in accordance with rules 3.2 and 3.3.

3.2　The *SRA* may impose conditions under rule 3.1 if it is satisfied that the *authorised body*, or a *manager*, *compliance officer*, *employee*, *owner*, or *interest holder* of the *authorised body*:

(a)　is unsuitable to undertake certain activities or engage in certain business or practising arrangements;

(b)　is putting or is likely to put at risk the interests of *clients*, third parties or the public;

(c)　will not comply with the *SRA*'s *regulatory arrangements*, or requires monitoring of compliance with the *SRA*'s *regulatory arrangements*; or

(d)　should take specified steps conducive to the *regulatory objectives*.

3.3　The conditions imposed by the *SRA* under rule 3.1 may:

(a)　specify certain requirements that must be met or steps that must be taken;

(b) restrict the carrying on of particular activities or holding of particular roles; or

(c) prohibit the taking of specified steps without its approval.

Rule 4: Duration of authorisation

4.1 A body's authorisation takes effect from the date the certificate of authorisation is issued to it by the *SRA*.

4.2 A body's authorisation shall cease to have effect:

(a) subject to Part 5, if the body ceases to exist; or

(b) if the body is a *licensed body* and is issued with a licence by another *approved regulator*.

4.3 The *SRA* may revoke or suspend a body's authorisation, if:

(a) it is satisfied that the authorisation was granted as a result of error, misleading or inaccurate information, or fraud;

(b) the body is or becomes ineligible to be authorised, or the grounds for refusal of an application under rule 2.2 are met;

(c) the body has failed to provide any information the *SRA* has reasonably requested;

(d) the body has failed to pay any *prescribed* fee to the *SRA*;

(e) the body makes an application to the *SRA* for its authorisation to be revoked, but the *SRA* may refuse the application if the applicant is subject to any proceedings, investigation or consideration of their conduct or practice by the *SRA* or the *Tribunal*;

(f) the body has failed to comply with any obligations under the *SRA's regulatory arrangements*;

(g) the body, or an *owner*, *interest holder*, *manager* or *employee* of the body fails to comply with any duty imposed on them by sections 90 or 176 of the *LSA*;

(h) a *relevant insolvency event* has occurred in relation to the body, or the sole principal is made the subject of bankruptcy proceedings or makes a proposal for an individual voluntary arrangement;

(i) the *SRA* has decided to exercise its powers of *intervention* in relation to the body or a *solicitor's* practice within the body; or

(j) for any other reason, it considers it to be in the public interest to do so.

4.4 In the case of a *licensed body*, the *SRA* may revoke or suspend the body's authorisation:

(a) as a result of a *person* who holds an *interest* in the *licensed body* taking a step in circumstances where that constitutes an offence under paragraph 24(1) of

Schedule 13 to the *LSA* (whether or not the *person* is charged with or convicted of an offence under that paragraph);

(b) where such a *person* is in breach of conditions imposed under paragraphs 17, 28 or 33 of that Schedule; or

(c) where a *person's* holding of an *interest* in the *licensed body* is subject to an objection by the *SRA* under paragraph 31 or 36 of that Schedule.

4.5 The *SRA* must not revoke or suspend a body's authorisation other than under rule 4.3(e) unless it has first given the body no less than 28 days' notice of its intention to revoke or suspend the authorisation, inviting representations regarding the issues giving rise to the proposed revocation or suspension.

PART 3: EFFECT OF AUTHORISATION AND CONDITIONS OF PRACTICE

Rule 5: Effect of authorisation

5.1 If you are a *recognised body* or a *recognised sole practice* authorised by the *SRA* you are entitled to carry on:

(a) all *reserved legal activities* except notarial activities; and

(b) *immigration work*.

5.2 If you are a *licensed body* you are entitled to carry on the activities set out in rule 5.1, in accordance with the terms of your licence.

5.3 An *authorised body* may only carry on a *reserved legal activity* through a *person* who is entitled to do so.

GENERAL CONDITIONS OF PRACTICE

Rule 6: Restrictions on services provided by a recognised body or recognised sole practice

6.1 If you are a *recognised body* or *recognised sole practice*, your business may consist only of the provision of:

(a) professional services of the sort provided by individuals practising as *solicitors* and/or *lawyers* of other jurisdictions; and

(b) the services set out in annex 2 (whether or not they are also included in paragraph (a)),

and if you have a notary public as a *manager* or *employee*, then professional services of the sort provided by notaries public.

Rule 7: Payment of periodical fees

7.1 Every *authorised body* must pay to the *SRA* a periodical fee in the amount, and by the date *prescribed*.

Rule 8: Compliance officers

8.1 An *authorised body* must at all times have an individual who is designated as its *COLP* and an individual who is designated as its *COFA*, and whose designations the *SRA* has approved.

8.2 Subject to rule 8.3, an individual who is designated under rule 8.1 must:

(a) be a *manager* or *employee* of the *authorised body*;

(b) consent to the designation;

(c) not be disqualified from acting as a *HOLP* or *HOFA* under section 99 of the *LSA*; and

(d) in the case of a *COLP*, be an individual who is authorised to carry on *reserved legal activities* by an *approved regulator*.

8.3 An *authorised body* is not required to comply with rule 8.2(a) where an individual who is designated under rule 8.1:

(a) is currently approved by the *SRA* as a *compliance officer* for an *authorised body* with a *manager* or *owner* in common with the body; and

(b) is a *manager* or *employee* of that related *authorised body*.

Rule 9: Management, control, and supervision

9.1 Subject to rules 9.2 and 9.3, an *authorised body* must ensure that the *SRA* has approved any *manager* or *owner* of the *authorised body* under Part 4.

9.2 A sole principal whose practice has been authorised as a *recognised sole practice* is not required to be approved separately as a *manager* of that practice.

9.3 If the *SRA* is satisfied that a *manager* of an *authorised body* is not involved in any of the following:

(a) the day to day or strategic management of the *authorised body*;

(b) compliance by the *authorised body* with the *SRA's regulatory arrangements*; or

(c) the carrying on of *reserved legal activities*, or the provision of legal services in England and Wales,

the *SRA* may decide that the *authorised body* is not required to comply with rule 9.1 in respect of that *manager*.

9.4 An *authorised body* must have at least one *manager* or *employee*, or must procure the services of an individual, who:

(a) is a *lawyer* and has practised as such for a minimum of three years; and

(b) supervises the work undertaken by the *authorised body* (or, if the body is a licensed body, the work undertaken by the body that is regulated by the *SRA* in accordance with the terms of the body's licence).

Rule 10: Restrictions on employment and remuneration of certain individuals

10.1 An *authorised body* must not employ or remunerate, or permit to be a *manager, owner* or *interest holder* of the body, a person:

(a) who is subject to an order under section 43 of the *SA*, without the *SRA's* written permission;

(b) whose name has been struck off the roll, or who is suspended from practising as a *solicitor*, without the *SRA's* written permission;

(c) in respect of whom there is a direction in force under section 47(2)(g) of the *SA*, without the *SRA's* written permission; or

(d) who has been disqualified from the relevant role.

Rule 11: Information return and notification events

11.1 An *authorised body* must complete and deliver to the *SRA* an annual return by the date and in the form *prescribed*.

Rule 12: Modification of terms and conditions

12.1 The *SRA* may at any time, extend, revoke or vary any terms or conditions on a body's authorisation, imposed in accordance with rule 3 or otherwise, either on the application of the *authorised body* or on the *SRA's* own initiative.

PART 4: APPROVAL OF ROLE HOLDERS

Rule 13: Approval of role holders

13.1 Subject to rules 13.2 to 13.4, the *SRA* may approve a *person's* designation as a *COLP* or *COFA* or to be a *manager* or *owner* of an *authorised body* if it is satisfied that the individual is fit and proper to undertake the role, in accordance with the SRA Assessment of Character and Suitability Rules.

13.2 The *SRA* will deem a *person* to be fit and proper to be a *manager* or *owner* of an *authorised body* if the *person* is:

(a) a *solicitor*, an *REL, RFL* or an *authorised body*; or

(b) a *person* who has previously been approved by the *SRA* under rule 13.1 and is:

(i) authorised and regulated by another *approved regulator*; or

(ii) authorised and regulated by a regulatory body which operates a regulatory regime recognised by the *SRA* as reasonably equivalent to that of an *approved regulator*, and who is not subject to a regulatory or disciplinary investigation, or adverse finding or decision of the *SRA*, the *Tribunal* or another regulatory body.

13.3 A *person* who meets the conditions under rule 13.2, shall be deemed to be approved to be designated as a *manager* or *owner* of any *authorised body*.

13.4 An *authorised body* must notify the *SRA* promptly in the *prescribed* form of the designation as a *manager* or *owner* of that body of a *person* who has been deemed to be approved under rule 13.3.

13.5 The *SRA* will deem an individual to be fit and proper to be a *compliance officer* of an *authorised body* if:

(a) that individual is a *lawyer* and a *manager* of the *authorised body*;

(b) the *authorised body* has an annual turnover of no more than £600,000;

(c) they are not a *compliance officer* of any other *authorised body*; and

(d) they are not subject to a regulatory or disciplinary investigation, or adverse finding or decision of the *SRA*, the *Tribunal* or another regulatory body.

13.6 An *authorised body* must notify the *SRA* promptly, in the *prescribed* form, of the identity of a *compliance officer* whose fitness and propriety has been deemed under rule 13.5, and the *SRA* shall approve their designation to undertake the role in that body accordingly.

13.7 Approval of a *person's* designation under rule 13.1 or 13.6:

(a) takes effect from the date of the decision unless otherwise stated;

(b) remains effective only if the *person* takes up the designated role within the period specified in the notice of approval, or the period of one year if no period is specified; and

(c) expires when the *person* ceases to carry out the designated role;

(d) expires when the *person* ceases to be eligible under rule 8.2.

13.8 The *SRA* may at any time, on granting approval for the designation of a *person* under this Part, or otherwise, make the holding of a *material interest* in a *licensed body* subject to conditions in accordance with paragraphs 17, 28 or 33 of Schedule 13 to the *LSA*.

13.9 The *SRA* may at any time withdraw approval of a *person's* designation under rule 13.1, 13.3 or 13.6 if it is not satisfied that the *person* is fit and proper to undertake the designated role.

13.10 A *person* whose designation has been approved under rule 13.1, 13.3 or 13.6, must notify the *SRA* promptly of any information in relation to them which would be relevant to an assessment of their fitness and propriety under the SRA

Assessment of Character and Suitability Rules, and may be required to provide a self-declaration of their fitness and propriety on request by the *SRA*.

13.11 In respect of a *person* whose designation has been approved under rule 13.3, the obligation to notify under rule 13.10 applies when the *person* is holding an approved post and extends to information relating to matters taking place at any time, following their approval, irrespective of whether they were holding an approved post at the time.

13.12 Where the *SRA* withdraws approval for the designation of a *person* who is the *director* of a *company*, the *SRA* may set separate dates for the individual ceasing to be a *director* and disposing of their shares.

PART 5: SUCCESSION, LOSS OF ELIGIBILITY AND TEMPORARY EMERGENCY AUTHORISATION

Rule 14: Loss of eligibility

14.1 If the last remaining *legally qualified manager* of an *authorised body* whose role ensures the body's compliance with the eligibility requirements for its authorisation under rule 1:

(a) is sentenced to imprisonment;

(b) becomes unable to carry on their role because of incapacity;

(c) abandons the business;

(d) is made subject to a restriction, condition or other regulatory decision by the *SRA* or another regulatory body which would prevent or restrict them acting as a *manager*; or

(e) is unable to fulfil the role for any other reason,

the body must inform the *SRA* within seven days of becoming aware of the relevant event and, within 28 days of becoming aware of the event, must either become eligible for authorisation (without reference to the *manager* in question), or cease to carry on *reserved legal activities* and to hold themselves out as an *authorised body*.

14.2 Subject to any *prescribed* application requirements, the *SRA* may:

(a) transfer a body's authorisation to another body where the first body ceases to exist and the second body succeeds to the whole or substantially the whole of its business;

(b) substitute a body's authorisation for another type of authorisation where it is satisfied that the body is materially carrying on the same practice, notwithstanding a change in its management or control; and

(c) permit any *person* previously approved as a *manager*, *owner*, or *compliance officer* of the body to continue to act in their designated role, notwithstanding the transfer or substitution.

Rule 15: Temporary emergency authorisation or approval

15.1 An application for temporary emergency authorisation may be made:

(a) within seven days of any change in the management or control of an *authorised body* which brings into being a new unauthorised body or practice;

(b) within 28 days of the death or incapacity of a *sole practitioner* by a *solicitor* or an *REL* who is:

    (i) the *sole practitioner's* executor, personal representative, attorney under a lasting power of attorney, or Court of Protection deputy (as appropriate);

    (ii) a practice manager appointed by the *sole practitioner's* executor, personal representative, attorney under a lasting power of attorney, or Court of Protection deputy (as appropriate); or

    (iii) an *employee* of the practice.

15.2 An application for temporary emergency approval of a *compliance officer* may be made within seven days of an *authorised body* ceasing to have a *COLP* or *COFA* whose designation is approved under Part 4.

15.3 The *SRA* will only grant an application under rule 15.1(a) or 15.2 if it is satisfied that:

(a) the body or its *managers* could not reasonably have commenced a substantive application for authorisation under Part 2 in advance of the events giving rise to the application;

(b) in relation to an application under rule 15.1(a) the body meets the eligibility requirements under rule 1.1 and will comply with our *regulatory arrangements* as they apply to *authorised bodies*; or

(c) in relation to an application under rule 15.2, it has no reason to believe that the individual to which the application relates is not fit and proper to be a *compliance officer* of the *authorised body*.

15.4 Temporary emergency authorisation or approval:

(a) shall be granted for an initial period of 28 days from the date specified;

(b) may be extended for such period as the *SRA* thinks fit;

(c) shall be extended, if a substantive application for authorisation or approval is made during the period of temporary emergency authorisation or approval, pending determination of the substantive application;

(d) may be revoked, withdrawn, or made subject to such conditions as the *SRA* considers appropriate, in the public interest,

save that, if the *SRA* grants temporary emergency authorisation under rule 15.1(b), the authorisation will be deemed to run from the date of death or incapacity and will cease to have effect on the earliest of the date of the winding up of the estate or 12 months from the date of death or incapacity.

Rule 16: Apportionment of periodical fees on succession

16.1 An *authorised body* which:

(a) has taken over the whole or a part of one or more *authorised bodies*; or

(b) has split or ceded part of its practice to another *authorised body* and wishes the *SRA* to take this into account in determining its periodical fee,

must within 28 days of the change taking place deliver to the *SRA* a notice in the *prescribed* form.

ANNEXES

Annex 1: Transitional arrangements under paragraph 7(3) of Schedule 5 to the LSA

1. A *licensable body* will be eligible to be a *recognised body* if as at 6 October 2011, it has been recognised by the *SRA* under section 9 of the *AJA* but has an *interest holder* or *manager* that is not a *lawyer* or a legally qualified body. It shall continue to be treated as a *recognised body* for the purposes of these rules and the *SRA's regulatory arrangements* until:

(a) such time as it ceases to comply with the management and control requirements set out in paragraph 2 below; or

(b) the end of the transitional period under Part 2 of Schedule 5 to the *LSA*, or such earlier time as the body may elect,

at which time it must apply for authorisation as a *licensed body*.

2. The management and control requirements are:

(a) at least 75% of the body's *managers* must be:

(i) individuals who are, and are entitled to practise as, *lawyers of England and Wales*, advocates or solicitors in Scotland, members of the Bar of Northern Ireland, solicitors of the Court of Judicature of Northern Ireland or *RFLs*; or

(ii) bodies corporate which are legally qualified bodies,

although a legally qualified body cannot be a *director* of a body which is a *company*;

(b) individuals who are, and are entitled to practise as, *lawyers of England and Wales*, advocates or solicitors in Scotland, members of the Bar of Northern Ireland, solicitors of the Court of Judicature of Northern Ireland or *RFLs* must make up at least 75% of the ultimate beneficial ownership of the body; and

(c) individuals who are, and are entitled to practise as, *lawyers of England and*

Wales, advocates or solicitors in Scotland, members of the Bar of Northern Ireland, solicitors of the Court of Judicature of Northern Ireland or *RFLs*, and/or legally qualified bodies, must:

    (i)   exercise or control the exercise of at least 75% of the *voting rights* in the body; and

    (ii)   if the body is a *company* with shares, hold (as registered members of the *company*) at least 75% of the shares.

(d)   every *interest holder* of the *recognised body*, and every *person* who exercises or controls the exercise of any *voting rights* in the body, must be:

    (i)   an individual who is, and is entitled to practise as, a *lawyer of England and Wales*, an advocate or solicitor in Scotland, a member of the Bar of Northern Ireland, a solicitor of the Court of Judicature of Northern Ireland or an *RFL*;

    (ii)   a legally qualified body; or

    (iii)   an individual who is approved by the *SRA*, and is a *manager* of the body;

(e)   an individual who is not entitled under paragraph 2(d)(i) may be an *interest holder* of a *recognised body* without being a *manager* of the body if:

    (i)   the *recognised body* is a *company* which is wholly or partly owned by a *partnership* or *LLP* which is a legally qualified body;

    (ii)   the individual is approved by the *SRA* and is a *manager* of the *partnership* or *LLP*; and

    (iii)   the individual is precluded under the *partnership* agreement or *members'* agreement from exercising or authorising any vote in relation to the *company*.

For the purposes of this annex, "legally qualified body" means a body which is:

(A)   a recognised body;

(B)   an authorised non-SRA firm of which individuals who are, and are entitled to practise as, lawyers of England and Wales, advocates or solicitors in Scotland, members of the Bar of Northern Ireland or solicitors of the Court of Judicature of Northern Ireland or RFLs make up at least 75% of the ultimate beneficial ownership.

Annex 2: Professional services

The professional services referred to in rule 6.1(b) are:

1.   Alternative dispute resolution.

2.   Financial services.

3.   Estate agency.

4. Management consultancy.

5. Company secretarial services.

6. Other professional and specialist business support services including human resources, recruitment, systems support, outsourcing, transcription and translating.

7. Acting as a parliamentary agent.

8. Practising as a lawyer of another jurisdiction.

9. Acting as a bailiff.

10. Accountancy services.

11. Education and training activities.

12. Authorship, journalism and publishing.

Supplemental notes

Made by the SRA Board on 30 May 2018.

Made under sections 31 of the Solicitors Act 1974, sections 9 and 9A of the Administration of Justice Act 1985, and section 83 of, and Schedule 11 to, the Legal Services Act 2007.

[Last updated: 31 December 2020]

SRA Authorisation of Individuals Regulations

INTRODUCTION

These regulations set out the SRA's requirements relating to the authorisation of individuals as solicitors in terms of admission, and the issuing of practising certificates and the registration of individuals as an REL or RFL. They set out the effect of SRA authorisation on how an individual may practise, the requirements for and how the SRA will decide applications for authorisation, the conditions that apply during authorisation, and how authorisation may be revoked.

If you are unsure whether you are eligible for authorisation, or need to be authorised, please see our guidance.

They also set out the education and training requirements in place for those seeking to be admitted as solicitors, and to exercise higher rights of audience in the higher courts of England and Wales. Education and training underpins the regulation of solicitors and it seeks to ensure the development of competent and ethical practitioners.

The regulations also govern the qualification process for solicitors and barristers or other UK qualified lawyers seeking admission as a solicitor of England and Wales from another jurisdiction.

This introduction does not form part of the SRA Authorisation of Individuals Regulations.

PART 1: ADMISSION AS A SOLICITOR

[Not yet in force: Eligibility for admission

1.1   You will be eligible for admission as a *solicitor* if the *SRA* is satisfied:

(a)   you have successfully and satisfactorily passed an assessment which is designed to assess your competence against the *prescribed* competences for solicitors and is conducted by an assessment organisation appointed by the *SRA* for the purpose;

(b)   you hold a *degree* or qualifications or experience which the *SRA* is satisfied are equivalent to a *degree*;

(c)   you have completed qualifying work experience which meets the requirements of regulation 2; and

(d)   as to your *character and suitability* to be a *solicitor*.]

[Not yet in force: Qualifying work experience

2.1   Qualifying work experience must:

(a) comprise experience of providing legal services which provides you the opportunity to develop the *prescribed* competences for *solicitors*;

(b) be of a duration of a total of at least two years' full time or equivalent; and

(c) be carried out under an arrangement or employment with no more than four separate firms, educational institutions or other organisations.

2.2   In respect of each organisation under regulation 2.1(c) above, you must arrange for confirmation in the *prescribed* form of the matters set out in regulation 2.3 to be given by a person specified in (a) to (c) below who has taken sufficient steps to satisfy themselves as to those matters:

(a) the organisation's *COLP*;

(b) a *solicitor* working within the organisation; or

(c) if neither (a) or (b) are applicable, a *solicitor* working outside of the organisation who has direct experience of your work and who has, in order to be so satisfied:

    (i) undertaken a review of the work you have done during the relevant period of work experience, which may include review of a training diary or portfolio of work; and

    (ii) received feedback from the person or persons supervising your work.

2.3   The matters in respect of which confirmation by a person specified in regulation 2.2 must be given are:

(a) details of the period of work experience carried out;

(b) that it provided you with the opportunity to develop some or all of the *prescribed* competences for *solicitors*; and

(c) that no issues arose during the period of work experience that raise a question as to your *character and suitability* to be admitted as a *solicitor*, or if such confirmation cannot be given, then details of any such issues.]

[Not yet in force: Eligibility for admission of qualified lawyers

3.1   You will be eligible for admission as a solicitor if the *SRA* is satisfied:

(a) you hold a legal professional qualification that is recognised by the *SRA*, which confers rights to practise in England and Wales or in an *overseas* jurisdiction; and

(b) subject to regulation 3.2, you meet the criteria in regulation 1.1(a), (b) and (d).

3.2   If you hold a qualification recognised under regulation 3.1(a) and the *SRA* is satisfied that your qualifications or experience demonstrate that you meet some or all of the *prescribed* competences, the *SRA* may decide you are not required to pass the assessment under regulation 1.1(a) or such parts of it as it considers appropriate.]

Eligibility requirements

3A.1 You will be eligible for admission as a *solicitor* if the *SRA* is satisfied:

(a) you have successfully and satisfactorily completed:

(i) an apprenticeship leading to qualification as a *solicitor*; or

(ii) the *academic stage of training* and the *vocational stage of training*; and

(b) as to your *character and suitability* to be a *solicitor*.

3A.2 The *SRA* may decide that it is satisfied that you have completed all or any part of the *academic stage of training* or the *vocational stage of training* by equivalent means.

Apprenticeships

3B.1 To complete an apprenticeship for the purposes of regulation 3A.1(a)(i), you must meet the requirements set out in the assessment plan for the Apprenticeship Standard for a Solicitor (England) approved by the Department for Business, Innovation and Skills, or set out in the Apprenticeship Framework specified in the Level 7 Higher Apprenticeship in Legal Practice (Wales). This must include successfully passing an assessment, which the *SRA* either conducts or approves as suitable for the purpose of admission as a *solicitor*.

3B.2 If at any time the *SRA* is not satisfied that you have successfully and satisfactorily completed an apprenticeship it may:

(a) refuse to recognise all or any part of that apprenticeship; or

(b) require you to take certain steps or undertake further training, subject to such conditions as it considers appropriate.

Academic stage

3C.1 Your eligibility to commence the *academic stage of training* will be determined according to the requirements, which may be approved by the *SRA*, of the relevant *approved education provider*.

3C.2 You may be entitled to credit for prior certified or experiential learning, which may entitle you to exemption from assessment in some subjects required by the *Joint Statement*. You must make any application for credit for prior learning to the *approved education provider*.

Vocational stage

3D.1 Your eligibility to commence the *Legal Practice Course* will be determined according to the requirements, approved by the *SRA*, of the relevant *authorised education provider*.

3D.2 Subject to regulation 3A.2, to complete the *vocational stage of training* you must complete:

   (a) the *Legal Practice Course*;

   (b) a *period of recognised training*; and

   (c) the Professional Skills Course.

Recognised training

3E.1 In order to satisfactorily complete your *period of recognised training*, you must maintain a *record of training* which:

   (a) contains details of the work you have performed;

   (b) records how you have applied and developed the skills, as set out in the *Practice Skills Standards*;

   (c) records your reflections on, and your *training principal's* appraisal of, your performance and development against, and your attainment of the skills set out in the *Practice Skills Standards*; and

   (d) is verified by the individual supervising you.

3E.2 If at any time the *SRA* is not satisfied that you have received, or are receiving, training that meets regulation 3E.1 above and regulation 4.1 of the SRA Education, Training and Assessment Provider Regulations, the *SRA* may:

   (a) refuse to recognise all or any part of that training; or

   (b) require you to take certain steps or undertake further training, subject to such conditions as it considers appropriate.

Admission of qualified lawyers

3F.1 Subject to regulation 4.1, you will be eligible for admission as a *solicitor* if the *SRA* is satisfied that you are:

   (a) (i)   a *barrister*; or

        (ii) a qualified lawyer in a *recognised jurisdiction* and you:

              (A) have followed the full route to qualification in the *recognised jurisdiction*; and

              (B) are entitled to practise as a qualified lawyer of the *recognised jurisdiction*;

   (b) of the *character and suitability* to be admitted as a *solicitor*; and

(c) have passed all relevant Qualified Lawyers Transfer Scheme assessments in accordance with this regulation.

3F.2 Unless regulation 3F.3A, 3F.3B or 3F.4 applies, you must pass all the Qualified Lawyers Transfer Scheme assessments.

3F.3A If you are:

(a) a solicitor or barrister qualified in Northern Ireland;

(b) a solicitor or advocate qualified in Scotland; or

(c) a *barrister*,

the *SRA* may grant you an exemption from one or more of the QLTS assessments, or parts of them, as we consider appropriate based upon your qualification and experience.

3F.3B If regulation 3F.3A does not apply, the *SRA* may grant you an exemption from such of either those QLTS assessments which together comprise the multiple choice test, or those QLTS assessments which together form the objective structured clinical examination, or both, as we consider appropriate based upon your qualifications and experience.

3F.4 If you have passed the *Legal Practice Course*, the *SRA* may grant you an exemption from the multiple-choice test of the Qualified Lawyers Transfer Scheme assessments.

European Communities (Lawyer's Practice) Regulations 2000

4.1 If you are an *REL* or you were an *REL* immediately before the end of IP completion day, you will be eligible for admission as a *solicitor* under Part V of the European Communities (Lawyer's Practice) Regulations 2000 to the extent that they continue to have effect in accordance with the Services of Lawyers and Lawyer's Practice (Revocation etc.) (EU Exit) Regulations 2020, if:

(a) you satisfy the requirements of those regulations; and

(b) the *SRA* is satisfied as to your *character and suitability* to be a *solicitor*.

Admission, retention, removal, and restoration to the roll

Application for admission

5.1 You may apply for admission in writing in the *prescribed* form. Following an application for admission, the *SRA* will issue you with a certificate of satisfaction if it is satisfied that you have met the eligibility requirements for admission as a *solicitor* set out in this Part.

5.2 At any time before making an application for admission, you may apply to the *SRA* for an early assessment of your *character and suitability* to be a *solicitor*. The

SRA is not bound, in any subsequent application for admission, by any decision it makes as to your *character and suitability* to be a *solicitor* as a result of an early assessment.

5.3   As soon as reasonably practicable after the *SRA* has issued a certificate of satisfaction, you will be admitted as a *solicitor* and your name entered on the roll, unless the *SRA* receives information in writing that it is satisfied demonstrates that you should not be admitted. If so, the *SRA* will give you written notice, providing you with the information it has received, and the opportunity to provide written representations within the period of 28 days from the date of the notice, following which it may decide not to admit you as a *solicitor*.

Retention

5.4   If you are a *solicitor*, the *SRA* will write to you at the last notified version of your postal or email address, to ask you whether you wish your name to remain on the roll, at appropriate intervals as prescribed if you do not hold a practising certificate.

5.5   If, following an enquiry under regulation 5.4, you wish your name to remain on the roll, you shall be required to pay such fee as may be *prescribed* in regulations.

Removal from and restoration to the roll

5.6   The *SRA* may remove your name from the roll if:

   (a)   following an enquiry made by the *SRA* under regulation 5.4:

      (i)   you tell the *SRA* that you do not wish to remain on the roll;

      (ii)   you do not, within eight weeks from the date of the notice, reply to the *SRA* and pay the fee specified under regulation 5.5, or

   (b)   you apply to have your name removed from the roll.

5.7   Where regulation 5.6(a)(ii) applies, the *SRA* must not remove your name from the roll until it has given notice to you that it intends to do so.

5.8   The *SRA* shall remove your name from the roll on your death.

5.9   If your name has been removed from the roll, you may apply to the *SRA* for your name to be restored to the roll and the *SRA* may, if it considers it appropriate to do so in reaching a decision on an application made under this regulation, assess your *character and suitability* to be a *solicitor*.

5.10   The *SRA* may decide not to remove your name from, or restore your name to, the roll under this regulation if you are subject to any proceedings, investigation, or consideration of your conduct or practice by the *SRA*. The *SRA* must not remove your name from, or restore your name to, the roll if you are the subject of disciplinary proceedings (either in progress or pending) before the senior *courts* or the *Tribunal*.

PART 2: PRACTISING CERTIFICATES FOR SOLICITORS AND REGISTRATION AS A EUROPEAN OR FOREIGN LAWYER

Eligibility requirements

6.1 The *SRA* shall only grant an application for a practising certificate, or registration in the *register of European lawyers* or the *register of foreign lawyers* if you meet the eligibility requirements in this regulation.

6.2 You will be eligible to apply for a practising certificate if:

(a) your name is on the roll;

(b) you have sufficient knowledge of written and spoken English or Welsh; and

(c) you are not suspended from practice as a *solicitor*.

6.3 Subject to regulation 3A you will be eligible for registration in the *register of European lawyers* if:

(a) you are a European lawyer as defined in the European Communities (Lawyer's Practice) Regulations 2000 and you are a Swiss lawyer as defined in paragraph 2 of regulation 6 of The Services of Lawyers and Lawyer's Practice (Revocation etc.) (EU Exit) Regulations 2020;

(b) you intend to commence practice under your Swiss professional title as defined in the European Communities (Lawyer's Practice) Regulations 2000 on a permanent basis in England and Wales or Northern Ireland, and are legally entitled to do so;

(c) you have provided the *SRA* with a certificate which is no more than three months old, confirming your registration with the competent authority in Switzerland under whose home professional title you intend to practise;

(d) you are not struck off or suspended from the *register*, or subject to a direction from the *Tribunal* prohibiting your restoration to the *register*; and

(e) the *SRA* is satisfied as to your *character and suitability* to be an *REL*.

6.3A At the end of the period of four years beginning with IP completion day, you will be eligible for registration in the *register of European lawyers* if you satisfy the requirements of regulation 6.3 and you fall within paragraph 4 but not paragraph 5 of regulation 6 of The Services of Lawyers and Lawyer's Practice (Revocation etc.) (EU Exit) Regulations 2020.

6.4 You will be eligible for registration in the *register of foreign lawyers* if:

(a) you are a *foreign lawyer* of a legal profession which the *SRA* is satisfied is so regulated as to make it appropriate for members of that profession to be *managers* of *recognised bodies*;

(b) you are not struck off or suspended from the *register*, or subject to a direction from the *Tribunal* prohibiting your restoration to the *register*; and

(c) the *SRA* is satisfied as to your *character and suitability* to be an *RFL*.

Determination of applications

7.1   If the *SRA* considers it to be in the public interest to do so, it must:

(a) refuse your application for a practising certificate, or your application for registration or renewal of registration, in the *register of European lawyers* or the *register of foreign lawyers*; or

(b) at any time, whether on grant of such an application or at the end of a period of suspension of a practising certificate or registration, or otherwise, impose such conditions on your certificate or registration as it thinks fit in accordance with regulations 7.2 and 7.3.

7.2   The *SRA* may impose conditions under regulation 7.1(b) if it is satisfied that you:

(a) are unsuitable to undertake certain activities or engage in certain business or practising arrangements;

(b) are putting, or are likely to put, at risk the interests of *clients*, third parties or the public;

(c) will not comply with the *SRA's regulatory arrangements* or require monitoring of compliance with the *SRA's regulatory arrangements*; or

(d) should take specified steps conducive to the *regulatory objectives*.

7.3   The conditions imposed by the *SRA* under regulation 7.1(b) may:

(a) specify certain requirements that must be met or steps that must be taken;

(b) restrict the carrying on of particular activities or holding of particular roles; or

(c) prohibit the taking of specified steps without its approval.

7.4   The *SRA* may vary or revoke any conditions on your practising certificate or registration.

7.5   Before imposing or varying any conditions on your practising certificate or registration, the *SRA* shall give you no less than 28 days' notice of its intention to do so, inviting representations regarding the issues giving rise to the proposed conditions.

7.6   The *SRA* may shorten or dispense with the 28 days' notice under regulation 7.5 where conditions are imposed on grant of your practising certificate or registration, or otherwise if it is satisfied that it is in the public interest to do so.

7.7 If the *SRA* issues you with a practising certificate or registers you, or renews your registration, in the *register of European lawyers* or the *register of foreign lawyers*, you must pay the *prescribed* fee.

Commencement, replacement, and renewal

8.1 The commencement date for a practising certificate or for registration in the *register of European lawyers* or *register of foreign lawyers* shall be the date specified by the *SRA* on the practising certificate or the register.

8.2 The replacement date for a practising certificate is 31 October following the issue of the certificate.

8.3 The renewal date for registration in the *register of European lawyers* or *register of foreign lawyers* is the first 31 October following initial registration, and 31 October in each successive year.

Revocation and expiry

8.4 The *SRA* may revoke a practising certificate, or withdraw registration in the *register of European lawyers* or the *register of foreign lawyers*, at any time, if the *SRA* is satisfied:

(a) that the practising certificate or registration was granted or renewed as a result of error, misleading or inaccurate information, or fraud;

(b) that the replacement or renewal date has passed and an application has not been made for replacement of the practising certificate or renewal of the registration;

(c) that a *solicitor*, an *REL* or *RFL* has failed to pay the *prescribed* fee required under regulation 7.7;

(d) subject to regulation 8.7(c), in the case of an *REL* or *RFL* that the eligibility requirements under regulations 6.3 and 6.4 are no longer met; or

(e) that an application for a replacement practising certificate or renewal of registration has been refused under regulation 7.1(a).

8.5 The *SRA* must not revoke a practising certificate or withdraw registration under regulation 8.4(a), (c) or (d) unless it has first given the person no less than 28 days' notice of its intention to do so, inviting representations regarding the issues giving rise to the proposed revocation or withdrawal of registration.

8.6 The *SRA* shall revoke a practising certificate or withdraw registration on the application of the person concerned, unless the applicant is subject to any proceedings, investigation, or consideration of their conduct or practice by the *SRA* or the *Tribunal*.

8.7 A practising certificate or registration will expire:

(a) on the death of the *solicitor*, *REL* or *RFL*;

(b) if a *solicitor*, an *REL* or *RFL* is removed from, or struck off, the roll or *register* or their registration is withdrawn;

(c) if an *REL* or *RFL* is no longer eligible for registration under 6.3(a) or 6.4(a) respectively;

(d) in the case of a practising certificate, when the *SRA* issues a replacement certificate;

(e) in the case of a practising certificate which is suspended, on its replacement date, or if the replacement date has passed, 14 days after the suspension took effect; or

(f) in the case of a registration which is suspended, on its next renewal date, or if a suspension takes effect after a renewal date but before renewal has been granted in respect of that renewal date, 14 days after the suspension took effect.

What authorisation entitles you to do

Reserved legal activities

9.1 Subject to regulations 9.2, 9.3, 9.5 to 9.10 and 10.2(b), if you are a *solicitor* with a current practising certificate, or an *REL*, you are entitled to carry on all *reserved legal activities* except notarial activities.

9.2 If you are an *REL* you may only exercise a right of audience before a *court*, conduct litigation or prepare court documents, in conjunction with a *solicitor* or *barrister* who is authorised to do so.

9.3 If you are an *REL* you may only:

(a) prepare instruments for remuneration creating or transferring an interest in land, and lodge documents relating to a transfer or charge of land, if you have a home professional title listed under Regulation 12 of the European Communities (Lawyer's Practice) Regulations 2000;

(b) carry on probate activities for remuneration if you have a home professional title listed under Regulation 13 of the European Communities (Lawyer's Practice) Regulations 2000.

9.4 If you are an *RFL* you may only:

(a) undertake advocacy in chambers in England and Wales under instructions given by a person who is authorised to do so;

(b) under the direction and supervision of a person qualified to supervise:

(i) prepare *court* documents;

(ii) prepare instruments and the lodging of documents relating to the transfer or charge of land;

(iii) prepare papers on which to found or oppose a grant of probate, or a grant of letters of administration;

(iv) prepare trust deeds disposing of capital if you also are eligible to act as a *lawyer of England and Wales*;

(c) in relation to *immigration work*:

(i) undertake advocacy before immigration tribunals;

(ii) have conduct of, and prepare documents for, immigration tribunal proceedings.

Immigration work

9.5 Subject to regulation 9.7, if you are a *solicitor*, an *REL* or *RFL* you may undertake *immigration work*, provided that such work is undertaken:

(a) through an *authorised body*;

(b) through an *authorised non-SRA firm* that is a qualified person under the Immigration and Asylum Act 1999;

(c) as an employee, for your employer or work colleagues; or

(d) through a non-commercial advice service which is registered with the Office of the Immigration Services Commissioner. or is otherwise a qualified person under the Immigration and Asylum Act 1999.

9.6 Where you undertake work under regulation 9.5(c) or (d) above, this must be undertaken by you personally and not by another person on your or your employer's behalf unless such person is a qualified person under the Immigration and Asylum Act 1999 other than under section 84(2)(e) of that Act.

9.7 If you undertake *immigration work* through a body which is registered with the Office of the Immigration Services Commissioner, other than as permitted under regulation 9.5(d), you must be registered as an individual with the Office of the Immigration Services Commissioner or otherwise qualified to provide such services under the Immigration and Asylum Act 1999 and must undertake such work in that capacity.

9.7A For the purposes of regulation 9.7, you are not otherwise qualified to provide services under the Immigration and Asylum Act 1999 by virtue of your authorisation by the SRA to practise as a *solicitor*, an *REL* or *RFL*.

9.7B Where you are undertaking work under 9.7 above, in the event of any conflict between the *SRA's regulatory arrangements* and any requirements placed on you by the Office of the Immigration Services Commissioner, the latter shall prevail.

9.7C Nothing in regulations 9.5 to 9.7B restrict you from undertaking *immigration work* if you fall within section 84(6) of the Immigration and Asylum Act 1999.

Regulated claims management activities

9.8   If you are a *solicitor*, an *REL* or *RFL* you may carry on *regulated claims management activities* or activities that would be *regulated claims management activities* but for the exclusion in article 89N of the *Regulated Activities Order*, provided that such work is undertaken through:

(a) a body authorised to carry on *reserved legal activities*; or

(b) if the work does not comprise *reserved legal activities*

(i)   a body which has been granted permission to carry on *regulated claims management activities* by the *FCA* under Part 4A of *FSMA*; or

(ii) as permitted under an exemption made in or under *FSMA*, to the general prohibition set out in section 19 of *FSMA*.

Financial services activities

9.9   If you are a *solicitor*, an *REL* or *RFL* you may carry on *regulated financial services activities* under the SRA Financial Services (Scope) Rules, provided that such activities are undertaken through an *authorised body*.

Higher rights of audience

9.10 If you are a *solicitor* or an *REL* you may exercise civil or criminal advocacy in the *higher courts* if the *SRA* is satisfied you have successfully and satisfactorily completed the appropriate *higher courts advocacy qualification* and that you have done so after the date of your admission as a *solicitor* or initial registration as an *REL*, or you are:

(a) an *REL* or *lawyer* to whom the European Union (Recognition of Professional Qualifications) Regulations 2015 applies and you have applied for a qualification to exercise rights of audience in the *higher courts*, and you have undertaken any further steps as the *SRA* specifies in order to gain the qualification; or

(b) authorised by another *approved regulator* to exercise civil or criminal advocacy in the *higher courts*.

Practising on your own

10.1 Subject to regulation 10.2, if you are a *solicitor* or an *REL* you must not act as a *sole practitioner* unless your practice is authorised as a *recognised sole practice*.

10.2 If you otherwise would be, you will not be regarded as acting as a *sole practitioner* and you will not therefore need to be authorised as a *recognised sole practice* if:

(a) your practice consists entirely of carrying on activities which are not *reserved legal activities*; or

(b) any *reserved legal activities* you carry on are provided through an *authorised body* or an *authorised non-SRA firm*, or in circumstances in which you:

(i)   have practised as a *solicitor* or an *REL* for a minimum of three years since admission or registration;

(ii)   are self-employed and practise in your own name, and not through a trading name or service company;

(iii)   do not employ anyone in connection with the services that you provide;

(iv)   are engaged directly by the *client* with your *fees* payable directly to you;

(v)   have a practising address in the *UK*;

(vi)   take out and maintain indemnity insurance that provides adequate and appropriate cover in respect of the services that you provide or have provided, whether or not they comprise *reserved legal activities*, taking into account any alternative arrangements you or your *clients* may make; and

(vii)   do not hold *client money*, save that you may hold money which falls within the category of *client money* set out in rule 2.1(d) of the SRA Accounts Rules so long as:

(A)   any money held for *disbursements* relates to costs or expenses incurred by you on behalf of your *client* and for which you are liable; and

(B)   you have informed your *client* in advance of where and how the money will be held,

and you choose for your practice not to be authorised as a *recognised sole practice*.

Commencement, revocation, and transitional provisions

11.1 Regulations 1.1 to 3.3 come into force on a date to be determined in an order made by the *SRA* Board.

11.2 Subject to regulations 11.3 to 11.7, regulations 3A.1 to 3F.4 shall be revoked on the date determined in accordance with regulation 11.1.

11.3 Regulations 3A.1 to 3E.2 shall continue to have effect, in respect of those individuals falling within regulation 11.5, and for the purposes of regulation 11.6, until 31 December in the year of the eleventh anniversary of the date determined in accordance with regulation 11.1.

11.4 Regulation 3F shall continue to have effect, in respect of those individuals who have passed the multiple-choice test of the Qualified Lawyers Transfer Scheme assessments at the date determined in accordance with regulation 11.1, until the first anniversary of that date.

11.5 Regulation 11.3 applies to any individual who has, at the date determined in accordance with regulation 11.1, started, or who has entered into a contractual agreement or made a non-refundable financial commitment to start, any of the following:

(a) a *Qualifying Law Degree*;

(b) a *CPE*;

(c) an *Exempting Law Degree*;

(d) an *Integrated Course*;

(e) the *Legal Practice Course*; or

(f) a *period of recognised training*, and has not yet been admitted as a *solicitor*.

11.6 An individual who falls within regulation 11.5 will be eligible to be admitted as a *solicitor* under either regulations 3A.1 to 3E.2, or under regulations 1.1 to 3.3.

11.7 Where an individual has made an application for admission on the basis of eligibility under either regulation 3A or regulation 3F, and it has not been determined at the point those regulations are revoked (and any continuation under regulation 11.3 has come to an end), then the application shall continue to be determined under those regulations as if they were still in force.

11.8 If you are:

(a) an *RFL*;

(b) were an *REL* immediately prior to IP completion day; and

(c) have made an application under regulation 29 of the European Communities (Lawyer's Practice) Regulations 2000 to which regulation 9 of The Services of Lawyers and Lawyer's Practice (Revocation etc.) (EU Exit) Regulations 2020 applies

you are entitled to continue to carry on or undertake those activities and that work you were entitled to do immediately prior to IP completion day under regulation 9 of these regulations until your application referred to in (c) has been finally determined or withdrawn.

Future changes

Regulations not yet in force

Regulations not yet in force are contained in square brackets and are preceded by the words "Not yet in force".

Regulations 1.1 to 3.3 come into force on a date to be determined in an order made by the SRA Board.

Supplemental notes

Made by the SRA Board on 30 May 2018.

Made under sections 2, 13, 28 and 31 of the Solicitors Act 1974 and section 89 of, and paragraphs 2 and 3 of Schedule 14 to, the Courts and Legal Services Act 1990.

[Last updated: 1 April 2021]

SRA Education, Training and Assessment Provider Regulations

INTRODUCTION

These regulations set out the requirements governing organisations which are providing or intending to provide education and training, and the delivery of assessments to those seeking to be admitted as solicitors.

This introduction does not form part of the SRA Education, Training and Assessment Provider Regulations.

PART 1: REQUIREMENTS FOR EDUCATION PROVIDERS

Regulation 1: Education providers

1.1   Only an *approved education provider* may provide and assess:

(a)   a *Qualifying Law Degree*;

(b)   a *CPE*;

(c)   an *Exempting Law Degree*; or

(d)   an *Integrated Course*.

1.2   Only an *authorised education provider* may provide and assess the *Legal Practice Course* or the Professional Skills Course.

1.3   An organisation may apply to the *SRA* in such manner as may be *prescribed* to be an *approved education provider* or an *authorised education provider*.

1.4   The *SRA* may, in relation to an application for approval or authorisation:

(a)   grant the application, subject to such conditions and for such period as it considers appropriate; or

(b)   refuse the application.

1.5   If the *SRA* considers that an *approved education provider* or an *authorised education provider* has failed to comply with any obligation placed on it under these regulations, the *SRA* may:

(a)   revoke the organisation's approval or authorisation, as appropriate; or

(b)   make the approval or authorisation subject to such conditions as it considers appropriate.

PART 2: REQUIREMENTS FOR AUTHORISED TRAINING PROVIDERS

Regulation 2: Authorised training providers

2.1   Only an *authorised training provider* may provide a *period of recognised training* to *trainees*.

2.2   An organisation may apply for authorisation as an *authorised training provider* and its application must demonstrate that it will meet the requirements of regulations 3 to 5 below.

2.3   The *SRA* may, in relation to an application for approval or authorisation:

   (a) grant the application, subject to such conditions and for such period as it considers appropriate; or

   (b) refuse the application.

2.4   If the *SRA* considers that an *authorised training provider* or a *training principal* has failed to comply with any obligation placed on it under these regulations, the *SRA* may:

   (a) revoke the organisation's authorisation;

   (b) make the authorisation subject to such conditions as it considers appropriate; or

   (c) require the *authorised training provider* to appoint a new *training principal*.

Regulation 3: Requirements for authorised training providers

3.1   An *authorised training provider* must:

   (a) have in place a *training principal* for the whole duration of any *period of recognised training*, who meets the requirements of regulation 5 and whose identity has been notified to the *SRA* in the *prescribed* form; and

   (b) pay the fees and expenses for each *trainee's* first attempt at the Professional Skills Course.

Regulation 4: Requirements for recognised training

4.1   A *period of recognised training* must:

   (a) unless regulation 4.2 applies, be of a duration of a total of at least two years full time, or equivalent;

   (b) ensure that the *trainee* has applied and developed the skills as set out in the *Practice Skills Standards*;

   (c) be appropriately supervised by *solicitors* and other individuals who have adequate legal knowledge and experience in the practice area they are supervising and the necessary skills to provide effective supervision; and

(d) include regular appraisal of the *trainee's* performance and development, and review of the *trainee's record of training*.

4.2 An *authorised training provider* may recognise previous work-based experience the *trainee* has undertaken as satisfying up to six months of the required *period of recognised training*, provided:

(a) the experience was gained in the three years preceding the commencement of the *period of recognised training*;

(b) the experience enabled the *trainee* to apply and develop one or more of the skills as set out in the *Practice Skills Standards*; and

(c) the *trainee* was supervised, and was subject to an appraisal of their performance and development, during the period of work-based experience.

Regulation 5: Training principals

5.1 The *training principal* for an *authorised training provider* must:

(a) be a *solicitor* holding a current practising certificate or be a practising *barrister*;

(b) notify the *SRA* in the *prescribed* form before any individual commences a *period of recognised training* or if this is not possible then as soon as practicable thereafter;

(c) ensure that the training provided meets the requirements of regulation 4;

(d) ensure that the *trainee* maintains a *record of training* which will meet the requirements set out at regulation 3E.1 of the SRA Authorisation of Individuals Regulations; and

(e) certify to the *authorised training provider* in the *prescribed* form at the end of any *period of recognised training* whether, in their opinion, the *trainee*:

(i) is of the proper *character and suitability* to be admitted as a *solicitor*; and

(ii) has completed training which complies with regulation 4 of these regulations,

and inform the *SRA* of any previous experience recognised under regulation 4.2.

PART 3: REQUIREMENTS FOR HIGHER RIGHTS OF AUDIENCE ASSESSMENT PROVIDERS

Regulation 6: Higher rights of audience assessment providers

6.1 Only an organisation approved by the *SRA* may provide assessments in *higher courts* civil advocacy and *higher courts* criminal advocacy conferring a *higher courts advocacy qualification*.

6.2   An organisation may apply to the *SRA* in such manner as may be *prescribed* to be approved to provide such assessments.

6.3   The *SRA* may, in relation to an application for approval:

(a)   grant the application, subject to such conditions as it considers appropriate; or

(b)   refuse the application.

6.4   The *SRA* shall issue guidelines and standards for the provision of competence assessments against which the competence of those applying for a *higher court advocacy qualification* must be assessed.

6.5   If the *SRA* considers that an assessment provider has failed to comply with any obligation placed on it under these regulations, the *SRA* may:

(a)   revoke the provider's approval; or

(b)   make the approval subject to such conditions and for such period as it considers appropriate.

PART 4: MONITORING AND INSPECTION

Regulation 7: Monitoring and inspection

7.1   In order to protect and promote the standards of legal education and training, the *SRA* may:

(a)   monitor the relevant programmes of study provided by an *approved education provider* and an *authorised education provider*, the training provided by an *authorised training provider* or the assessments provided by an assessment provider approved under regulation 6;

(b)   visit the provider's premises, at such intervals and on such grounds as it may consider appropriate;

(c)   require the provider to respond promptly, fully and accurately to any request by the *SRA* for explanations, information or documents;

(d)   require the provider to ensure that relevant information or documents it holds, or that a third party holds on its behalf are available for inspection.

PART 5: TRANSITIONAL PROVISIONS

Regulation 8: Transitional provisions

8.1   Any approval, authorisation or recognition granted under the Monitoring of Courses Regulations 1991, the SRA Training Regulations 2011, the SRA Higher Rights of Audience Regulations 2011 or the SRA Training Regulations 2014 – Qualification and Provider Regulations, will continue as if granted under these regulations.

8.2   A *period of recognised training* entered into before these regulations come into force will continue to be governed by the SRA Training Regulations 2014 – Qualification and Provider Regulations.

Supplemental notes

Made by the SRA Board on 30 May 2018.

Made under section 2 of the Solicitors Act 1974.

[Last updated: 25 November 2019]

[10] SRA Financial Services (Scope) Rules

INTRODUCTION

The SRA, through the Law Society, is a designated professional body under Part 20 of FSMA. This means that firms (including sole practices) authorised by us may carry on certain regulated financial services activities without being regulated by the FCA if they can meet the conditions in section 327 of FSMA. The purpose of these rules is to set out the scope of the regulated financial services activities that may be undertaken by firms authorised by us and not regulated by the FCA.

These rules do not apply to solicitors, RELs or RFLs practising outside firms authorised by us.

This introduction does not form part of the SRA Financial Services (Scope) Rules.

Rule 1: Application

1.1 These rules apply to *authorised bodies* that are not regulated by the *FCA*, their *managers* and *employees* and references to "you" in these rules should be read accordingly.

1.2 Where an *authorised body* is a *licensed body*, these rules apply only in relation to the activities regulated by the *SRA* in accordance with the terms of the body's licence.

Rule 2: Basic conditions

2.1 If you carry on any *regulated financial services activities* you must ensure that:

(a) you satisfy the conditions in section 327(2) to (5) of *FSMA*;

(b) the activities arise out of, or are complementary to, the provision of a particular *professional service* to a particular *client*;

(c) there is not in force any order or direction of the *FCA* under sections 328 or 329 of *FSMA* which prevents you from carrying on the activities; and

(d) the activities are not otherwise prohibited by these rules.

Rule 3: Prohibited activities

3.1 You must not carry on, or agree to carry on, any of the following activities:

(a) an activity that is specified in an order made under section 327(6) of *FSMA*;

(b) an activity that relates to an investment that is specified in an order made under section 327(6) of *FSMA*;

(c) entering into a *regulated credit agreement* as lender except where the *regulated credit agreement* relates exclusively to the payment of *disbursements* or professional fees due to you;

(d) exercising, or having the right to exercise, the lender's rights and duties under a *regulated credit agreement* except where the *regulated credit agreement* relates exclusively to the payment of *disbursements* or professional fees due to you;

(e) entering into a *regulated consumer hire agreement* as owner;

(f) exercising, or having the right to exercise, the owner's rights and duties under a *regulated consumer hire agreement*;

(g) operating an electronic system in relation to lending within the meaning of article 36H of the *Regulated Activities Order*;

(h) providing credit references within the meaning of article 89B of the *Regulated Activities Order*;

(i) insurance distribution activities in relation to insurance-based investment products; or

(j) creating, developing, designing or underwriting a *contract of insurance*.

Rule 4: Corporate finance

4.1   You must not act as any of the following:

(a) sponsor to an issue in respect of *securities* to be admitted for dealing on the London Stock Exchange;

(b) nominated adviser to an issue in respect of *securities* to be admitted for dealing on the Alternative Investment Market of the London Stock Exchange; or

(c) corporate adviser to an issue in respect of *securities* to be admitted for dealing on the ICAP Securities and Derivatives Exchange or any similar exchange.

Rule 5: Insurance distribution activities

5.1   You may only carry on *insurance distribution activities* as an *ancillary insurance intermediary*.

5.2   You must not carry on any *insurance distribution activities* unless you:

(a) are registered in the *Financial Services Register*; and

(b) have appointed an *insurance distribution officer* who will be responsible for your *insurance distribution activities*.

5.3   If you are carrying on, or proposing to carry on, *insurance distribution activities* you must notify the *SRA* in the *prescribed* form.

5.4   The *SRA* may give the *FCA* any of the information collected on the *prescribed* form and you must notify the *SRA* without undue delay of any changes to this information or to any information about you that appears on the *Financial Services Register*.

5.5 Rule 5.3 does not apply to you if you have been registered in the *Financial Services Register* and are able to carry on insurance mediation activities before 1 October 2018.

Rule 6: Credit-related regulated financial services activities

6.1 You must not enter into any transaction with a *client* in which you:

(a) provide the *client* with credit card cheques, a credit or store card, *credit tokens, running account credit,* a current account or *high-cost short-term credit*;

(b) hold a *continuous payment authority* over the client's account; or

(c) take any article from the *client* in *pledge* or *pawn* as security for the transaction.

6.2 You must not:

(a) enter into a *regulated credit agreement* as lender; or

(b) exercise, or have the right to exercise, the lender's rights and duties under a *regulated credit agreement,*

which is secured on land by a *legal or equitable mortgage*.

6.3 You must not:

(a) enter into a *regulated credit agreement* as lender; or

(b) exercise, or have the right to exercise, the lender's rights and duties under a *regulated credit agreement,*

which includes a variable rate of interest.

6.4 You must not provide a *debt management plan* to a *client*.

6.5 You must not charge a separate fee for, or attribute any element of your fees to, *credit broking* services.

Supplemental notes

Made by the SRA Board on 30 May 2018.

Made under section 31 of the Solicitors Act 1974, section 9 of the Administration of Justice Act 1985, section 83 of the Legal Services Act 2007 and section 332 of the Financial Services and Markets Act 2000.

[Last updated: 25 November 2019]

[11] SRA Financial Services (Conduct of Business) Rules

INTRODUCTION

The SRA, through the Law Society, is a designated professional body under Part 20 of FSMA. This means that firms (including sole practices) authorised by us may carry on certain regulated financial services activities without being regulated by the FCA if they can meet the conditions in section 327 of FSMA.

The SRA Financial Services (Scope) Rules set out the scope of the regulated financial services activities that may be undertaken by firms authorised by us and not regulated by the FCA. These rules regulate the way in which firms carry on such exempt regulated financial services activities and the way in which firms that are dually regulated by us and the FCA carry on their non-mainstream regulated activities.

These rules do not apply to solicitors, RELs and RFLs practising outside firms that are authorised by us.

This introduction does not form part of the SRA Financial Services (Conduct of Business) Rules.

PART 1: APPLICATION

Rule 1: Application

1.1   Apart from rule 2 (Status Disclosure), these rules apply to:

(a) *authorised bodies* which are not regulated by the *FCA*;

(b) *authorised bodies* which are regulated by the *FCA*, but only in respect of their *non-mainstream regulated activities*; and

(c) the *managers* and *employees* of *authorised bodies* in (a) and (b) above,

and references to "you" in these rules should be read accordingly.

1.2   Where an *authorised body* is a *licensed body*, these rules apply only in relation to the activities regulated by the *SRA* in accordance with the terms of the body's licence.

1.3   Rule 2 applies only to *authorised bodies* which are not regulated by the *FCA*.

PART 2: RULES

Rule 2: Status disclosure

2.1   Notwithstanding the wider information obligations in the *SRA Codes of Conduct*, you must give the *client* the following information in writing in a manner that is clear, fair and not misleading before providing a service which includes the carrying on of a *regulated financial services activity* and in good time before the conclusion of a *contract of insurance*:

(a) a statement that you are not authorised by the *FCA*;

(b) your name and practising address;

(c) the nature of the *regulated financial services activities* carried on by you, and the fact that they are limited in scope;

(d) a statement that you are authorised and regulated by the *SRA*; and

(e) a statement explaining that complaints and redress mechanisms are provided through the *SRA* and the *Legal Ombudsman*.

2.2   Before you provide a service, which includes the carrying on of an *insurance distribution activity* with or for a *client* and in good time before the conclusion of a *contract of insurance*, you must state that you are an *ancillary insurance intermediary* and make the following statement in writing to the *client* in a way that is clear, fair and not misleading:

"[This firm is]/[We are] not authorised by the Financial Conduct Authority. However, we are included on the register maintained by the Financial Conduct Authority so that we can carry on insurance distribution activity, which is broadly the advising on, selling and administration of insurance contracts. This part of our business, including arrangements for complaints or redress if something goes wrong, is regulated by the Solicitors Regulation Authority. The register can be accessed via the Financial Conduct Authority website at www.fca.org.uk/firms/financial-services-register."

Rule 3: Execution of transactions

3.1   You must ensure that where you have agreed or decided in your discretion to effect a *transaction*, you must do so as soon as possible, unless you reasonably believe that it is in the *client's* best interests not to.

Rule 4: Records of transactions

4.1   Where you receive instructions from a *client* to effect a *transaction*, or make a decision to effect a *transaction* in your discretion, you must keep a record of:

(a) the name of the *client*;

(b) the terms of the instructions or decision; and

(c) in the case of instructions, the date on which they were received.

4.2   Where you give instructions to another person to effect a *transaction*, you must keep a record of:

(a) the name of the *client*;

(b) the terms of the instructions;

(c) the date on which the instructions were given; and

(d) the name of the other person instructed.

Rule 5: Record of commissions

5.1 Where you receive commission which is attributable to your *regulated financial services activities*, you must keep a record of:

(a) the amount of the commission; and

(b) how you have accounted to the *client*.

Rule 6: Safekeeping of clients' investments

6.1 Where you undertake the *regulated financial services activity* of safeguarding and administering investments, you must operate appropriate systems, including the keeping of appropriate records, which provide for the safekeeping of *assets* entrusted to you by *clients* and others.

6.2 Where such *assets* are passed to a third party:

(a) you should obtain an acknowledgement of receipt of the property; and

(b) if they have been passed to a third party on the *client's* instructions, you should obtain such instructions in writing.

Rule 7: Execution-only business

7.1 If you arrange for a *client* on an *execution-only* basis any *transaction* involving a *retail investment product*, you must send the *client* written confirmation to the effect that:

(a) the *client* had not sought and was not given any advice from you in connection with the *transaction*; or

(b) the *client* was given advice from you in connection with that *transaction* but nevertheless persisted in wishing the *transaction* to be effected,

and in either case the *transaction* is effected on the *client's* explicit instructions.

Rule 8: Retention of records

8.1 Each record which is made under these rules shall be kept for at least six years from the date it is made.

PART 3: INSURANCE DISTRIBUTION ACTIVITIES

Rule 9: Communication and disclosure

9.1 You must ensure that, in relation to *insurance distribution*:

(a) you communicate all information, including marketing communications, in a way that is clear, fair and not misleading.

(b) your marketing communications are always clearly identifiable as such.

Rule 10: General information to be provided

10.1 In good time before the conclusion of a *contract of insurance*, you must disclose the following information to *clients*:

(a) whether you provide a *personal recommendation* about the insurance products offered;

(b) the procedures allowing *clients* and other interested parties to register complaints about you and information about the out-of-court complaint and redress procedures available for the settlement of disputes between you and your *clients*;

(c) whether you are representing the *client* or acting for and on behalf of the *insurer*;

(d) whether you have a direct or indirect holding representing 10% or more of the *voting rights* or capital in a relevant *insurance undertaking*;

(e) whether a given *insurance undertaking* or its parent undertaking has a direct or indirect holding representing 10% or more of the *voting rights* or capital in the *authorised body*.

Rule 11: Scope of service

11.1 Where you propose, or give a *client* a *personal recommendation* for, a *contract of insurance*, then in good time before the conclusion of an initial *contract of insurance* and if necessary on its amendment or renewal, you must provide the *client* with information on whether you:

(a) give a *personal recommendation* on the basis of a fair and personal analysis;

(b) are under a contractual obligation to conduct *insurance distribution* exclusively with one or more *insurance undertakings*, in which case you must provide the names of those *insurance undertakings*; or

(c) are not under a contractual obligation to conduct *insurance distribution* exclusively with one or more *insurance undertakings* and do not give advice on the basis of a fair and personal analysis, in which case you must provide the names of the *insurance undertakings* with which you may and do conduct business.

11.2 If you inform a *client* that you give a *personal recommendation* on the basis of a fair and personal analysis:

(a) you must give that personal recommendation on the basis of an analysis of a sufficiently large number of insurance contracts available on the market to enable it to make that recommendation; and

(b) that personal recommendation must be in accordance with professional criteria regarding which contract of insurance would be adequate to meet the client's needs.

Rule 12: Demands and needs

12.1 Prior to the conclusion of a *contract of insurance*, you must specify on the basis of information obtained from the *client*, the demands and needs of that *client*.

12.2 The details must be adapted according to the complexity of the *contract of insurance* proposed and the individual circumstances of the *client*.

12.3 You must give the *client* a statement of the *client's* demands and needs prior to the conclusion of a *contract of insurance*.

12.4 Any *contract of insurance* proposed by you must be consistent with the *client's* demands and needs and where you have given a *personal recommendation* to the *client*, you must, in addition to the statement of the demands and needs, provide the *client* with a personalised explanation of why a particular *contract of insurance* would best meet the *client's* demands and needs.

Rule 13: Use of intermediaries

13.1 You must not use, or propose to use, the services of another *person* consisting of:

(a) *insurance distribution*;

(b) *reinsurance distribution*;

(c) *insurance distribution activity*; or

(d) *home finance mediation activity*,

unless the *person*:

(i) has permission to carry on the activity under Part 4A *FSMA*;

(ii) is permitted to carry on the activity under an exemption made in or under *FSMA*, to the general prohibition set out in section 19 of *FSMA*;

(iii) in relation to *insurance distribution activity*, is not carrying on this activity in the *UK*; or

(iv) in relation to *home finance mediation activity*, is not carrying on this activity in the *UK*.

13.2 Before using the services of the intermediary, you must check the *Financial Services Register* and use the services of that person only if the relevant register indicates that the person is registered for that purpose.

Rule 14: Treating complaints fairly

14.1 Notwithstanding your complaints handling obligations in the *SRA Code of Conduct for Firms*, you must have in place and operate appropriate and effective procedures for registering and responding to complaints from a person who is not a *client*.

Rule 15: Remuneration and the client's best interests

15.1 You must not:

(a) be *remunerated*; or

(b) *remunerate* or assess the performance of the firm's *employees*,

in a way that conflicts with their duty to act in each *client's* best interest.

15.2 In particular, you must not make any arrangement by way of *remuneration*, sales target or otherwise that could provide an incentive to the firm or its *employees* to recommend a particular *contract of insurance* to a *client* when it could offer a different *contract of insurance* which would better meet its *client's* needs.

Rule 16: Remuneration disclosure

16.1 In good time before the conclusion of the initial *contract of insurance* and if necessary, on its amendment or renewal, you must provide the *client* with information:

(a) on the nature of the *remuneration* received in relation to the *contract* of *insurance*;

(b) about whether in relation to the contract you work on the basis of:

(i) a fee, that is *remuneration* paid directly by the *client*;

(ii) a commission of any kind, that is *remuneration* included in the premium;

(iii) any other type of *remuneration*, including an economic benefit of any kind offered or given in connection with the contract; or

(iv) a combination of any type of *remuneration* set out above in (i), (ii) and (iii).

Rule 17: Fee disclosure: additional requirements

17.1 Where a fee is payable, you must inform the *client* of the amount of the fee before the *client* incurs liability to pay the fee, or before conclusion of the *contract of insurance*, whichever is earlier.

17.2 To the extent that it is not possible for the amount in rule 17.1 to be given, you must give the *client* the basis for its calculation.

17.3 This rule applies to all such fees that may be charged during the life of the *policy*.

Rule 18: Means of communication to clients

18.1 Rule 18 applies to all information required to be provided to a *client* in this Part.

18.2 You must communicate information to the *client* on paper or using any of the following means:

(a) a *durable medium* other than paper where the following conditions are satisfied:

    (i) the use of a *durable medium* other than paper is appropriate in the context of the business conducted between the firm and the *client*; and

    (ii) the *client* has been given the choice between information on paper and on a *durable medium* other than paper and has chosen a *durable medium* other than paper; or

(b) on a website (where it does not constitute a *durable medium*) where the following conditions are satisfied:

    (i) the provision of that information by means of a website is appropriate in the context of the business conducted between you and the *client*;

    (ii) the *client* has consented to the provision of that information by means of a website;

    (iii) the *client* has been notified electronically of the address of the website, and the place on the website where that information can be accessed; and

    (iv) you ensure that the information remains accessible on the website for such period of time as the *client* may reasonably need to consult it.

18.3 For the purposes of rules 18.2(a)(i) and (b)(i), the provision of information using a *durable medium* other than paper or by means of a website shall be regarded as appropriate in the context of the business conducted between you and the *client* if there is evidence that the *client* has regular access to the internet. The provision by the *client* of an e-mail address for the purposes of that business is sufficient evidence.

18.4 You must communicate the information:

(a) in a clear and accurate manner, comprehensible to the *client*;

(b) in an official language of the Member State in which the insured risk, or proposed insured risk, is situated or in any other language agreed upon by the parties; and

(c) free of charge.

18.5 Where you communicate the information using a *durable medium* other than paper or by means of a website, you must, upon request and free of charge, send the *client* a paper copy of the information.

18.6 You must ensure that a *client's* choice or consent to receive the information by means of a website (whether a *durable medium* or where the conditions under rule 18.2(b) are satisfied) is an active and informed choice or consent.

18.7 In the case of services supplied to the *client* by telephone that are subject to the Financial Services (Distance Marketing) Regulations 2004:

(a) the information must be given in accordance with those regulations; and

(b) if prior to the conclusion of the *contract of insurance* the information is provided:

    (i) orally; or

    (ii) on a *durable medium* other than paper,

you must also provide the information to the *client* in accordance with rule 18.2 immediately after the conclusion of the *contract of insurance*.

Rule 19: Cross-selling requirements where insurance is the ancillary product

19.1 When you offer a non-insurance ancillary product or service as part of a package or in the same agreement with an insurance product, you must:

(a) inform the *client* whether it is possible to buy the components separately and, if so must provide the *client* with an adequate description of:

    (i) the different components;

    (ii) where applicable, any way in which the risk or insurance coverage resulting from the agreement or package differs from that associated with taking the components separately; and

(b) provide the *client* with separate evidence of the charges and costs of each component.

19.2 When you offer an insurance product ancillary to and as part of a package or in the same agreement with a non-insurance product or service, you must offer the *client* the option of buying the non-insurance goods or services separately.

19.3 Rule 19.2 does not apply where the non-insurance product or service is any of the following:

(a) investment service or activities;

(b) a *credit agreement* as defined in point 3 of article 4 of the *MCD* which is:

    (i) an *MCD credit agreement*;

    (ii) an exempt *MCD credit agreement*;

    (iii) a *CBTL credit agreement*; or

    (iv) a *credit agreement* referred to in articles 72G(3B) and (4) of the *Regulated Activities Order*; or

(c) a payment account as defined in point 3 of Article 2 of Directive 2014/92/EU.

19.4 Rule 19 shall not prevent the distribution of insurance products which provide coverage for various types of risks (multi-risk insurance policies).

19.5 In the cases referred to in rules 19.1 and 19.2, you must still comply with other provisions in this Part relating to the offer and sale of insurance products that form part of the package or agreement, including specifying the demands and needs of the *client* in accordance with rule 12.

Rule 20: Professional and organisational requirements

20.1 You must ensure that:

(a) the firm and each relevant *employee* possesses appropriate knowledge and ability in order to complete their tasks and perform duties adequately; and

(b) that all the persons in its management structure and any staff directly involved in *insurance distribution activities* are of good repute.

20.2 In considering a person's good repute, you must as a minimum ensure that the person:

(a) has a clean criminal record or any other national equivalent in relation to serious criminal offences linked to crimes against property or other crimes related to financial activities; and

(b) has not previously been declared bankrupt,

unless they have been rehabilitated in accordance with national law.

Rule 21: Insurance product information document and appropriate information

21.1 You must ensure that the *client* is given objective and relevant information about a *policy* in good time prior to the conclusion of the *policy*, so that the *client* can make an informed decision.

21.2 You must provide the information in rule 21.1 to the *client*:

(a) whether or not you give a *personal recommendation*; and

(b) irrespective of the fact that the *policy* is offered as part of a package with:

(i) a non-insurance product or service; or

(ii) another *policy*.

21.3 You must ensure that the level of information provided takes into account the complexity of the *policy* and the individual circumstances of the *client*.

21.4 When dealing with a *client* who is an individual and who is acting for purposes which are outside his trade or profession the information provided under rule 21.1 must include an *Insurance Product Information Document*.

21.5 You must provide the information required in rule 21.4 by way of an *Insurance Product Information Document* for each *policy* (other than a *pure protection contract*).

21.6 Where you distribute *contracts of insurance*, you must have in place adequate arrangements to:

(a) obtain from the manufacturer of the *contract of insurance*:

   (i)   all appropriate information on the *contract of insurance* and the product approval process; and

   (ii) the identified target market of the *contract of insurance*; and

(b) understand the characteristics and the identified target market of each *contract of insurance*.

Rule 22: Exclusions for large risks

22.1 Only rules 9, 13, 14, 18, 19, 20 and 22 apply where you carry on *insurance distribution activities* for commercial *clients* in relation to *contracts of insurance* covering risks within the following categories:

(a) railway rolling stock, aircraft, ships (sea, lake, river and canal vessels), goods in transit, aircraft liability and liability of ships (sea, lake, river and canal vessels);

(b) credit and suretyship, where the policyholder is engaged professionally in an industrial or commercial activity or in one of the liberal professions, and the risks relate to such activity;

(c) land vehicles (other than railway rolling stock), fire and natural forces, other damage to property, motor vehicle liability, general liability, and miscellaneous financial loss, in so far as the policyholder exceeds the limits of at least two of the following three criteria:

   (i)   balance sheet total: £6.2 million;

   (ii) net turnover: £12.8 million;

   (iii) average number of employees during the financial year: 250.

PART 4: CREDIT–RELATED REGULATED FINANCIAL SERVICES ACTIVITIES

Rule 23: Disclosure of information

23.1 Where you undertake *credit-related regulated financial services activities* for a *client*, you must ensure that information in connection with such activities and any agreements to which they relate are communicated to the *client* in a way that is clear, fair and not misleading.

23.2 Where you carry on the activity of *credit broking*, you must indicate in any advertising and documentation intended for consumers or *clients* the extent and scope of your *credit broking* activities, in particular whether you work exclusively with one or more lenders or as an independent broker.

Rule 24: Regulated credit agreements

24.1 Where you carry on a *credit-related regulated financial services* activity involving a proposed *regulated credit agreement*, you must:

(a) provide adequate explanations to the *client* in order to enable the *client* to assess whether the proposed *regulated credit agreement* is suitable to the *client's* needs and financial situation; and

(b) when providing such explanations, comply with the requirements of the *FCA* Consumer Credit sourcebook 4.2.5R.

24.2 Before entering into a *regulated credit agreement* as lender, you must assess the *client's* creditworthiness on the basis of sufficient information to enable you to make the assessment, where appropriate such information will be obtained from the *client* and, where necessary, from a credit reference agency.

24.3 After entering into a *regulated credit agreement* where you are the lender, if the parties agree to change the total amount of credit, you must update the financial information you hold concerning the *client* and assess the *client's* creditworthiness before any significant increase in the total amount of credit.

24.4 In the event of you assigning to a third party your rights as lender in relation to a *regulated credit agreement*, you must inform the *client* of the assignment.

Rule 25: Appropriation of payments

25.1 Where you are entitled to payments from the same *client* in respect of two or more *regulated credit agreements*, you must allow the *client* to put any payments made, in respect of those agreements, towards the satisfaction of the sum due under any one or more of the agreements in such proportions as the *client* thinks fit.

Rule 26: Consumer credit guidance

26.1 Where you undertake *credit-related regulated financial services activities*, you must have regard to any guidance issued by the *SRA* from time to time relating to such activities.

Supplemental notes

Made by the SRA Board on 30 May 2018.

Made under section 31 of the Solicitors Act 1974, section 9 of the Administration of Justice Act 1985, section 83 of the Legal Services Act 2007 and section 332 of the Financial Services and Markets Act 2000.

[Last updated: 31 December 2020]

SRA Overseas and Cross-border Practice Rules

INTRODUCTION

Part A of these rules sets out provisions for those who have established to provide legal services outside of England and Wales, for example as an overseas representative, or a branch office or subsidiary of an authorised firm. The rules set out in Part A are a modified version of the SRA Principles, together with key standards relating to client money and assets, and information and reporting requirements.

Authorised firms are required to ensure that those overseas practices for which they are responsible, and those who manage and own those overseas practices, meet the principles and standards set out in Part A of these rules. Regulated individuals who are established overseas must also meet the principles and standards set out in Part A of these rules, in place of the SRA Principles and Code of Conduct for Individuals. These rules do not apply to those who are providing services on a temporary basis from outside the jurisdiction; instead, the SRA Principles and Code of Conduct for Individuals will apply to them.

This reflects the fact that detailed regulatory requirements are less appropriate in a situation where the services are being provided from outside the jurisdiction, and where there will be different legal, regulatory and cultural practices. However, authorised firms will themselves be required to meet the full requirements of our regulatory arrangements and individuals established overseas will need to meet those requirements of our other rules and regulations which apply to them as solicitors or RELs (for example in respect of their character and suitability, and authorisation requirements).

The Cross-border Practice Rules set out in Part B of these rules apply to those who are engaged in professional activities in another State that is a member of the Council of the Bars and Law Societies of Europe (CCBE) and those who are in professional contact with a lawyer of another CCBE State whether or not they are physically present in that State.

This introduction does not form part of the SRA Overseas and Cross-border Practice Rules.

PART A: OVERSEAS RULES

Rule 1: Application

1.1 The Overseas Rules apply to you:

   (a) as a *regulated individual* who is *practising overseas*, in place of the SRA Principles and the *SRA Code of Conduct for Individuals*; or

   (b) as a *responsible authorised body* in that you must ensure that your *overseas practice* and the individual *managers*, *members* and *owners* that are involved in the day to day or strategic management of your *overseas practice*, comply with the Overseas Rules. Your *overseas practice* and these individual *managers*, and *members* and *owners* of your *overseas practice* are together referred to as those "for whom you are responsible" for the purposes of these rules.

1.2 In the event of any conflict between the Overseas Rules and any requirements placed on you or on those for whom you are responsible by local law or regulation, then local law or regulation must prevail, with the exception of Overseas Principle 2 which must be observed at all times.

1.3 Notwithstanding rule 1.1, the SRA Principles and the *SRA Code of Conduct for Individuals* will apply instead of the Overseas Rules if you are a *solicitor* or an *REL*, and your practice predominantly comprises the provision of legal services to *clients* within England and Wales, or in relation to *assets* located in England and Wales.

Rule 2: Overseas Principles

2.1 You act:

1. in a way that upholds the constitutional principle of the rule of law and the proper administration of justice in England and Wales.

2. in a way that upholds public trust and confidence in the *solicitors'* profession of England and Wales and in legal services provided by authorised *persons*.

3. with independence.

4. with honesty.

5. with integrity.

6. in a way that encourages equality, diversity and inclusion having regard to the legal, regulatory and cultural context in which you are *practising overseas*.

7. in the best interests of each client.

Rule 3: Dealings with client money

3.1 In all dealings you have with *client money (overseas)* you must:

(a) safeguard *client* money and *assets* entrusted to you;

(b) keep *client money (overseas)*, separate from money which belongs to you;

(c) on receipt, pay *client money (overseas)* promptly into, and hold it in, an *overseas client account*, unless:

    (i) to do so would conflict with your obligations under local law or regulation or with any obligation relating to any specified office or appointment you hold; or

(ii)   you agree in the individual circumstances an alternative arrangement in writing with your *client* or the third party for whom the money is held;

(d) only withdraw *client money (overseas)* from an *overseas client account*:

(i)   for the purposes for which it is being held; or

(ii)   following receipt of instructions from the *client*, or the third party for whom the money is held.

(e) return *client money (overseas)* promptly to the *client* or third party for whom money is held as soon as there is no longer any proper reason to retain those funds;

(f) have effective accounting systems and proper controls over those systems in order to ensure compliance with these rules;

(g) keep and maintain for at least six years accurate, contemporaneous and chronological *accounting records* in order to provide details of all money received and paid from all *overseas client accounts* and to show a running balance of all *client money (overseas)* held in those accounts; and

(h) account to *clients* or third parties for a fair sum of *interest* on any *client money (overseas)* held by you on their behalf, as required by local law and customs of the jurisdiction in which you are practising and otherwise when it is fair and reasonable to do so in all circumstances. You may by a written agreement come to a different arrangement with the *client* or the third party for whom the money is held as to the payment of *interest*, but you must provide sufficient information to enable them to give informed consent.

Rule 4: Reporting, cooperation and accountability

4.1   You must cooperate with the *SRA*, other regulators, ombudsmen and those bodies in England and Wales, with a role overseeing and supervising the delivery of, or investigating in relation to, legal services.

4.2   You must monitor compliance with these rules, and report any serious breach to the *SRA* when this occurs, or as soon as reasonably practicable thereafter.

4.3   You must notify the *SRA* promptly if:

(a) you become aware that you or anyone for whom you are responsible is convicted by any *court* of a criminal offence or becomes subject to disciplinary action by another regulator; or

(b) you have grounds to believe that you or anyone for whom you are responsible is in serious financial difficulty.

4.4   You must respond promptly to the *SRA* and:

(a) provide full and accurate explanations, information and documentation in response to any requests or requirement; and

(b) ensure that relevant information which is held by you, or by third parties carrying out functions on your behalf which are critical to the delivery of your legal services, is available for inspection by the *SRA*.

4.5 If you are a *responsible authorised body*, the *SRA* may, on reasonable notice, require you to obtain an accountant's report in respect of your *overseas practice*. The report must:

(a) confirm whether the report should be qualified on the basis of a failure to comply with these rules, such that money belonging to *clients* or third parties is, or has been, or is likely to be placed, at risk; and

(b) be signed by a qualified accountant approved by the *SRA*.

4.6 Any obligation under this section to notify or provide information to the *SRA* will be satisfied if you provide information to your firm's *COLP* or *COFA*, as and where appropriate, on the understanding that they will do so.

PART B: CROSS-BORDER PRACTICE RULES

Rule 5: Cross-border Practice Rules

5.1 This Part applies to *European cross-border practice* from any office by:

(a) *solicitors*;

(b) *managers* of *authorised bodies* who are not authorised by an *approved regulator* (other than the *SRA*) under the *LSA*; and

(c) *authorised bodies*.

5.2 These rules apply to *European cross-border practice* from an office in England and Wales by:

(a) *RELs*; and

(b) *RFLs* who are *managers* or *employees* of an *authorised body*.

5.3 When engaged in *European cross-border practice* you must ensure that you comply with any applicable provisions of the Council of the Bars and Law Societies of Europe's Code of Conduct for European lawyers.

Supplemental notes

Made by the SRA Board on 30 May 2018.

Rules made under sections 31, 32, 33A and 34 of the Solicitors Act 1974, section 9 of the Administration of Justice Act 1985 and section 83 of, and paragraph 20 of Schedule 11 to, the Legal Services Act 2007.

[Last updated: 25 November 2019]

SRA Regulatory and Disciplinary Procedure Rules

INTRODUCTION

These rules set out how we investigate and take disciplinary and regulatory action, for breaches of our rules and regulatory requirements. They apply to solicitors, RELs, and RFLs as well as the firms we authorise and those who work for them.

The sanctions and controls we can impose as a result of our investigation will depend on the scope of our statutory powers and will be determined in accordance with our Enforcement Strategy.

This introduction does not form part of the SRA Regulatory and Disciplinary Procedure Rules.

Rule 1: Assessing reports

1.1 The *SRA* shall assess any allegation which comes to, or is brought to, its attention in respect of a relevant *person* to decide if it should be considered under rule 3.

1.2 A matter is an allegation in respect of a *person* for the purpose of these rules if it raises a question that the *person*:

(a) is a *solicitor*, an *REL* or *RFL* and has committed professional misconduct;

(b) has committed or is responsible for a serious breach of any regulatory obligation placed on them by the *SRA's regulatory arrangements*, section 56 of the Legal Aid, Sentencing and Punishment of Offenders Act 2012, section 58 of the Criminal Justice and Courts Act 2015, section 6 of the Civil Liability Act 2018, the Money Laundering, Terrorist Financing and Transfer of Funds Regulations 2017, the Financial Guidance and Claims Act 2018 or any equivalent legislative requirements that may succeed the same;

(c) is a *manager* or employee of an *authorised body* and is responsible for a serious breach by the body of any regulatory obligation placed on it by the *SRA's regulatory arrangements*;

(d) is not a *solicitor* and has been convicted of a criminal offence, or been involved in conduct related to the provision of legal services, of a nature that indicates it would be undesirable for them to be involved in legal practice;

(e) in relation to a *licensed body*, has committed or substantially contributed to a serious breach of any regulatory obligation of a nature that indicates it is undesirable for them to carry out activities as a *HOLP*, *HOFA*, *manager* or employee of an *authorised body*;

(f) has otherwise engaged in conduct that indicates they should be made subject to a decision under rule 3.1.

Rule 2: The investigation process

2.1 The *SRA* may carry out such investigations, and in doing so may exercise any of its investigative powers, as it considers appropriate:

(a) to identify whether a matter comprises an allegation under rule 1.2, or

(b) to the consideration of an allegation under rule 3.

2.2 As soon as reasonably practicable after commencing an investigation under rule 2.1(b), the *SRA* will inform the relevant *person* accordingly and their employer, unless and to the extent that it considers that it would not be in the public interest to do so.

2.3 Before making a decision under rule 3, the *SRA* shall give notice to the relevant *person*:

(a) setting out the allegation and the facts in support;

(b) summarising any regulatory or other history relating to the relevant *person*, or any associated *person*, which is relevant to the allegation, including to the question of propensity;

(c) where appropriate, making a recommendation as to the decision to be made under rule 3, regarding publication under rule 9, and costs under rule 10; and

(d) accompanied by any evidence or documentation that the *SRA* considers to be relevant to the allegation, and

inviting the person to respond with written representations within such period as the *SRA* may specify (which must be no less than 14 days from the date of the notice).

2.4 At any stage, an *authorised decision maker* may decide to take no further action in respect of an allegation and to close the matter. If so, the *authorised decision maker* may decide to issue advice to the relevant *person*, or a warning regarding their future conduct or behaviour, but it must give notice under rule 2.3 before doing so.

2.5 The *SRA* may dispense with the giving of notice under rule 2.3 or 2.4 where:

(a) it intends to include a further allegation in a matter already subject to an application or ongoing proceedings before the *Tribunal*;

(b) it intends to make an application to the *Tribunal* in a case in which it is exercising its powers of *intervention* as a matter of urgency; or

(c) it is otherwise in the public interest to do so.

2.6 The *SRA* must inform the relevant *person*, their employer (where they were informed of the investigation under rule 2.2) and, where practicable, any person who reported the allegation to the *SRA*, of any decision to close a matter under rule 2.4, together with reasons.

2.7 At any stage the *SRA* may decide to exercise its powers of *intervention* or to take action in relation to the approval of a person or the holding of an interest in accordance with rule 13.8 or 13.9 of the SRA Authorisation of Firms Rules or Schedule 13 to the *LSA*.

Rule 3: Consideration by authorised decision makers

3.1 On finding that an allegation is proved (save for sub-paragraph (g)), an *authorised decision maker* may decide as appropriate in respect of a relevant *person* to:

   (a) give a written rebuke, in accordance with section 44D(2)(a) of the *SA* or paragraph 14B(2)(a), Schedule 2 to the *AJA*;

   (b) direct the payment of a financial penalty in accordance with section 44D(2)(b) of the *SA*, paragraph 14B(2)(b) of Schedule 2 to the *AJA* or section 95 of the *LSA*, together with the amount of any penalty;

   (c) disqualify a person from acting as a *HOLP* or *HOFA*, *manager* or employee of a body licensed under the *LSA* in accordance with section 99 of the *LSA*;

   (d) make an order to control the person's activities in connection with legal practice, in accordance with section 43(2) of the *SA*;

   (e) impose a condition on the practising certificate of a *solicitor*, the registration of an *REL* or *RFL* or the authorisation of a body for such period as may be specified, in accordance with section 13A(1) of the *SA*, paragraph 2A(1) of Schedule 14 to the Courts and Legal Services Act 1990, section 9(2G) of the *AJA* or section 85 of the *LSA* and regulation 19 of The European Communities (Lawyer's Practice) Regulations 2000;

   (f) revoke or suspend authorisation to practise under the SRA Authorisation of Firms Rules;

   (g) make an application to the *Tribunal* under section 47 of the *SA* for the allegation to be considered.

3.2 At any stage, an *authorised decision maker* may:

   (a) pending a final decision under rule 3.1 or by the *Tribunal*, impose interim conditions on the practising certificate of a *solicitor*, the registration of an *REL* or *RFL* or the authorisation of a body, where satisfied it is necessary for the protection of the public or in the public interest to do so; or

   (b) following an application to the *Tribunal* under section 47 of the *SA* in circumstances in which the *solicitor*, *REL* or *RFL* has been convicted of an indictable offence or an offence involving dishonesty or deception, suspend or continue a suspension of their practising certificate or registration in accordance with section 13B of the *SA*.

3.3 As soon as reasonably practicable, the *SRA* shall give notice to the relevant *person* of any decision made under this rule, together with reasons, and will inform the *person* of any right they may have to apply for a review or appeal of the decision.

3.4 A decision is made on the date notice of it is given under rule 3.3.

3.5 Conditions imposed under rule 3.2(a) shall take effect immediately or on such other date as may be specified by the *authorised decision maker.*

Rule 4: Decisions to impose a financial penalty

4.1 An *authorised decision maker* may decide to direct the payment of a financial penalty under rule 3.1(b), where this is appropriate to:

(a) remove any financial or other benefit arising from the conduct;

(b) maintain professional standards; or

(c) uphold public confidence in the *solicitors'* profession and in legal services provided by *authorised persons.*

4.2 Where the *SRA* recommends the imposition of a financial penalty on a relevant *person*, it may, by notice, require the *person* to provide a statement as to their financial means which includes a statement of truth, within such period as the *SRA* may specify (which must be no less than 14 days from the date of the notice).

4.3 Where an *authorised decision maker* has directed a *person* to pay a financial penalty:

(a) such penalty shall be paid within a time and in the manner *prescribed*;

(b) the *SRA* may direct that the payment of all or part of the penalty be suspended on such terms as *prescribed.*

Rule 5: Decisions to disqualify a person

5.1 An *authorised decision maker* may decide to disqualify a *person* under rule 3.1(c) only where they are satisfied that it is undesirable for the *person* to engage in the relevant activity or activities.

Rule 6: Applications to the Tribunal

6.1 An *authorised decision maker* may decide to make an application to the *Tribunal* in respect of a firm or an individual under rule 3.1(g) only where they are satisfied that:

(a) there is a realistic prospect of the *Tribunal* making an order in respect of the allegation; and

(b) it is in the public interest to make the application.

6.2 Where an *authorised decision maker* has made an application to the *Tribunal*, the *SRA* may carry out such further investigations, and in doing so may exercise any of its investigative powers, as it considers appropriate.

Rule 7: Applications for termination of certain orders

7.1 Where a *person* has been:

(a) disqualified from acting as a *HOLP* or *HOFA*, or a *manager* or employee of a body licensed under the *LSA*;

(b) made subject by the *SRA* to an order under section 43(2) of the *SA*; or

(c) made subject by the *SRA* to an order suspending their practising certificate or registration in the *register of European lawyers* or the *register of foreign lawyers*,

where there has been a material change in circumstances, the relevant *person* may apply to the *SRA* seeking a decision that the disqualification or order should cease to be in force.

7.2 An *authorised decision maker* may decide that a disqualification should cease to be in force if they are satisfied that it is no longer undesirable for the disqualified person to engage in the relevant activity or activities.

Rule 8: Evidential and procedural matters

8.1 The *SRA* may vary the procedure set out in these rules where it considers that it is in the interests of justice, or in the overriding public interest, to do so.

8.2 A decision under rule 3 may be made by agreement between the relevant *person* and the *SRA*.

8.3 Before reaching a decision under rule 3, an *authorised decision maker* or adjudication panel may give directions for the fair and effective disposal of the matter.

8.4 Decisions of an adjudication panel are made by simple majority.

8.5 Where an allegation is being considered by an adjudication panel, the proceedings will generally be conducted in private by way of a meeting. However, the panel may decide to conduct a hearing, which it may decide should be held in public, if it considers it in the interests of justice to do so.

8.6 Where an adjudication panel have decided to consider an allegation at a hearing:

(a) the *SRA* shall send a notice informing the relevant *person* of the date, time and venue of the hearing, no less than 28 days before the date fixed for the hearing;

(b) the relevant *person* and the *SRA* shall have the right to attend and be represented; and

(c) the panel may, at any time, whether of its own initiative or on the application of a party, adjourn the hearing until such time and date as it thinks fit.

8.7 The civil standard of proof applies to all decisions made under these rules.

8.8 An *authorised decision maker* may admit any evidence they consider fair and relevant to the case before them, whether or not such evidence would be admissible in a *court*. This may include regulatory or other history relating to the relevant *person*, or any associated *person*, which is relevant to the allegation, including to the question of propensity.

8.9 A certificate of conviction, or a finding by a *court* or disciplinary or regulatory body, certified by a competent officer of the *court*, or relevant body in the *UK* or *overseas*, shall be conclusive evidence of the offence committed or finding reached, and the facts relied upon.

Rule 9: Disclosure and publication

9.1 The *SRA* may disclose or publish any information arising from or relating to an investigation, either in an individual case or a class of case, where it considers it to be in the public interest to do so.

9.2 The *SRA* shall publish any decision under rule 3.1 or 3.2, when the decision takes effect or at such later date as it may consider appropriate, unless it considers the particular circumstances outweigh the public interest in publication.

9.3 The *SRA* shall notify the Legal Services Board as soon as reasonably practicable:

(a) of any decision to disqualify a *person* under rule 3.1(c);

(b) of the results of any review of any decision to disqualify a *person* under rule 7; and

(c) of any decision that a *person's* disqualification should cease to be in force.

Rule 10: Costs

10.1 An *authorised decision maker* may require a *person* who is the subject of a decision under rule 3.1(a) to (f) to pay a charge in accordance with Schedule 1 to these rules.

10.2 The *authorised decision maker* may decide to charge less than the amount that would be payable in accordance with Schedule 1 if they consider that it would be just in all the circumstances to do so.

10.3 Any charge must be paid by the *person* in such time and manner as may be specified by the *authorised decision maker*.

SCHEDULE 1

1. This schedule sets out the basis for calculating the charges payable under rule 10.

2. The *SRA* will record the amount of time spent by the *SRA* or its agents in

investigating the matter, including time spent on correspondence, evidence gathering and analysis, and report writing.

3. The standard charges are as follows:

Number of hours spent investigating matter	Standard Charge
Under 2 hours	£300
2 hours or more but under 8 hours	£600
8 to 16 hours	£1350

4. In addition to the fixed charge of £1,350, where the time recorded under paragraph 2 above amounts to more than 16 hours, an extra charge of £75 for every additional hour spent will be applied (rounded up or down to the nearest half hour).

Supplemental notes

Made by the SRA Board on 30 May 2018.

Made under sections 31, 44C and 44D of the Solicitors Act 1974, section 9 of, and paragraphs 14A and 14B of Schedule 2 to, the Administration of Justice Act 1985, section 83 of, and paragraph 20 of Schedule 11 to, the Legal Services Act 2007 and the Legal Services Act 2007 (The Law Society and the Council of Licensed Conveyancers) (Modification of Functions) Order 2011.

[Last updated: 31 May 2021]

[14] SRA Statutory Trust Rules

INTRODUCTION

These rules set out what the SRA does with money it takes possession of following an intervention into a firm's and/or an individual's practice. We hold this money on trust for the people it belongs to. This type of trust is called a statutory trust. The people that the money belongs to are beneficiaries of the trust. We have produced guidance on the way that we deal with this money.

This introduction does not form part of the SRA Statutory Trust Rules.

PART 1: GENERAL

Rule 1: Holding statutory trust monies

1.1 The *SRA* shall place all *statutory trust monies* in an identifiable *statutory trust account*.

1.2 All interest earned on the funds held in any *statutory trust account* shall be paid into that account.

Rule 2: Identifying beneficial entitlements

2.1 The *SRA* will create a *reconciled list* or a *best list* in respect of *statutory trust monies* held, using the information which it has available.

2.2 In creating a *reconciled list* or a *best list*, any sums of money which are identified within a *statutory trust account* as being payments on account of *fees* or unpaid *disbursements*, or which are equivalent to the *costs* incurred in a matter to which the funds relate, will be treated as due to the *client* rather than the *intervened practitioner*, unless there is sufficient evidence of a bill or other written notification of *costs* having been sent to the *client*.

2.3 The *SRA* will attempt to contact all *persons* identified as having a potential beneficial interest in the *statutory trust monies* and invite them to submit a claim in accordance with rule 4.

Rule 3: Minimum level of funds

3.1 The *SRA* may set a minimum level of funds to which a *beneficiary* may be entitled within a *statutory trust account* below which it will not attempt to identify or locate potential *beneficiaries* on the basis that, in the opinion of the *SRA*, it would be unreasonable or disproportionate to do so.

3.2 The level in rule 3.1 applies to the sum identified as relating to a particular *beneficiary*, after the application of any pro-rata adjustment which may be made under rule 6.2 but without including any interest under rule 7.3.

PART 2: CLAIMS

Rule 4: Claimants to money

4.1   Unless the *SRA* agrees otherwise, every *claimant* must submit to the *SRA* a claim in the *prescribed* form accompanied by any documentation and other evidence as may be required by the *SRA*, and which must include, if requested by the *SRA*, a statement of truth.

Rule 5: Verification of claims

5.1   The *SRA* may verify the individual potential beneficial entitlements claimed under rule 4 by examining all available evidence.

Rule 6: Shortfall in statutory trust account

6.1   In cases where a shortfall is revealed between *statutory trust monies* held, and the beneficial entitlements shown in a *reconciled list* or *best list*, the *SRA* may rectify the position, in whole or in part, by the use of other monies taken into its possession in consequence of the intervention to which that list relates.

6.2   Where, having applied additional funds under rule 6.1, a shortfall still exists on a *statutory trust account*, the *SRA* will decide on the method for calculating how to distribute the funds that are available in the account to *beneficiaries*.

Rule 7: Distribution of beneficial entitlements

7.1   In a case where the accounting records of the *intervened practitioner* are *reconciled accounts*, payments to *beneficiaries* will be made on the basis of the *reconciled list*.

7.2   In a case where the accounting records of the *intervened practitioner* are not *reconciled accounts*, payments to *beneficiaries* will be made on the basis of the *best list*.

7.3   Any interest which has accrued on a *statutory trust account* under rule 1.2, will be distributed to *beneficiaries* on a pro-rata basis in proportion to the payments made to them under rule 7.1 or 7.2.

Rule 8: Residual balances

8.1   The *SRA* may use any funds which remain in a *statutory trust account* following the distribution to *beneficiaries* under rule 7 to reimburse any costs, charges, or other expenses, which it has incurred in establishing the beneficial entitlements to the *statutory trust monies* and in distributing the monies accordingly.

8.2   If funds remain in a *statutory trust account* after payment to *beneficiaries* and the reimbursement of costs, charges and expenses in accordance with rule 8.1, the *SRA* may transfer such remaining funds into the compensation fund held by the *SRA* and any claim to such funds under these rules shall be extinguished.

Rule 9: Interim payments

9.1 The *SRA* may make an interim payment to a *beneficiary* before the full distribution of funds in a *statutory trust account* takes place provided that the *SRA* is satisfied that the payment can be made without prejudicing other claims to those funds.

Supplemental notes

Made by the SRA Board on 30 May 2018.

Made under paragraph 6B of Schedule 1 to the Solicitors Act 1974, paragraphs 32 to 34 of Schedule 2 to the Administration of Justice Act 1985, and paragraph 6 of Schedule 14 to the Legal Services Act 2007, governing the treatment of sums vested in the Law Society under paragraphs 6 or 6A of Schedule 1 to the Solicitors Act 1974 and under paragraphs 3 or 4 of Schedule 14 to the Legal Services Act 2007.

[Last updated: 25 November 2019]

SRA Roll, Registers and Publication Regulations

INTRODUCTION

These regulations set out the nature and contents of the registers and the roll that the SRA is required to keep. They contain certain information about the individuals and firms that the SRA regulates and how we make this information available to the public.

This introduction does not form part of the SRA Roll, Registers and Publication Regulations.

Regulation 1: The roll and registers

1.1 The *SRA* shall keep in electronic form:

(a) the roll;

(b) a register of all *solicitors* who hold practising certificates;

(c) the *register of European lawyers*;

(d) the *register of foreign lawyers*; and

(e) a register of *authorised bodies*.

Regulation 2: Information in respect of individuals

2.1 The roll, and the registers in regulation 1.1(b) to (d) shall contain the following information in respect of each individual included in the same:

(a) their full name;

(b) their authorisation number;

(c) the date of their admission as a *solicitor* or commencement of their registration, as appropriate;

(d) in respect of *solicitors* that hold a current practising certificate, the fact that they do so and the commencement date of the certificate;

(e) in respect of *solicitors* whose practising certificate has expired, the expiry date;

(f) their main practising address;

(g) the name of all organisations through which they practise, and whether the organisation is authorised by the *SRA*, by another *approved regulator*, or is not authorised under the *LSA*. If they are not practising through an organisation, the fact that this is the case, and whether they are practising in accordance with regulation 10.2(a) of the SRA Authorisation of Individuals Regulations or the circumstances set out in 10.2(b)(ii) to (vii) of the same;

    (h) if they are not practising, an address for correspondence;

    (i) details of:

        (i) any conditions on their practising certificate or registration to which they are subject;

        (ii) any current suspension of their practising certificate or registration;

        (iii) any other decision subject to publication under rule 9.2 of the SRA Regulatory and Disciplinary Procedure Rules;

        (iv) any other order made by the *Tribunal*; and

        (v) the exercise by the *SRA* of any powers of *intervention* in relation to their practice.

Regulation 3: Information in respect of authorised bodies

3.1   The register of *authorised bodies* under regulation 1.1(e) shall contain the following information in respect of each body included within it:

    (a) the name under which the body is authorised;

    (b) the body's authorisation number;

    (c) the body's main practising address in the *UK*;

    (d) all the body's other practising addresses including addresses of its *overseas practices*;

    (e) any previous name under which the body has been authorised by the *SRA*;

    (f) any other trading styles used by the body;

    (g) the date from which the body's authorisation has effect;

    (h) the *prescribed* categories of work that the body provides;

    (i) the *reserved legal activities* that the body is authorised to carry on;

    (j) whether the body is a *recognised body*, a *recognised sole practice* or a *licensed body*;

    (k) details of:

        (i) any current condition to which the body's authorisation is subject;

        (ii) any suspension or revocation of the body's authorisation;

        (iii) any other decision subject to publication under rule 9.2 of the SRA Regulatory and Disciplinary Procedure Rules;

        (iv) any other order made by the *Tribunal*; and

        (v) the exercise by the *SRA* of any powers of *intervention* in relation to the body.

3.2   For each *licensed body* the register of *authorised bodies* must contain:

(a) the name of the individual who is designated as the body's *HOLP*, together with details of the *approved regulator* with whom that person is authorised;

(b) the name of the individual who is designated as the body's *HOFA*; and

(c) the body's registered office and registered number if it is an *LLP* or *company* and if it is a *charity*, its *charity* number.

Regulation 4: General provisions

4.1 The *SRA* may include in the roll or registers such other *prescribed* information it considers conducive to help it meet the *regulatory objectives*.

4.2 The *SRA* shall keep and publish lists of:

(a) orders made by the *Tribunal* and disciplinary or regulatory decisions made under the SRA Regulatory and Disciplinary Procedure Rules, in respect of individuals who are not *solicitors*, *RELs* or *RFLs* (including former *solicitors*, *RELs* or *RFLs*); and

(b) individuals whose practising certificate has expired or who have been struck off the roll, or whose registration has been revoked, together with details of any relevant decision.

Regulation 5: Publication of information

5.1 The *SRA* shall publish all entries on the roll or registers, except for any address included under regulation 2.1(h).

5.2 If the *SRA* considers that it would be in the public interest to do so, it may withhold from publication any or all of the information subject to publication under regulation 5.1.

5.3 The *SRA* may publish such further information or classes of information as it may consider in the public interest to do so.

Supplemental notes

Made by the SRA Board on 30 May 2018.

Made under section 28 of the Solicitors Act 1974, section 89 of, and paragraphs 2 and 3 of Schedule 14 to, the Courts and Legal Services Act 1990, section 9 of the Administration of Justice Act 1985 and section 83 of, and Schedule 11 to, the Legal Services Act 2007.

[Last updated: 25 November 2019]

INTRODUCTION

These rules set out the information authorised firms, and individuals providing services to the public from outside authorised firms, should make available to clients and potential clients.

The rules aim to ensure people have accurate and relevant information about a solicitor or firm when they are considering purchasing legal services and will help members of the public and small businesses make informed choices, improving competition in the legal market.

This introduction does not form part of the SRA Transparency Rules.

Rule 1: Costs information

1.1 An *authorised body*, [or an individual practising in the circumstances set out in regulation 10.2(b)(i) to (vii) of the SRA Authorisation of Individuals Regulations,] who publishes as part of its usual business the availability of any of the services set out at rule 1.3 to individuals or at rule 1.4 to businesses, must, in relation to those services, publish on its website cost information in accordance with rule 1.5 and 1.6.

1.2 Rule 1.1 does not apply to publicly funded work.

1.3 The services in relation to individuals are:

(a) the conveyance of residential real property or real estate which comprise:

(i) freehold or leasehold sales or purchases; or

(ii) mortgages or re-mortgages;

(b) the collection and distribution of *assets* belonging to a person following their death, where these are within the *UK* and the matters are not contested;

(c) the preparation and submission of immigration applications, excluding asylum applications;

(d) the provision of advice and representation at the First-tier Tribunal (Immigration and Asylum Chamber) in relation to appeals against Home Office visa or immigration decisions, excluding asylum appeals;

(e) the provision of advice and representation at the Magistrates Court in relation to summary only road traffic offences dealt with at a single hearing;

(f) the provision of advice and representation to employees in relation to the bringing of claims before the Employment Tribunal against an employer for unfair dismissal or wrongful dismissal.

1.4   The services in relation to businesses are:

    (a)   the provision of advice and representation to employers in relation to defending claims before the Employment Tribunal brought by an employee for unfair dismissal or wrongful dismissal;

    (b)   debt recovery up to the value of £100,000;

    (c)   the provision of advice and assistance and representation in relation to licensing applications for business premises.

1.5   Costs information must include:

    (a)   the total cost of the service or, where not practicable, the average cost or range of costs;

    (b)   the basis for your charges, including any hourly rates or fixed fees;

    (c)   the experience and qualifications of anyone carrying out the work, and of their supervisors;

    (d)   a description of, and the cost of, any likely *disbursements*, and where the actual cost of a *disbursement* is not known, the average cost or range of costs;

    (e)   whether any fees or *disbursements* attract VAT and if so the amount of VAT they attract;

    (f)   details of what services are included in the price displayed, including the key stages of the matter and likely timescales for each stage, and details of any services that might reasonably be expected to be included in the price displayed but are not; and

    (g)   if you use conditional fee or damages based agreements, the circumstances in which *clients* may have to make any payments themselves for your services (including from any damages).

1.6   Cost information published under this rule must be clear and accessible and in a prominent place on your website.

Rule 2: Complaints information

2.1   An *authorised body*, or an individual practising in the circumstances set out in regulation 10.2(b)(i) to (vii) of the SRA Authorisation of Individuals Regulations, must publish on its website details of its complaints handling procedure including, details about how and when a complaint can be made to the *Legal Ombudsman* and to the *SRA*.

Rule 3: Publication

3.1   An *authorised body*, or an individual practising in the circumstances set out in regulation 10.2(b)(i) to (vii) of the SRA Authorisation of Individuals Regulations, that does not have a website, must make the information set out in rules 1 to 2 available on request.

Rule 4: Regulatory information

4.1 An *authorised body* must display in a prominent place on its website (or, in the case of a *licensed body*, the website relating to its legal services, if separate) its *SRA* number and the *SRA's* digital badge.

4.2 An *authorised body's* letterhead and e-mails must show its *SRA* authorisation number and the words "authorised and regulated by the Solicitors Regulation Authority".

4.3 A *solicitor*, an *REL* or *RFL* who is providing legal services to the public or a section of the public other than through a firm that is regulated by the *SRA*:

(a) where they are not required to meet the *MTC*, must before engagement inform all *clients* of this fact and specify that alternative insurance arrangements are in place if this is the case (together with information about the cover this provides, if requested); and

(b) where applicable, must inform all *clients* that they will not be eligible to apply for a grant from the SRA Compensation Fund.

4.4 Rule 4.3 does not apply to a *solicitor*, an *REL* or *RFL* that is working in an *authorised non-SRA firm* or a *non-commercial body*.

Supplemental notes

Made by the SRA Board on 30 May 2018.

Made under section 31 of the Solicitors Act 1974, section 9 of the Administration of Justice Act 1985 and section 83 of, and Schedule 11 to, the Legal Services Act 2007.

[Last updated: 25 November 2019]

SRA Indemnity (Enactment) Rules 2012

PART 1: THE ENACTMENT RULES

Rule 1: Authority

1.1 These Rules are made on 22 June 2012 by the Solicitors Regulation Authority Board under sections 37, 79 and 80 of the Solicitors Act 1974, section 9 of the Administration of Justice Act 1985, and paragraph 19 of Schedule 11 to the Legal Services Act 2007, with the approval of the Legal Services Board under paragraph 19 of Schedule 4 to the Legal Services Act 2007.

Rule 2: Commencement and application

2.1 The Solicitors' Indemnity Rules 1987 as amended from time to time shall be further amended with effect from 1 October 2012 and shall continue in force thereafter in the form annexed hereto in which form they may be known as the SRA Indemnity Rules 2012.

2.2 The Solicitors' Indemnity (Incorporated Practice) Rules 1991 as amended from time to time shall continue in force only in respect of the *indemnity periods* commencing on 1 September 1991 and 1 September 1992.

2.3 The *contributions* payable in respect of the *indemnity periods* commencing prior to 1 September 1996 shall remain unaltered.

2.4 In respect of any *indemnity periods* commencing on or after 1 September 1996 the *Society* shall retain the power under Rule 35 of the Solicitors' Indemnity Rules 1996 to determine supplementary *contributions* in respect of any such period.

2.5 The indemnity available in respect of the *indemnity periods* commencing prior to 1 October 2012 shall remain unaltered.

2.6 In these Rules the terms in italics will have the meaning set out in Rule 3.1 of the SRA Indemnity Rules 2012 annexed hereto.

Supplemental notes

These rules consist of one part split into two rules. The SRA Indemnity Rules 2012 form the annex to these rules.

[Last updated: 25 November 2019]

[18] **SRA Indemnity Rules 2012**

These rules form the annex to the SRA Indemnity (Enactment) Rules 2012.

PART 1: GENERAL PROVISIONS AND INTERPRETATION

Rule 1: Authority

1.1 These Rules are made on 22 June 2012 by the Solicitors Regulation Authority Board under sections 37, 79 and 80 of the Solicitors Act 1974, section 9 of the Administration of Justice Act 1985, and paragraph 19 of Schedule 11 to the Legal Services Act 2007, with the approval of the Legal Services Board under paragraph 19 of Schedule 4 to the Legal Services Act 2007.

1.2 These Rules regulate indemnity provision in respect of the practices of *solicitors*, *recognised bodies*, *RELs*, *RFLs*, and *licensed bodies* in respect of their *regulated activities* and certain other European lawyers, carried on wholly or in part in England and Wales.

Rule 2: Citation

2.1 These Rules may be cited as the SRA Indemnity Rules 2012.

Rule 3: Definitions and interpretation

3.1 The SRA Handbook Glossary 2012 (the Glossary) shall apply and unless the context otherwise requires:

   (a) all italicised terms shall be defined in accordance with the Glossary;

   (b) terms shall be interpreted in accordance with the Glossary;

   (c) a reference to a Rule is to a Rule forming part of these Rules, except in relation to Schedule 1 where a reference to a rule is to a rule in the Solicitors' Indemnity Rules 1999;

   (d) the Schedule to these Rules forms part of these Rules; and

   (e) these Rules will be governed by and interpreted in accordance with English law.

Rule 4: Establishment and maintenance of fund

4.1 The *Society* shall maintain the *fund* in accordance with these Rules.

4.2 The purpose of the *fund* is to provide indemnity against loss as mentioned in section 37 of the *SA* as extended by section 9 of the *AJA*, Schedule 4 paragraph 1(3) of the European Communities (Lawyer's Practice) Regulations 2000 and section 89 of the Courts and Legal Services Act 1990 in the circumstances, to the extent and subject to the conditions and exclusions specified by the Solicitors' Indemnity Rules 1987 as the same have been and are in force and amended and applied from time to time and by any future Rules continuing, amending, adding to, applying or re-enacting such or other Rules to provide such indemnity in respect of annual *indemnity periods* (starting in 1987) unless and until otherwise determined by future Rules.

4.3   The *fund* shall be maintained by *contributions* previously made by or on behalf of *solicitors*, *recognised bodies*, *RELs* and *RFLs* in respect of each *indemnity period* in accordance with Part III of the SRA Indemnity Rules 2011 (or any earlier corresponding provisions), and by any additional *contributions* in accordance with Rule 16.

4.4   The *Society* may maintain the *fund* as a single continuous *fund*, and any deficiency in respect of one *indemnity period* may be met in whole or part from *contributions* in respect of another *indemnity period* or *indemnity periods* and any balance in respect of one *indemnity period* may be applied to the benefit of any other *indemnity period* or *indemnity periods*.

4.5   The *fund* shall be held, managed and administered in accordance with Part IV of these Rules by Solicitors Indemnity Fund Limited, a company set up by the *Society* for this purpose, or by such other *person* or *persons* (including the *Society* itself) as the *Society* may designate for such purpose, in place of Solicitors Indemnity Fund Limited. References in these Rules to Solicitors Indemnity Fund Limited shall include any such other *person* or *persons*.

Rule 5: Indemnity Periods before 1 September 1987

5.1   The policies taken out and maintained and the certificates issued by the *Society* pursuant to the Solicitors' Indemnity Rules 1975 to 1986 shall continue to provide cover subject to and in accordance with their terms in respect of their respective periods up to and including 31 August 1987. They shall not provide cover in respect of any subsequent period.

Rule 6: Application of the Rules

6.1   These Rules shall apply to a *practice* carried on by:

(a)   a sole *solicitor*;

(b)   an *REL* practising as a *sole practitioner*;

(c)   a *recognised body*;

(d)   a *partnership* consisting of one or more *solicitors* and/or *RELs* and/or *recognised bodies* and/or *licensed bodies*;

(e)   a *partnership* consisting of one or more *solicitors* and/or *RELs*, together with one or more *RFLs*;

(f)   a *partnership* consisting of one or more *RELs* with or without one or more

RFLs, together with one or more *non-registered European lawyers* practising from one or more offices in any state to which the *Establishment Directive* applies, but outside England and Wales; and

(g) a *licensed body* in respect of its *regulated activities*.

Rule 7: Scope of indemnity

7.1 The following *persons*, namely:

(a) *solicitors*, former *solicitors*, *RELs*, *persons* formerly practising as *RELs*, *RFLs* practising in *partnership* with *solicitors* or *RELs*, *persons* formerly practising as *RFLs* in *partnership* with *solicitors* or *RELs*, *non-registered European lawyers* practising in *partnership* with *RELs*, and *persons* formerly practising as *non-registered European lawyers* in *partnership* with *RELs*;

(b) employees and former employees of the above;

(c) *recognised bodies* and former *recognised bodies*;

(d) officers and employees and former officers and employees of *recognised bodies* and former *recognised bodies*;

(e) *licensed bodies* and former *licensed bodies* in respect of their *regulated activities*; and

(f) *regulated persons*, including officers and employees and former officers and employees of *licensed bodies*,

shall be provided with indemnity out of the *fund* against loss arising from claims in respect of civil liability incurred in *private practice* in their aforesaid capacities or former capacities in the manner set out in Rule 10 and in the circumstances, to the extent and subject to the conditions and exclusions set out in Part II of these Rules and not otherwise.

PART 2: INDEMNITY COVER

Rule 8: Indemnity

Indemnity for ceased practices

8.1 Any *member* of a *previous practice* which ceased on or before 31 August 2000 who has at any time been either:

(a) an assured as a result of the issue of a certificate under one or more of the *master policies*, or

(b) a *person* entitled to be indemnified by virtue of the issue of a receipt under the Solicitors' Indemnity Rules 1987–1990 or a payment of Contribution and Value Added Tax thereon as stated in the Solicitors' Indemnity Rules 1991–1999, and who is not, at the time during the *indemnity period* when a claim is first made or intimated against him or her or when circumstances which might give rise to such a claim are first notified by him or her to Solicitors Indemnity Fund Limited, a *person* entitled or required to be indemnified in respect of claims arising from that *previous practice* by a policy of *qualifying insurance* or otherwise under the *SIIR*,

and the *previous practice*

shall be entitled to indemnity out of the *fund* in the manner, to the extent and subject to the conditions and exclusions set out in these Rules against:

(a) all loss (including liability for third party claimants' costs) incurred by the *previous practice* or any *member* thereof at any time arising directly from:

(i) any claim(s) first made or intimated against the *previous practice* or any *member* thereof during the *indemnity period* in respect of any description of civil liability whatsoever which may have been incurred in *private practice* by the *previous practice* or by a *member* as a *member* of such *previous practice*;

(ii) any claim in respect of any such description of civil liability as aforesaid, made or intimated against the *previous practice* or any *member* thereof, whether during or subsequent to the *indemnity period* arising out of circumstances notified to Solicitors Indemnity Fund Limited during the *indemnity period* as circumstances which might give rise to such a claim; and

(b) all costs and expenses incurred with the consent of Solicitors Indemnity Fund Limited (such consent not to be unreasonably withheld) in the defence or settlement or compromise of any such claim as aforesaid.

Eligible former principals

8.2 Rule 8.1 shall apply in addition in respect of any *principal* of a *previous practice* that is an *eligible former principal*.

8.3 In respect of any claim referred to in Rule 8.2 made by an *eligible former principal*, the extent of the indemnity (if any) to be provided by Solicitors Indemnity Fund Limited shall be limited to an amount equal to the lesser of:

(a) the Due Proportion of the Deductible (excluding any Penalty Deductible) in respect of the *eligible former principal* that would have been disregarded by Solicitors Indemnity Fund Limited in relation to the claim had it been made under the Solicitors' Indemnity Rules 1999; and

(b) such amount if any which the *relevant successor practice* is entitled to and seeks to recover from the *eligible former principal* in relation to the claim.

8.4 For the purposes of Rule 8.3, "Due Proportion", "Deductible" and "Penalty Deductible" shall have the meanings respectively given to them by the Solicitors' Indemnity Rules 1999, as set out in Schedule 1 to these Rules.

Expired run-off claims

8.5 Any firm or *person* shall be entitled to indemnity out of the *fund* in the manner, to the extent and subject to the conditions and exclusions set out in this Rule 8.5, in relation to an *expired run-off claim*, provided that:

(a) such claim is first notified to Solicitors Indemnity Fund Limited at any time between 1 September 2007 and 30 September 2021; and

(b) there is no *preceding qualifying insurance* which provides cover for such claim; and

(c) such claim does not relate to or arise out of any *claim* first made against an *insured* or *circumstances* first notified to the provider of such *preceding qualifying insurance*, in either case at a time when such *preceding qualifying insurance* was required to provide cover in respect thereof; and

(d) such *person* was an *insured* under the relevant *preceding qualifying insurance*.

Notwithstanding any other provision of these Rules:

(a) the obligations of the *fund* and/or any *insured* in respect of an *expired run-off claim* shall be in accordance with, and limited to, the *expired run-off cover*; and

(b) any obligation owed by any *insured* under the *preceding qualifying insurance* to the qualifying insurer which issued such insurance shall be deemed to be owed to Solicitors Indemnity Fund Limited in place of such qualifying insurer, unless and to the extent that Solicitors Indemnity Fund Limited in its absolute discretion otherwise agrees.

Rule 9: Exclusions from cover

9.1 The *fund* shall not afford any indemnity in respect of any loss arising out of any claim:

(a) for death, bodily injury, physical loss or physical damage to property of any kind whatsoever (other than property in the care, custody and control of the *previous practice* or *member* thereof in connection with its, his or her *private practice* for which it, he or she is responsible, not being property occupied or used by it, him or her for the purposes of the *previous practice*);

(b) for any alleged breach or other relief in respect of any *partnership* or *partnership* agreement between the *principals* in the *previous practice* or between any *principal* therein and any other *person* as *principals* in any other *previous practice*;

(c) for wrongful dismissal or termination of articles of clerkship or training contract or any other alleged breach or any other relief by either party in respect of any contract of employment by the *previous practice* or any *member* thereof; and/or for wrongful termination or any other alleged breach or any other relief by either party in respect of any contract for supply to or use by the *previous practice* or any *member* thereof of services and/or materials and/or equipment and/or other goods;

(d) for the payment of a trading debt incurred by the *previous practice* or any *member* thereof;

(e) in respect of any undertaking given by any *principal* in the *previous practice* or by a *recognised body* or *licensed body* or on his, her or its behalf (whether in his, her or its own name or in the name of the *previous practice*) to any *person* in connection with the provision of finance, property, assistance or other advantage whatsoever to or for the benefit of such *principal* or any other *principal* or of his or her or any other *principal's* spouse or children or of such *recognised body* or *licensed body* or of any business, firm, company, enterprise, association or venture owned or controlled by him, her or it or any other *principal* or in a beneficial capacity whether alone or in concert with others, EXCEPT to the extent that the *person* seeking indemnity shall establish that he, she or it was unaware that the undertaking was or was likely to be connected with the provision of any such finance, property, assistance or other advantage;

(f) in respect of any dishonest or fraudulent act or omission, but nothing in this exclusion shall prevent any particular *member* of the *previous practice* who was not concerned in such dishonesty or fraud being indemnified in accordance with these Rules in respect of any loss arising out of any claim in respect of any dishonest or fraudulent act or omission by any other such *member*;

(g) in respect of any liability incurred in connection with an *overseas practice*. In relation to a *previous practice* having any *overseas* offices deemed by paragraph (ii) of the definition of *separate practice* in Rule 3.1 to form a *separate practice*, a liability shall be deemed to have been incurred in connection with the office where or from which the major part of the work out of which the loss arose in respect of which indemnity is sought was being done. In the event of doubt as to which (if any) office satisfies this requirement, the liability shall be deemed to have been incurred in connection with the office to which the *person* who accepted the initial instructions was most closely connected;

(h) in respect of any liability incurred in connection with a *previous practice* in relation to which the obligation to pay *contribution* has been exempted under Rule 27 of the Solicitors' Indemnity Rules 2006 (or any earlier corresponding Rule) or, unless otherwise provided by the terms of the waiver, waived by the *Council* under Rule 19 (or under any corresponding earlier Rule);

(i) arising out of any circumstances or occurrences which have been notified under the *master policy* or any certificate issued under the *master policy* or any other insurance existing prior to 1 September 1987;

(j) in respect of any adjustment by way of claims loading or loss of discount which may at any future date or in respect of any future period be made by reference to any claim or claims first made or intimated during any *indemnity period*;

(k) in respect of any liability incurred by any *person* in his, her or its capacity as a shareholder or beneficial owner of a share in a body corporate that is either a *recognised body* or *licensed body* notwithstanding the definition of *principal* in Rule 3.1;

(l) in respect of any act or omission on the part of any *principal* whilst acting on behalf of the *previous practice* or any *member* thereof in connection with any matter affecting the business of the *previous practice* provided that at the time of such act or omission such *principal* was a *principal* in the *previous practice*;

(m) where the *previous practice* or any *member* thereof is entitled to indemnity under any insurance except in respect of any amount greater than the amount which would have been payable under such insurance in the absence of the indemnity provided by the *fund*.

9.2 For the avoidance of doubt, any claim or claims by any *member* or former *member* of any *previous practice* against any *member* or former *member* of any such *previous practice* for the payment of the whole or any part of the deductible paid or due in respect of a claim already notified or made under these Rules or any previous Rules is not a loss arising within the meaning of Rule 8 and shall in no event be recoverable hereunder.

9.3 The exclusions set out in this Rule 9 shall not apply in relation to an *expired run-off claim*, in respect of which the provisions of Rule 8.5 shall apply.

Rule 10: Manner of indemnity

10.1 Such indemnity shall be provided, according to the decision of Solicitors Indemnity Fund Limited as set out in Rule 10.2, in any one or any combination of the following ways:

(a) by payment, in or towards satisfaction of the claim and/or claimant's costs and expenses, to or to the order of the claimant making the claim;

(b) by payment, in respect of the claim and/or claimant's costs and expenses and/or costs and expenses incurred in respect of the defence or settlement or compromise of the claim, to or to the order of the *person* against whom the claim is made;

(c) by payment, in or towards discharge of costs and expenses incurred in respect of the defence or settlement or compromise of the claim, to or to the order of the legal advisers, adjusters or other persons by whom or in respect of whose services such costs and expenses were incurred;

(d) by payment to any firm or *person* in relation to an *expired run-off claim* who was an *insured* under the relevant *preceding qualifying insurance*.

10.2 Solicitors Indemnity Fund Limited shall in any particular case, and notwithstanding the insolvency or bankruptcy of any *person* for whom indemnity is provided, have the sole and absolute right to decide in which way or combination of ways indemnity is provided.

Rule 11: Source of indemnity

11.1 Any such indemnity shall be provided and any claim thereto shall lie and be made exclusively out of and against the *fund*.

11.2 Solicitors Indemnity Fund Limited shall have no obligation to provide indemnity save to the extent that the same can be provided out of the *fund*.

11.3 In no circumstances shall any claim to indemnity lie or be made against the *Society* or the *Council* or the Legal Services Board.

11.4 Save as provided in Rule 21, the *fund* shall be available exclusively for the purpose specified in Rule 4.2.

11.5 In no circumstances shall the *fund* or any part thereof be available or be treated by any *person* as available (whether by virtue of any claim, attachment, execution or proceeding or otherwise howsoever) for or in connection with any other purpose.

Rule 12: Maximum liability of the fund

12.1 The liability of the *fund* as stated in Rule 8.1(c) shall in no event exceed in respect of each such claim the indemnity limit for the *relevant indemnity period*.

12.2 All claims arising from the same act or omission (whether or not made or intimated or arising out of circumstances notified during the same *indemnity period* and whether or not involving the same or any number of different *practices* or *previous practices* and/or *members* of such *practices* or *previous practices*) shall be regarded as one claim.

12.3 If a payment exceeding the indemnity limit is made to dispose of any such claim (or, in circumstances within Rule 12.2, claims) for loss (including claimants' costs) such as stated in Rule 8.1(c), then any liability of the *fund* for costs and expenses under Rule 8.1(d) shall be limited to such proportion of such costs and expenses as the indemnity limit bears to the amount of the payment so made.

12.4 The provisions of this Rule 12 shall not apply in relation to an *expired run-off claim*, in respect of which the provisions of Rule 8.5 shall apply.

Rule 13: Indemnity limit

13.1 Save in relation to an *expired run-off claim*, in respect of which the provisions of Rule 8.5 shall apply, the indemnity limit shall be £1,000,000 each and every claim (including claimants' costs).

Rule 14: Conditions

14.1 The *previous practice* and each *member* thereof shall procure that notice to Solicitors Indemnity Fund Limited shall be given in writing as soon as practicable of:

(a) any claim(s) the subject of Rule 8 made or intimated during the *relevant indemnity period* against it, him or her of any claim for or likely to be for more than £500; or

(b) the receipt by it, him or her of notice of any intention to make any such claim(s).

14.2 The *previous practice* and any *member* thereof may also give notice in writing to Solicitors Indemnity Fund Limited of any circumstances of which it, he or she shall become aware which may (whether during or after the *relevant indemnity period*) give rise to any such claim(s).

14.3 Any notice given under Rule 14.2, will be effective only if, at the date when such notice was given, the circumstances known to and notified by the *previous practice* and/or *member* thereof, represent sufficient ground for a genuine and reasonable supposition on the part of the *previous practice* or *member* that those circumstances may give rise to a claim the subject of indemnity under Rule 8.

14.4 If notice is given to Solicitors Indemnity Fund Limited under Rule 14.1(b) or 14.2, any claim subsequently made (whether during or after the *relevant indemnity period*) pursuant to such an intention to claim or arising from circumstances so notified shall be deemed to have been made at the date when such notice was given.

14.5 The *previous practice* and each *member* thereof shall not admit liability for, or settle, any claim falling within Rule 8 or incur any costs or expenses in connection therewith without the prior consent of Solicitors Indemnity Fund Limited (such consent not to be unreasonably withheld).

14.6 Subject to Rule 14.7:

(a) the *previous practice* and each *member* thereof shall procure that Solicitors Indemnity Fund Limited shall be entitled at the *fund's* own expense at any time to take over the conduct in the name of the *previous practice* or *member* of the defence or settlement of any such claim, including any claim in respect of which the *previous practice* or *member* may become entitled to partial indemnity under any insurance with any insurers; and

(b) Solicitors Indemnity Fund Limited may after taking over the defence or settlement of any such claim conduct the same as it may in its absolute discretion think fit notwithstanding any dispute or difference, whether or not referred to arbitration under Rule 15, which may exist or arise between it and the *previous practice* or *member*.

14.7 No *previous practice* or *member* thereof shall be required to contest any legal proceedings unless a Queen's Counsel (to be mutually agreed upon or failing agreement to be appointed by the President of the *Society* for the time being) shall advise that such proceedings should be contested.

14.8 Without prejudice to Rules 14.5, 14.6 and 14.7, the *previous practice* and each *member* thereof shall keep Solicitors Indemnity Fund Limited informed in writing at all times, whether or not Solicitors Indemnity Fund Limited shall specifically so request, as to the development and handling of any claim, intimated claim, notice or circumstances the subject of or arising subsequent to any notice given to Solicitors Indemnity Fund Limited under Rule 14.1 or 14.2; and shall consult and co-operate with Solicitors Indemnity Fund Limited in relation thereto as Solicitors Indemnity Fund Limited may request, whether or not Solicitors Indemnity Fund Limited shall take over the conduct thereof.

14.9 The *fund* waives any rights of subrogation against any *member* of the *previous practice* save where those rights arise in connection with

(a) a dishonest or criminal act by that *member*; or

(b) the provision of indemnity under the exception to Rule 9.1(e); or

(c) a claim to indemnity in circumstances where that *member* has received a net benefit to which he or she was not entitled as a consequence of another *member* being provided with indemnity out of the *fund*;

and save as otherwise expressly provided in these Rules.

14.10 If the *previous practice* or any *member* thereof shall prefer any claim to indemnity out of the *fund* knowing the same to be false or fraudulent as regards amount or otherwise, it, he or she shall forfeit any claim to any such indemnity in respect of any claim or future claim against the *previous practice* or *member* to which the false or fraudulent claim to indemnity out of the *fund* may have related or relate.

14.11 Where there has been a failure to pay any instalment of any *contribution* due or any Value Added Tax payable in accordance with the Solicitors' Indemnity Rules 1987 to 2007 or the SRA Indemnity Rules 2011 or 2012 and a claim has been made or intimated against the *previous practice* or any *member* thereof in respect of which such *previous practice* or *member* would otherwise have been entitled to be provided with indemnity, Solicitors Indemnity Fund Limited shall provide such indemnity by payment (up to the indemnity limit) in or towards satisfying, or enabling the *previous practice* or *member* concerned to satisfy, the claim and claimants' costs and such *previous practice* shall thereafter upon request reimburse to Solicitors Indemnity Fund Limited on behalf of the *fund* the whole or such part as Solicitors Indemnity Fund Limited may request of any payment so made and of any costs and expenses incurred in its defence, settlement or compromise, and each *principal* therein shall be jointly and severally responsible to Solicitors Indemnity Fund Limited for such reimbursement accordingly. Provided always that Solicitors Indemnity Fund Limited shall require such reimbursement only to the extent of (a) any increase which in its opinion may have occurred in the total payable out of the *fund* (including costs and expenses) as a result of such failure, together with (b) such amount as may be necessary to satisfy any unpaid *contribution* and Value Added Tax and interest thereon at the rate of 4% above Barclays Bank base rate with quarterly rests or at such other rate as the *Society* may from time to time publish in the Law Society's Gazette.

14.12 Where non-compliance with any provision of these Rules by any *previous practice* or any *member* thereof claiming to be entitled to indemnity out of the *fund* has resulted in prejudice to the handling or settlement of any claim in respect of which such *previous practice* or *member* is entitled to indemnity hereunder, such *previous practice* or *member* shall reimburse to Solicitors Indemnity Fund Limited on behalf of the *fund* the difference between the sum payable out of the *fund* in respect of that claim and the sum which would have been payable in the absence of such prejudice. Provided always that it shall be a condition precedent of the right of the *fund* to such reimbursement that it shall first have provided full indemnity for such *previous practice* or *member* by payment (up to the indemnity limit) in or towards satisfying, or enabling such *previous practice* or *member* to satisfy, the claim and claimants' costs in accordance with the terms hereof.

14.13 In respect of any loss arising from any claim or claims as described by Rule 8.1(c) arising out of any dishonest or fraudulent act or omission of any *member* of the *previous practice*, the *fund* shall nonetheless be available to afford indemnity in accordance with these Rules to the *previous practice* and any *member* thereof, other than and excluding in each case the particular *member* concerned in such dishonesty or fraud. Provided always that at the request of Solicitors Indemnity Fund Limited, the *previous practice* or *member* being indemnified shall:

(a) take or procure to be taken at the *fund's* expense all reasonable steps to obtain reimbursement for the benefit of the *fund* from or from the personal representatives of any such *member* concerned in such dishonesty or fraud, and

(b) procure that any reimbursement so obtained together with any monies which but for such fraud or dishonesty would be due to such *member* concerned in such dishonesty or fraud shall be paid to the *fund* up to but not exceeding the amounts paid by the *fund* in respect of such claim together with any expenditure reasonably incurred by the *fund* in obtaining such reimbursement.

14.14 In the event of indemnity being afforded under the exception to Rule 9.1(e), the *previous practice* or *member* being indemnified shall take or procure to be taken at the *fund's* expense all reasonable steps to obtain reimbursement for the benefit of the *fund* from any *person* to whom any benefit arising from the giving of any undertaking accrues in the circumstances set out in Rule 9.1(e). Provided always that such reimbursement shall not exceed:

(a) the amount paid by the *fund* by way of indemnity together with any expenditure reasonably incurred by the *fund* in obtaining such reimbursement, or

(b) the amount of any benefit accruing to such *person*,

whichever is the lesser.

14.15 In respect of any claim to indemnity, Solicitors Indemnity Fund Limited may appoint *panel solicitors* to act on its behalf and on behalf of the *previous practice* or any *member* thereof, and *panel solicitors* shall:

(a) act at the sole direction of the *fund* for any purpose falling within the scope of these Rules, including acting on the Court record for the *previous practice* or any *member* thereof, and

(b) disclose to Solicitors Indemnity Fund Limited as required any statement or information given to or which becomes known to *panel solicitors* in the course of so acting, and such disclosure shall be treated as having been made directly to Solicitors Indemnity Fund Limited by the *previous practice* or *member*.

14.16 The provisions of this Rule 14 shall not apply in relation to an *expired run-off claim*, in respect of which the provisions of Rule 8.5 shall apply.

Rule 15: Arbitration

15.1 Any dispute or difference concerning any claim or the quantum of any claim to be provided with indemnity in accordance with these Rules shall be referred to the sole arbitrament, which shall be final and binding, of a *person* to be appointed on the application of either party in default of agreement by the President of the *Society* for the time being. Any such arbitration shall take place and be conducted between, on the one hand, the *person* for whom indemnity is provided, the party to the dispute or difference and, on the other hand, Solicitors Indemnity Fund Limited for and in respect of the *fund*.

PART 3: CONTRIBUTIONS

Rule 16: Power to require contributions

16.1 The *Society* shall have power to require *principals* to make *contributions* of such amount and on such basis as the *Society* may from time to time determine. Value Added Tax, to the extent chargeable on any relevant supply which takes or may be treated as taking place under or by virtue of these Rules, will be charged and payable in addition to and at the same time as any *contributions* payable hereunder.

16.2 Solicitors Indemnity Fund Limited may at any time give to any *practice* written notice correcting any inaccuracy in the calculation of any *contribution* under these Rules. Any reimbursement or any payment of *contribution* hereby required shall be made forthwith upon, respectively, issue or receipt of such a notice, together with any Value Added Tax applicable and (in the case of any amount payable to Solicitors Indemnity Fund Limited upon correction of an inaccuracy in calculation) interest at a rate of 4% above Barclays Bank base rate with quarterly rests or at such other rate as the *Society* may from time to time determine and publish in the Law Society's Gazette.

16.3 Solicitors Indemnity Fund Limited may at any time, to the extent that it is reasonably practicable for it to do so, recalculate any claims adjustment applicable to any *practice* under the Solicitors' Indemnity Rules 2006 (or any earlier corresponding Rules) as a result of the receipt by Solicitors Indemnity Fund Limited of any sum from any third party relating to any indemnity provided to that *practice* out of the *fund* under these Rules or any earlier corresponding Rules, after deduction of the reasonable costs and expenses incurred by Solicitors Indemnity Fund Limited.

16.4 Solicitors Indemnity Fund Limited shall not be entitled, at any time after 30 September 2008, to require any *practice* to make any *contribution* under the Solicitors' Indemnity Rules 2006 (or any earlier corresponding Rules) which would otherwise be payable by reason of an inaccuracy in calculation, unless that inaccuracy is attributable to a failure to provide information or to a material inaccuracy in information provided by or on behalf of that *practice* under Part III of the Solicitors' Indemnity Rules 2006 (or any earlier corresponding Rules).

16.5 The *Society's* decision shall be final and binding on all affected on any question arising as to:

(a) any obligation to make a *contribution*; or

(b) any sum due to any *person* out of the *fund*;

under this Rule 16.

PART 4: MANAGEMENT AND ADMINISTRATION OF THE FUND

Rule 17: Powers of the Society

17.1 Solicitors Indemnity Fund Limited shall hold, and have full power to manage and administer, the *fund*, subject only to:

(a) such directions, conditions and/or requirements as the *Society* may from time to time issue to or impose upon it expressly pursuant to this provision, and/or

(b) such further detailed arrangements as the *Society* may from time to time agree with it.

17.2 Without limiting the generality of Rule 17.1, the management and administration of the *fund* shall include power to:

(a) collect and recover *contributions* due to the *fund* in accordance with these Rules;

(b) deposit or invest in such manner as Solicitors Indemnity Fund Limited may determine all or any part of the *fund*, including any interest, dividends, profits, gains or other assets accruing to or acquired by the *fund*;

(c) arrange such insurances as Solicitors Indemnity Fund Limited may determine in respect of the *fund* and/or its assets and/or the *fund's* liability under these Rules to afford indemnity in respect of claims and costs and expenses; and to handle all aspects of any such insurances, including the payment of premiums thereon out of the *fund* and the making and recovery of claims thereunder;

(d) receive, investigate and handle claims to indemnity and other notices prescribed to be given to Solicitors Indemnity Fund Limited by these Rules, including settlement and compromise and making of ex gratia payments out of the *fund* in respect thereof and conduct of any dispute or difference referred to arbitration under Rule 15;

(e) receive, investigate and handle any claim made or intimated against any *person* in respect of which they are or may be entitled to be provided with indemnity out of the *fund* (whether or not a claim to indemnity hereunder has been made) and/or in respect of which the conduct is by these Rules assigned to Solicitors Indemnity Fund Limited, including settlement and compromise and making of ex gratia payments and conduct of any proceedings arising in respect of such claim;

(f) claim and recover reimbursement in respect of any sums paid by way of indemnity in any circumstances in which such reimbursement may under these Rules be claimed;

(g) exercise any right of subrogation save where such rights are waived in accordance with these Rules;

(h) maintain full and proper records and statistics (which subject to Rule 18, shall at all reasonable times be available on request to the *Society* for inspection and copying) as to the *fund* and all aspects of its management and administration;

(i) make to and review with the Council of the *Society* annually and at any other time that the *Council* may require, written and (if the *Council* so requires) oral reports as to the *fund* and, subject to Rule 18, its management and administration, including inter alia recommendations as to the *contributions* which are or may be required in respect of past, present and/or future *indemnity periods* and the circumstances in which, extent to which and conditions and exclusions subject to which indemnity should in any future *indemnity period* be afforded out of the *fund*;

(j) engage the assistance of any third party in respect of all or any aspect(s) of the management and administration of the *fund*;

(k) delegate to any third party all or any aspect(s) of the management and administration of the *fund*;

(l) institute and/or conduct such proceedings as it may consider necessary or appropriate for the due management and administration of the *fund* in its own name or (subject to prior consent of the *Society*) in the name of the *Society*;

(m) disburse and/or reimburse out of the *fund* all administrative and legal and other costs, overheads, fees and other expenses and liabilities incurred in respect of the *fund*, including without prejudice to the generality of the foregoing any such costs, overheads, fees and other expenses and liabilities incurred by the *Society* in respect of the establishment or maintenance, or the management, administration or protection, of the *fund*;

(n) disburse and/or reimburse out of the *fund* payments for any educational, charitable or other useful purpose which in its opinion is likely directly or indirectly to lead to the reduction or prevention of claims on the *fund* or otherwise to further the purpose or interests of the *fund*;

(o) disburse and/or reimburse out of the *fund* the costs, fees and expenses of the handling after 31 August 1987 of claims and potential claims against assureds notified under the *master policies* and *master policy* certificates;

(p) effect out of the *fund* or by arrangement with third parties the funding pending reimbursement by master policy insurers of such claims and potential claims and to bear out of the *fund* the costs, fees and expenses incurred thereby.

Rule 18: Use of information

18.1 Without prejudice to the *Society's* power under Rule 4.5 to designate itself as the *person* responsible for holding, managing and administering the *fund*, information and documents obtained by Solicitors Indemnity Fund Limited about any particular *practice* or *member* thereof in the course of investigating and handling any claim made or intimated or any circumstances notified as mentioned in Rule 21, may be utilised by Solicitors Indemnity Fund Limited for the purpose of preparation of general records, statistics, reports and recommendations (not identifying the particular *practice* or *member*) for or to the *Society*.

18.2 Solicitors Indemnity Fund Limited may bring to the attention of the *Society* at any time and without notice to the *practice* or *person* concerned:

(a) any failure to provide information in respect of any *practice* as required by Part III of the Solicitors' Indemnity Rules 2006 (or any earlier corresponding provisions) or any material omission or inaccuracy in such information;

(b) any failure to pay any *contribution* or other sum due when required to do so under these Rules (or any earlier corresponding Rules) or to reimburse any amount due by way of a Deductible, Due Proportion or Penalty Deductible, or (in the case of an *expired run-off claim*) which falls within a policy excess;

(c) a material inaccuracy in any proposal form submitted by or on behalf of a *practice*;

(d) (in the case of an *expired run-off claim*) any matter or circumstances that would permit the *expired run-off cover* to be avoided or but for the provisions of clause 4.1 of the *MTC* (and/or the corresponding of the *expired run-off cover*);

(e) any dishonesty or fraud suspected on the part of any *person* in relation to any *practice* or *member* thereof, or any other person subject to these Rules or any earlier corresponding Rules, or any *insured*; and

(f) any claim of inadequate professional services of which it becomes aware made against any such *practice*, *member* or *person* or any *insured*.

18.3 Such information and documents shall not otherwise be disclosed or available to the *Society* without the prior consent of the *practice* (or any subsequent or successor *practice* thereto) or *member* concerned, except where Solicitors Indemnity Fund Limited or the *Society* have reason to suspect dishonesty on the part of any *practice*, *previous practice*, subsequent or successor *practice* or any *member* or former *member* thereof, or *insured*.

18.4 Any information and documents held by Solicitors Indemnity Fund Limited about a particular *practice* or *member* thereof may be disclosed or available to the *Society* without the prior consent of the *practice* (or any subsequent or successor *practice* thereto) or *member* concerned where the *Society* has been requested by any *practice*, subsequent or successor *practice* or *member* thereof to grant, amend or revoke any waiver under Rule 19 or to make a determination under Rule 20.

18.5 Solicitors Indemnity Fund Limited may pass to the *Society* the name of any *practice* (including any subsequent, successor or *previous practice*) or any *member* or former *member* thereof in circumstances where Solicitors Indemnity Fund Limited has cause for concern having regard to:

(a) the nature, incidence or value of paid and/or reserved claims in respect of any such *practice* or *member*; or

(b) the existence of circumstances which are considered by the *fund* to create an increased risk of claims occurring in respect of that *practice* or *member*; or

(c) failure on the part of a *practice* or *member* thereof, or any *insured*, to comply with their obligations under these Rules (or any earlier corresponding Rules);

and for the purposes of paragraphs (b) and (c) above Solicitors Indemnity Fund Limited shall have the power to determine criteria which would indicate the likelihood of an increased risk of claims occurring and to specify those obligations in respect of which a failure to comply could form the basis for Solicitors Indemnity Fund Limited to pass on information.

18.6 In the exercise of the powers set out in Rule 18.5 Solicitors Indemnity Fund Limited may give details to the *Society* of the reasons for the decision to pass the name of the *practice* or *member* thereof to the *Society* including, in appropriate cases, releasing documentary information provided that no such documentary information will be released which could breach the general duty of confidentiality owed by a *practice* or *member* thereof to a client or former client.

18.7 In respect of any information that may be brought to the attention of the *Society* in accordance with Rules 18.1 to 18.6:

(a) the *Society* shall keep all such information confidential;

(b) the *Society* shall not (except where and to the extent required by law or in the proper performance by the *Society* of its regulatory functions) at any time reveal any such information to any *person* other than a duly authorised employee of the *Society* or any of its subsidiaries; and

(c) any privilege attaching to such information shall not be regarded as having been waived whether by virtue of such information having been provided to the *Society* or otherwise;

but the provisions of this Rule 18.7 shall not prevent the *Society* from making use of any such information for the purpose of bringing disciplinary proceedings against any *person*.

Rule 19: Waivers

19.1 The *Society* shall have power in any case or class of cases to waive in writing prospectively or retrospectively any obligation on any *solicitor*, *recognised body*, *licensed body* or *foreign lawyer* under these Rules and to amend or revoke any such waiver.

19.2 Any application by any *person* for:

(a) a waiver of any obligation under these Rules or under the Solicitors' Indemnity Rules 2001 or any Rules subsequent thereto; or

(b) a correction or recalculation of any sum paid or payable to the *fund* under these Rules, or under the Solicitors' Indemnity Rules 2001 or any Rules subsequent thereto;

must be made in writing to the *Society* no later than 3 calendar months from the date on which the relevant obligation has effect in relation to that *person*, or the date on which that *person* is notified thereof by Solicitors Indemnity Fund Limited, whichever is the earlier.

19.3 No application by any *person* for:

(a) a waiver of any obligation under the Solicitors' Indemnity Rules 2000 or any Rules made prior thereto; or

(b) a correction or recalculation of any sum paid or payable to the *fund* under the Solicitors' Indemnity Rules 2000 or any Rules made prior thereto;

may be considered unless it was made in writing to the *Society* as soon as practicable, and in any event no later than 28 February 2002.

19.4 Any appeal against any decision made by the *Society* in respect of any application for a waiver of any obligation under these Rules or any previous Rules, or in respect of any correction or recalculation of any sum paid or payable to the *fund* under these Rules or any previous Rules, must be made in writing to the *Society* within 21 days from the date of the decision.

19.5 An application for a waiver as contemplated by this Rule 19 or the making of an appeal against any decision made by the *Society* in respect of such application shall not relieve any *person* from any obligation under these Rules or any previous Rules pending the determination of any such application or appeal.

Rule 20: Decisions by the Society

20.1 The *Society* shall have power to treat any *person* as complying with any provision of these Rules for the purposes of the *SA* notwithstanding that the *person* has failed to comply with any provision of these Rules where such non-compliance is regarded by the *Society* in a particular case or cases as being insignificant.

PART 5: MAINTENANCE AND TERMINATION OF THE FUND

Rule 21: Maintenance and termination of the fund

21.1 The *fund* shall continue to be held, managed and administered by Solicitors Indemnity Fund Limited for so long as and to the extent that the *Society*, in the light of the reports made to it by Solicitors Indemnity Fund Limited, may consider necessary or appropriate for the purpose of providing indemnity in respect of any claim(s) made or intimated during any *indemnity period* and/or during or subsequent to any *indemnity period* arising out of circumstances notified during any *indemnity period* as circumstances which might give rise to such claim(s).

21.2 As and when the *Society* no longer considers it necessary or appropriate that all or any part of the *fund* should be so held, managed and administered, the *Society* may require all or any part of the *fund* not so required to be released to the *Society* which shall apply the same if and to the extent the *Society* considers it reasonably practicable for the purpose of providing indemnity in any other way permitted by section 37(2) of the *SA* and otherwise for the overall benefit of the *solicitors'* profession in such manner as it may decide.

Supplemental notes

[Last updated: 1 October 2020]

SRA Compensation Fund Rules 2021

INTRODUCTION

These rules govern the way that we operate the SRA Compensation Fund.

It is funded by contributions from individuals and firms authorised by us.

We have developed a statement setting out the purpose of the fund and guidance on the way we operate the fund.

PART 1: THE FUND

Rule 1: Maintenance of and contributions to the Fund

1.1 The *SRA* shall establish and maintain a fund for making grants in respect of applications made in accordance with these rules.

1.2 *Solicitors, RELs, RFLs, recognised bodies* and *licensed bodies* must make contributions to the *Fund* in such amounts and at such times as may be *prescribed*.

1.3 Any unpaid contributions may be recovered as a debt due to the *SRA*.

1.4 The *SRA* may at any time:

(a) borrow for the purposes of the *Fund*;

(b) charge investments which form part of the *Fund* as security for borrowing by the *SRA* for the purposes of the *Fund*.

Rule 2: Residual discretion and fund of last resort

2.1 The *Fund* is a discretionary fund of last resort and no *person* has a right to a grant enforceable at law. The *SRA* retains a discretion to refuse to consider an application or to make a grant notwithstanding that the conditions in these rules for making a grant are satisfied.

2.2 The circumstances in which the residual discretion in rule 2.1 may be exercised include, but are not limited to, circumstances in which the *SRA* considers that the loss suffered is not material in all the circumstances or has been appropriately compensated through another means.

2.3 The *SRA* may refuse or reduce a grant where the loss or part of the loss is, or was, capable of being made good or appropriately compensated by some other means, including another compensation scheme.

PART 2: PAYMENT OF GRANTS FROM THE FUND

Rule 3: Grants which may be made from the Fund

3.1   A *person* may apply for a grant out of the *Fund*, if the loss referred to in rule 3.3 relates to services provided:

(a)   by the *defaulting practitioner* for them; or

(b)   to, or as, a *trustee* where they are a beneficiary of the estate or trust.

3.2   A *person* who is not a client of the *defaulting practitioner* may apply for a grant out of the *Fund* if they:

(a)   were a party on the other side of a legal matter on which the *defaulting practitioner* was acting; and

(b)   have suffered, or are likely to suffer, financial loss in accordance with rule 3.3 arising as a result of the defaulting practitioner failing to apply funds for the purpose intended where they should have been used (whether on completion of certain conditions or otherwise) to complete a transaction for their benefit, or to make a settlement or other payment to them.

3.3   For any grant to be made out of the *Fund*, an *applicant* must satisfy the *SRA* that the *applicant* is eligible in accordance with rule 4 and (save in respect of a grant made under rule 3.4) has suffered, or is likely to suffer, financial loss directly resulting from:

(a)   the dishonesty of a *defaulting practitioner* or the employee or *manager* or *owner* of a *defaulting practitioner*; or

(b)   failure to account for money which has come into the hands of a *defaulting practitioner* or the employee or *manager* or *owner* of a *defaulting practitioner*, which may include the failure by a defaulting practitioner to complete work for which the *defaulting practitioner* was paid,

in the course of an activity of a kind which is part of the usual business of a *defaulting practitioner* and, in the case of a *defaulting licensed body*, the act or default arose in the course of performance of an activity regulated by the *SRA* in accordance with the terms of the body's licence.

3.4   The *SRA* may make a grant to alleviate direct losses suffered as a result of the civil liability of a *defaulting practitioner* or a *defaulting practitioner's* employee, *manager* or *owner* in circumstances where:

(a)   the *defaulting practitioner* in accordance with the SRA Indemnity Insurance Rules should have had, but did not have, in place a *policy* of *qualifying insurance*;

(b)   the liability of the *defaulting practitioner* or the *defaulting practitioner's* employee or *manager* would have been covered by a *policy* of *qualifying insurance*; and

(c) the loss is not covered by the *SIF*.

3.5 No grant will be made under rule 3.4 where due to the insolvency or cessation of the insurer the *defaulting practitioner's policy* of *qualifying insurance* has been disclaimed or otherwise ceases.

3.6 The *SRA* may make a grant as an interim measure in relation to part of an application before the application has been fully assessed.

Rule 4: Eligibility for a grant

4.1 A *person* is eligible to apply for a grant out of the *Fund* if, at the time the application is made, they are:

(a) an individual;

(b) a sole trader, *partnership*, body corporate, unincorporated association or mutual association with an annual *turnover* or *assets* of less than £2 million;

(c) a *charity* with annual income net of tax in the most recent financial year of less than £2 million; or

(d) a *trustee* of a trust with an asset value of less than £2 million.

4.2 The *SRA* may take into account such evidence as it sees fit when determining eligibility under rule 4.1 and may make a broad estimate of any relevant amount.

Rule 5: Defaulting practitioners

5.1 A *defaulting practitioner* means:

(a) a *solicitor* or an *REL* who at the date of the relevant act or omission was:

(i) practising in an *authorised body*; or

(ii) practising in a *non-commercial body*;

(b) a *solicitor* or an *REL* who at the date of the relevant act or omission:

(i) was self-employed and practising in their own name, and not through a trading name or service company;

(ii) did not employ anyone in connection with the services they provided; and

(iii) was engaged directly by their clients with their fees payable directly to them;

(c) an *RFL* who is a *manager* or *owner* of an *authorised body*;

(d) a *recognised body*; or

(e) a *licensed body*,

and the expressions "defaulting solicitor", "defaulting REL", "defaulting recognised body", "defaulting RFL" and "defaulting licensed body" shall be construed accordingly.

5.2 A grant may be made where, at the date of the relevant act or omission:

(a) a *defaulting solicitor* had no practising certificate in force;

(b) the registration of a *defaulting REL* or *defaulting RFL* had expired or been revoked;

(c) the authorisation of a *defaulting recognised body* or *defaulting licensed body* had been suspended or revoked;

provided that the *SRA* is satisfied that the *applicant* was unaware of the absence of a valid practising certificate or the relevant expiry, suspension or revocation (as the case may be).

Rule 6: Grants to defaulting practitioners

6.1 The *SRA* may make a grant to a *defaulting practitioner* who or which has suffered or is likely to suffer loss by reason of their liability to any client in direct consequence of an act or omission of:

(a) in the case of a *defaulting solicitor*, *defaulting REL* or *defaulting RFL*, any of their employees or any fellow *manager*;

(b) in the case of a *defaulting recognised body*, any of its employees or *managers* or *owners*;

(c) in the case of a *defaulting licensed body*, any of its employees or *managers* or *owners,* provided that such act or omission arose in the course of performance of an activity regulated by the *SRA* in accordance with the terms of the body's licence,

in circumstances where, but for the liability of the *defaulting practitioner*, a grant might have been made from the *Fund*

6.2 The *SRA* may make a grant under this rule by way of a loan upon such terms as the *SRA* specifies.

6.3 In the case of a *defaulting recognised body* or a *defaulting licensed body*, the *SRA* may make such grant payable to one or more of the *managers* or *owners* of the *defaulting recognised body* or *defaulting licensed body*. If a loan is made to more than one *person*, they shall be jointly and severally liable for the repayment of the loan.

Rule 7: Grants in respect of statutory trusts

7.1 The *SRA* may make a grant to alleviate a deficiency in a *statutory trust* held by the *SRA*.

7.2 The *SRA* may make a grant to a *person* where the money would have been due to that *person* but for their claim having been extinguished under rule 9.2 of the SRA Intervention Powers (Statutory Trust) Rules 2011 or rule 8.2 of the SRA Statutory Trust Rules.

Rule 8: Interest

8.1 In respect of any grants made under rules 3, 6 or 7 the *SRA* may make a supplementary grant by way of a sum in lieu of lost interest on the loss underlying the principal grant. Such interest will be calculated by the *SRA* in accordance with *prescribed* rates.

8.2 Where the application for the principal grant is in respect of a failure to redeem a mortgage, the *SRA* may also make a grant in respect of the additional interest accrued to the mortgage account as a result of the *defaulting practitioner's* failure to redeem.

Rule 9: Maximum grant

9.1 Unless the *SRA* is satisfied that there are exceptional circumstances in the public interest that justify a higher sum, the maximum grant that may be made is £2 million.

9.2 For the purposes of this rule, a single claim is an application, or applications, from an *applicant* for the loss incurred by them arising from a single event or set of connected underlying circumstances.

Rule 10: Capping payments of multiple applications

10.1 Where multiple applications are made to the *Fund*:

(a) that relate to the same or connected underlying circumstances; and

(b) the *SRA* is satisfied that the total amount of the grants made from the *Fund* in respect of such applications is likely to exceed £5 million,

the *SRA* may impose a limit on the total amount to be paid in respect of those applications of £5 million.

10.2 Where the *SRA* imposes a limit under rule 10.1, the amount paid may be apportioned between the *applicants* to whom the *SRA* is satisfied a grant is payable, in such of the following ways as the *SRA* considers appropriate in the circumstances:

(a) the amount to be apportioned equally between all those who have made an application within such reasonable time period for the purpose as shall be published by the *SRA*; or

(b) such percentage of loss or amount to be paid, as the *SRA* considers appropriate in all the circumstances.

Rule 11: Conduct of the applicant and contribution to loss

11.1 A grant may be refused or reduced to take account of:

(a) dishonest, improper or unreasonable conduct by the *applicant* or anyone acting on their behalf:

(i) in the circumstances that gave rise to the application;

(ii) in relation to the application itself; or

(b) failure to pursue the application promptly, co-operatively and in good faith.

11.2 A grant may be refused or reduced to take account of any act or omission by the *applicant* or anyone acting on their behalf that has contributed to or has failed to mitigate the loss.

Rule 12: Losses outside the remit of the Fund

12.1 For the avoidance of doubt, the *SRA* shall not make a grant in respect of losses that:

(a) arise solely by reason of professional negligence by a *defaulting practitioner*, or the employee or *manager* of a *defaulting practitioner*, save as provided for in rule 3.4;

(b) are indirect or consequential, save where the *SRA* exercises its discretion to make a grant:

(i) under rule 8;

(ii) for costs of completing or remedying work for which the *defaulting practitioner* has been paid; or

(iii) for loss where a client of a *defaulting practitioner* has been made personally liable for loss suffered by a third party as a result of the act or omission of that *defaulting practitioner*;

(c) are, or result from, the trading debts or liabilities of the *defaulting practitioner*, including claims for fees payable to the *applicant* for which the *defaulting practitioner* is liable;

(d) comprise legal or other professional costs incurred by the *applicant* in making an application to the *Fund*;

(e) are for costs of proceedings instituted by the *applicant* for recovery of their loss, save in exceptional circumstances;

(f) are for interest payable to the *applicant*, save where the *SRA* exercises its discretion to make a grant under rule 8;

(g) are suffered by the Legal Aid Agency as a result of making regular payments under the Agency's contracting schemes for civil or criminal work;

(h) are circumstances where the *applicant*:

(i) has been made bankrupt and any grant would vest in the trustee in bankruptcy;

(ii) has entered into a voluntary arrangement with their creditors and any grant would vest in the administrator of the arrangement; or

(iii) is in liquidation.

Rule 13: Foreign lawyers

13.1 The *SRA* shall not make a grant in respect of any act or omission of an *REL*, or the employee of an *REL*, where such act or omission took place outside the *UK*, unless the *SRA* is satisfied that the act or omission was, or was closely connected with, the act or omission of a *solicitor* or the employee of a *solicitor*, or that the act or omission was closely connected with the *REL's* practice in the *UK*.

13.2 The *SRA* shall not make a grant in respect of the act or omission of an *RFL*, or the employee of an *RFL*, where such act or omission took place outside England and Wales, unless the *SRA* is satisfied that the act or omission was, or was closely connected with, the act or omission of a *solicitor* or the employee of a *solicitor*, or that the act or omission was closely connected with practice in England and Wales.

Rule 14: Apportionment and multi-party issues

14.1 Where the loss has been sustained as a result of the act or omission of more than one party, the *SRA* will consider the role of each party in contributing to the *applicant's* loss in deciding whether to make a grant and, if so, the amount of any grant.

14.2 In the case of a *defaulting licensed body*, the *SRA* will consider the extent to which the loss is attributable to an act or omission which falls outside the performance of an activity regulated by the *SRA* in accordance with the terms of the body's licence in deciding whether to make a grant and, if so, the amount of any grant.

PART 3: APPLICATIONS AND PROCEDURES

Rule 15: Application and time limit

15.1 An *applicant* must make an application for a grant in the *prescribed* form, and within 12 months of the date they first became aware, or should reasonably have become aware, of the loss.

15.2 The *SRA* may extend the 12 month period in rule 15.1 if satisfied that there are circumstances which justify the extension of the time limit.

15.3 The *applicant* must provide information, documents and evidence requested by the *SRA*, which may include verification of matters by statement of truth or affidavit. Failure to provide such documentation or to co-operate with the *SRA* will be taken into account when determining the merits of the application.

Rule 16: Notice to defaulting practitioner

16.1 The *SRA* may not make a grant unless it has given not less than 8 days' notice to the *defaulting practitioner* informing them of the nature and value of the application, unless it appears to the *SRA* that it would not be reasonably practicable to give such notice, or the grant should be made urgently.

16.2 Where the *SRA* has made a grant urgently in accordance with rule 16.1, the *SRA* shall as soon as, and so long as, it is practicable to do so, give notice to the *defaulting practitioner* in the terms set out in rule 16.1 and may (insofar as any failure to give notice before the making of the grant has prejudiced the *defaulting practitioner*) waive in whole or in part the *Fund's* right of recovery under rule 18 against the *defaulting practitioner*.

Rule 17: Recovery and subrogation

17.1 Where the *SRA* makes a grant otherwise than by way of loan or if by way of loan repayments of the loan is waived or otherwise the borrower has failed to repay part or all of the loan, the *SRA* shall be subrogated to the rights and remedies of the *person* to whom or on whose behalf the grant is made to the extent of the amount of the grant.

17.2 Where rule 18.1 applies, the recipient must if required by the *SRA* whether before or after the grant has been made and upon the *SRA* giving the recipient a sufficient indemnity against costs, prove in any insolvency or winding up of the *defaulting practitioner* and sue for recovery of the loss in the name of the recipient but on behalf of the *SRA*.

17.3 The recipient of a grant must comply with all proper and reasonable requirements of the *SRA* for the purpose of giving effect to the *SRA's* rights under this rule, and shall permit the *SRA* to have conduct of any proceedings brought on its behalf.

Rule 18: Refusal of an application

18.1 If the *SRA* refuses to make a grant of either the whole or part of the amount applied for, the *applicant* will be informed in writing of the reasons for the decision.

18.2 The fact that an application has been rejected does not prevent a further application being submitted provided that material new relevant evidence or information is produced in support of the new application.

Supplemental notes

Made by the SRA Board on 14 July 2020.

Made under sections 36 and 36A of the Solicitors Act 1974, section 9 of, and paragraph 6 of Schedule 2 to, the Administration of Justice Act 1985, section 83 of, and paragraph

19 of Schedule 11 to, the Legal Services Act 2007 and the Legal Services Act 2007 (The Law Society and The Council of Licensed Conveyancers) (Modification of Functions) Order 2011.

[Last updated: 5 July 2021]

[The SRA Compensation Fund Rules were superseded on 5 July 2021 by the SRA Compensation Fund Rules 2021. The SRA Compensation Fund Rules still apply in respect of applications before 5 July 2021. For applications made before 5 July 2021 read the archived 2019 Compensation Fund Rules at **www.sra.org.uk/solicitors/ standards-regulations/compensation-fund-rules/compensation-fund-rules-archived.**]

[20] SRA Indemnity Insurance Rules

These rules require firms that are authorised by the *SRA* to take out and maintain professional indemnity insurance. They do not apply to solicitors, RELs and RFLs that practise outside SRA authorised firms.

PART 1: GENERAL

Rule 1: Application

1.1 These rules apply to *authorised bodies* and their *principals*.

PART 2: RESPONSIBILITY AND MONITORING

Rule 2: Obligation to effect insurance

2.1 An *authorised body* carrying on a *practice* during any *indemnity period* beginning on or after 25 November 2019 must take out and maintain *qualifying insurance* under these rules with a *participating insurer*.

2.2 In respect of its obligation under rule 2.1, an *authorised body* must obtain a *policy* of *qualifying insurance* prior to the expiry of the *policy period*, that provides cover incepting on and with effect from the expiry of the *policy period*.

2.3 If the *authorised body* has been unable to comply with rule 2.2, the *authorised body* must obtain a *policy* of *qualifying insurance* during or prior to the expiry of the *extended policy period* that provides cover incepting on and with effect from the expiry of the *policy period*.

2.4 If the *authorised body* has been unable to comply with either rule 2.2 or rule 2.3, the *authorised body* must cease *practice* promptly, and by no later than the expiry of the *cessation period*, unless the *authorised body* obtains a *policy* of *qualifying insurance* during or prior to the expiry of the *cessation period* that provides cover incepting on and with effect from the expiry of the *policy period* and covers all activities in connection with *private legal practice* carried out by the *authorised body* including, without limitation, any carried out in breach of rule 4.2.

Rule 3: Adequate and appropriate insurance

3.1 Notwithstanding rule 2.1 above, an *authorised body* must take out and maintain professional indemnity insurance that provides adequate and appropriate cover in respect of current or past practice taking into account any alternative arrangements the body or its *clients* may make.

3.2 An *authorised body* must ensure that its *clients* have the benefit of the indemnity insurance required under these rules and must not exclude or attempt to exclude liability below the minimum level of cover required under these rules.

Rule 4: Responsibility

4.1 Each *authorised body*, and any *principal* of such a body, must ensure that the *authorised body* complies with these rules.

4.2 Each *authorised body* that has been unable to obtain a *policy* of *qualifying insurance* prior to the expiration of the *extended policy period*, and any *principal* of such a body, must ensure that the *authorised body*, and each *principal* or *employee* of the body, undertakes no activities in connection with *private legal practice* and accepts no instructions in respect of any such activities during the *cessation period* save to the extent that the activity is necessary in connection with the discharge of its obligations within the scope of the *authorised body's existing instructions*.

Rule 5: Insolvency of participating insurer

5.1 If an *authorised body* is carrying on a *practice* which is being provided with *qualifying insurance* by a *participating insurer* (whether alone or together with another *participating insurer*) and that *participating insurer* is the subject of an *insolvency event* then the *authorised body* and any *principal* of the body must ensure that the *authorised body* has in place *qualifying insurance* with another *participating insurer* as soon as may be reasonably practicable and in any event within four weeks of such *insolvency event*.

Rule 6: Monitoring

6.1 The *SRA* may require from an *authorised body* or any *principal* in an *authorised body*, information and evidence it may reasonably require to satisfy itself that the body has complied with these rules.

Rule 7: RELs

7.1 The provisions contained in annex 2 to these rules apply to an *authorised body* that has at least one *principal* who is an *REL*.

PART 3: REPORTING

Rule 8: Use of information

8.1 Each *authorised body* must notify the *SRA* (or such *person* as the *SRA* may notify to the *authorised body* from time to time) and its *participating insurer* in writing as soon as reasonably practicable and in any event no later than five business days after the date on which:

(a) the *authorised body* enters an *extended policy period*;

(b) the *authorised body* has entered the *cessation period*; and

(c) where the *authorised body* is in the *extended policy period* or the *cessation period*, the *authorised body* has obtained a *policy* of *qualifying insurance*, and in such case the notification must include the name of the *participating insurer* who has issued the *policy* of *qualifying insurance* and the *policy* number.

8.2 The *SRA* may, without limitation and in its absolute discretion, disclose and make available for public inspection the identity of an *authorised body's participating insurer*.

Rule 9: Details of participating insurer

9.1 This rule is in addition to any obligations imposed on the *authorised body* under the Provision of Services Regulations 2009.

9.2 If a *claimant* asserts a *claim* against an *authorised body* or any person insured under that *authorised body's policy*, and the *claim* relates to any matter within the scope of cover of the *MTC*, the *authorised body*, and any person who is at the relevant time a *principal* in that *authorised body* must, upon request by that *claimant*, by any person insured under that *authorised body's policy*, or by any other person with a legitimate interest, provide the following details in relation to that *authorised body's policy*:

(a) the name of the *participating insurer* who issued the *policy*;

(b) the *policy* number; and

(c) the address and contact details of the *participating insurer* for the purpose of making a *claim* under the *policy*,

in each case in respect of the *policy* which it is reasonably believed to be the relevant *policy* to respond to the *claim*, or, if applicable, the fact that the *authorised body* or person against whom the *claim* is asserted is covered by *supplementary run-off cover*.

9.3 In the case of an *authorised body* which has ceased *practice*, any person who was a *principal* in that *authorised body* immediately before that body ceased *practice* must comply with rule 9.2.

PART 4: TRANSITIONALS

Rule 10: Transitionals and savings

10.1 For the purposes of the *SA* (including without limitation section 10 of that Act), any person who is in breach of any rule or part of any rule under the Solicitors' Indemnity Insurance Rules 2000 to 2010 or SRA Indemnity Insurance Rules 2011 to 2013 will be deemed, for so long as that person remains in breach, not to be complying with these rules.

ANNEX 1
SRA MINIMUM TERMS AND CONDITIONS OF PROFESSIONAL INDEMNITY INSURANCE

1   Scope of cover

1.1   *Civil liability*

Subject to the limits in clause 2, the insurance must indemnify each *insured* against civil liability to the extent that it arises from *private legal practice* in connection with the *insured firm's practice*, (including its *prior practice* and (unless run-off cover is provided in accordance with clause 5.3) any *successor practice*) provided that a *claim* in respect of such liability:

(a) is first made against an *insured* during the *period of insurance*; or

(b) is made against an *insured* during or after the *period of insurance* and arising from *circumstances* first notified to the *insurer* during the *period of insurance*.

1.2   *Defence costs*

The insurance must also indemnify the *insured* against *defence costs* in relation to:

(a) any *claim* referred to in clause 1.1; or

(b) any *circumstances* first notified to the *insurer* during the *period of insurance*; or

(c) any investigation or inquiry (save in respect of any disciplinary proceeding under the authority of the *SRA* and/or the *Tribunal*) during or after the *period of insurance* arising from any *claim* referred to in clause 1.1 or from *circumstances* first notified to the *insurer* during the *period of insurance*.

1.3   *The insured*

For the purposes of the cover contemplated by clause 1.1, the *insured* must include:

(a) the *insured firm*; and

(b) each service, administration, trustee or nominee *company* owned as at the date of occurrence of relevant *circumstances* by the *insured firm* and/or the *principals* of the *insured firm*; and

(c) each *principal*, each former *principal* and each *person* who becomes a *principal* during the *period of insurance* of the *insured firm* or a *company* referred to in paragraph (b); and

(d) each *employee*, each former *employee* and each *person* who becomes during the *period of insurance* an *employee* of the *insured firm* or a *company* referred to in paragraph (b); and

(e) the estate or legal personal representative of any deceased or legally incapacitated *person* referred to in paragraph (c) or (d).

1.4   *Award by regulatory authority*

The insurance must indemnify each *insured* against any amount paid or payable in accordance with the recommendation of the Office for Legal Complaints (including the *Legal Ombudsman* pursuant to section 137(2)(c) and section 137(4)(b) of the *LSA*) or any other regulatory authority to the same extent as it indemnifies the *insured* against civil liability provided that the *insurer* will have no liability in respect of any determination by the *Legal Ombudsman* pursuant to section 137(2)(b) of the *LSA* to refund any fees paid to the *insured*.

2   Limit of insurance cover

2.1   *Any one claim*

The *sum insured* for any one *claim* (exclusive of *defence costs*) must be, where the *insured firm* is a *relevant recognised body* or a *relevant licensed body* (in respect of activities regulated by the *SRA* in accordance with the terms of the body's licence) at least £3 million, and in all other cases, at least £2 million.

2.2   *Defence costs*

There must be no monetary limit on the cover for *defence costs*.

2.3   *Proportionate limit on defence costs*

Notwithstanding clauses 2.1 and 2.2, the insurance may provide that liability for *defence costs* in relation to a *claim* which exceeds the *sum insured* is limited to the proportion that the *sum insured* bears to the total amount paid or payable to dispose of the *claim*.

2.4   *No other limit*

The insurance must not limit liability to any monetary amount (whether by way of an aggregate limit or otherwise) except as contemplated by clauses 2.1 to 2.3 (inclusive).

2.5   *One claim*

The insurance may provide that, when considering what may be regarded as one *claim* for the purposes of the limits contemplated by clauses 2.1 to 2.3 (inclusive):

(a) all *claims* against any one or more *insured* arising from:

    (i)   one act or omission;

    (ii) one series of related acts or omissions;

    (iii) the same act or omission, in a series of related matters or transactions;

    (iv) similar acts or omissions, in a series of related matters or transactions, and

(b) all *claims* against one or more *insured* arising from one matter or transaction will be regarded as one *claim*.

2.6   *Multiple underwriters*

2.6.1 The insurance may be underwritten by more than one *insurer*, each of which must be a *participating insurer*, provided that the insurance is fully underwritten.

2.6.2 Where the insurance is underwritten jointly by more than one *insurer*, the insurance:

(a)   must state which *participating insurer* shall be the *lead insurer*;

(b)   may provide that each *insurer* shall be severally liable only for its respective proportion of liability in accordance with the terms of the insurance; and

(c)   (in addition to any proportionate limit on *defence costs* in accordance with clause 2.3), may provide that each *insurer's* liability for *defence costs* is further limited to the extent or the proportion of that *insurer's* liability (if any) in relation to the relevant *claim*.

2.6.3 The *insurer* stated to be the *lead insurer* shall act as such including without limitation being responsible for the conduct of *claims*, advancing *defence costs* (subject to clause 2.6.2(c)) and compromising and arranging the payment of *claims*. The liability of any *insurer* shall not be increased by virtue only of the fact that it is acting as *lead insurer*.

3   Excesses

3.1   The insurance may be subject to an *excess* of such monetary amount and on such terms as the *insurer* and the *insured firm* agree. Subject to clause 3.4, the *excess* may be 'self-insured' or partly or wholly insured without regard to these *MTC*.

3.2   The insurance must provide that the *excess* deductible does not reduce the limit of liability contemplated by clause 2.1.

3.3   The *excess* must not apply to *defence costs*.

3.4   The insurance must provide that, if an *insured* fails to pay to a *claimant* any amount which is within the *excess* within 30 days of it becoming due for payment, the *claimant* may give notice of the *insured's* default to the *insurer*, whereupon the *insurer* is liable to remedy the default on the *insured's* behalf. The insurance may provide that any amount paid by the *insurer* to remedy such a default erodes the *sum insured*.

3.5   The insurance may provide for multiple *claims* to be treated as one *claim* for the purposes of an *excess* contemplated by clause 3.1 on such terms as the *insured firm* and the *insurer* agree.

3.6   In the case of insurance written on an excess of loss basis, there shall be no *excess*; except in relation to the primary layer.

4   Special conditions

4.1   *No avoidance or repudiation*

The insurance must provide that the *insurer* is not entitled to avoid or repudiate the insurance on any grounds whatsoever including, without limitation, any breach of the duty to make a fair presentation of the risk, or any misrepresentation, in each case whether fraudulent or not.

4.2   *No adjustment or denial*

The insurance must provide that the *insurer* is not entitled to reduce or deny its liability under the insurance on any grounds whatsoever including, without limitation, any breach of any term or condition of the insurance, except to the extent that one of the exclusions contemplated by clause 6 applies.

4.3   *No cancellation*

The insurance must provide that it cannot be cancelled except (in the case of (a), (b) or (c) below) by the agreement of both the *insured firm* and the *insurer*, and in any event only in circumstances where:

(a)   the *insured firm's practice* is merged into a *successor practice*, provided that there is insurance complying with these *MTC* in relation to that *successor practice*, in which case cancellation shall have effect no earlier than the date of such merger; or

(b)   replacement insurance, complying with the *MTC* in effect at its commencement, commences, in which case cancellation shall have effect no earlier than the date on which such replacement insurance commences; or

(c)   it subsequently transpires that the *insured firm* is not required under the SRA Indemnity Insurance Rules to effect a *policy* of *qualifying insurance*, in which case cancellation shall have effect from the later of (a) the start of the relevant *policy period* and (b) the date on which the *insured firm* ceased to be required to effect a *policy* of *qualifying insurance*, or such later date as the *insured firm* and the *insurer* may agree.

Cancellation must not affect the rights and obligations of the parties accrued under the insurance prior to the date from which cancellation has effect.

4.4   *No set-off*

The insurance must provide that any amount payable by the *insurer* to indemnify an *insured* against civil liability to a *claimant* will be paid only to the *claimant*, or at the *claimant's* direction, and that the *insurer* is not entitled to set-off against any such amount any payment due to it by any *insured* including, without limitation, any payment of premium or to reimburse the *insurer*.

4.5   *No 'other insurance' provision*

The insurance must not provide that the liability of the *insurer* is reduced or excluded by reason of the existence or availability of any other insurance other than: (i) as contemplated by clause 6.1; or (ii) where the *insured*, having entered the *extended policy period* or *cessation period*, obtains a *policy* of *qualifying insurance* that incepts from and with effect from the expiration of the *policy period*. For the avoidance of doubt and subject to the provisions of the *participating insurer's agreement*, this requirement is not intended to affect any right of the *insurer* to claim contribution from any other *insurer* which is also liable to indemnify any *insured*.

4.6   *No retroactive date*

The insurance must not exclude or limit the liability of the *insurer* in respect of *claims* arising from incidents, occurrences, facts, matters, acts and/or omissions which occurred prior to a specified date.

4.7   *Successor practice – 'double insurance'*

The insurance may provide that, if the *insured firm's practice* is succeeded during the *period of insurance* and, as a result, a situation of 'double insurance' exists between two or more *insurers* of the *successor practice*, contribution between *insurers* is to be determined in accordance with the relative numbers of *principals* of the owners of the constituent *practices* immediately prior to succession.

4.8   *Resolution of disputes as to insurer of successor practice*

The insurance must provide that, if there is a dispute as to whether a *practice* is a *successor practice* for the purposes of clauses 1.1 or 5.5, the *insured* and the *insurer* will take all reasonable steps (including, if appropriate, referring the dispute to arbitration) to resolve the dispute in conjunction with any related dispute between any other party which has insurance complying with these *MTC* and that party's *insurer*.

4.8A   *Conduct of a claim pending dispute resolution*

The insurance must provide that, pending resolution of any coverage dispute and without prejudice to any issue in dispute, the *insurer* will, if so directed by the *SRA*, conduct any claim, advance *defence costs* and, if appropriate, compromise and pay the claim. If the *SRA* is satisfied that:

(a)   the party requesting the direction has taken all reasonable steps to resolve the dispute with the other party/ies;

(b)   there is a reasonable prospect that the coverage dispute will be resolved or determined in the *insured's* favour; and

(c)   it is fair and equitable in all the circumstances for such direction to be given,

it may in its absolute discretion make such a direction.

4.9   *Advancement of defence costs*

The insurance must provide that the *insurer* will meet *defence costs* as and when they are incurred, including *defence costs* incurred on behalf of an *insured* who is alleged to have committed or condoned dishonesty or a fraudulent act or omission, provided that the *insurer* is not liable for *defence costs* incurred on behalf of that *insured* after the earlier of:

(a) that *insured* admitting to the *insurer* the commission or condoning of such dishonesty, act or omission; or

(b) a court or other judicial body finding that that *insured* was in fact guilty of such dishonesty, act or omission.

4.10 *Variation of insurance terms*

The terms of the insurance must provide that the *insurer* shall vary the terms of the insurance to give effect to any variation to the SRA Indemnity Insurance Rules, the Glossary and the *MTC*, such variation to be implemented by the *insurer*:

(a) on the date of any renewal or replacement of the insurance or any extension to the *period of insurance* occurring in that *indemnity period*; or

(b) on each date falling in 18 month intervals from the commencement of the *policy period* where no variation has occurred by reason of clause 4.10(a) within the immediately preceding 18 month period.

save that no variation shall be required under clause 4.10(b) where the date on which variation would have been required is a date within the *extended policy period* or the *cessation period*.

4.11 *MTC to prevail*

The insurance must provide that:

(a) the insurance is to be construed or rectified so as to comply with the requirements of these *MTC* (including any amendment pursuant to clause 4.10); and

(b) any provision which is inconsistent with these *MTC* (including any amendment pursuant to clause 4.10) is to be severed or rectified to comply.

5 Extended policy period and run-off cover

5.1 *Extended policy period*

The insurance must provide cover complying with the *MTC* for the duration of the *extended policy period* where an *insured firm* has not, prior to the expiration of the *policy period*, obtained insurance complying with the *MTC* and incepting on and with effect from the day immediately following the expiration of the *policy period*.

5.2 *Cessation period*

The insurance must provide cover complying with the *MTC* for the duration of the *cessation period* where an *insured firm* has not, prior to the expiration of the *extended policy period*, obtained insurance complying with the *MTC* and incepting on and with effect from the day immediately following the expiration of the *policy period*.

5.3 *Run-off cover*

Subject to clause 5.7 the insurance must provide run-off cover:

(a) in the event of a *cessation* that occurs during or on expiration of the *policy period*;

(b) in the event of a *cessation* that occurs during the *extended policy period* or the *cessation period*; or

(c) from the expiration of the *cessation period*;

and for the purposes of this clause 5.3 and clause 5.7, an *insured firm's practice* shall (without limitation) be regarded as ceasing if (and with effect from the date upon which) the *insured firm* becomes a *non-SRA firm*.

5.4   Scope of run-off cover

The run-off cover referred to in clause 5.3 must:

(a) indemnify each *insured* in accordance with clauses 1.1 to 1.4;

(b) provide a minimum level of insurance cover in accordance with clauses 2.1 and 2.3;

(c) be subject to the exclusions and conditions of the insurance applicable in accordance with the *MTC*; and

(d) extend the *period of insurance* for an additional six years (ending on the sixth anniversary of the date upon which, but for this requirement, it would have ended, and for the avoidance of doubt, including the *extended policy period* and *cessation period*,) save that in respect of run-off cover provided under clause 5.3(c), such run-off cover shall not operate to indemnify any regulated *insured* for civil liability arising from acts or omissions of such *insured* occurring after the expiration of the *cessation period*.

5.5   Succession

The insurance must provide that, if there is a *successor practice* to the ceased *practice*, the *insured firm* may elect before its *cessation*, whether it wishes the ceased *practice*:

(a) to be insured under the run-off cover referred to in clause 5.3(a) or

(b) provided that there is insurance complying with these *MTC* in relation to that *successor practice*, to be insured as a *prior practice* under such insurance.

If the *insured firm* fails to make an election and/or fails to pay any premium due under the terms of the *policy*, before its *cessation*, clause 5.5(b) above shall apply.

5.6   Suspended practices

The insurance must provide that, where run-off cover has been activated in accordance with this clause 5, but where the *insured firm's practice* restarts, the *insurer* may (but shall not be obliged to) cancel such run-off cover, on such terms as may be agreed, provided that:

(a) there is insurance complying with these *MTC* in relation to that *insured firm* in force on the date of cancellation;

(b) the *participating insurer* providing such insurance confirms in writing to the *insured firm* and the *insurer* (if different) that:

   (i) it is providing insurance complying with these *MTC* in relation to that *insured firm* for the then current *indemnity period*; and

   (ii) it is doing so on the basis that the *insured firm's practice* is regarded as being a continuation of the *insured firm's practice* prior to *cessation* and that accordingly it is liable for *claims* against the *insured firm* arising from incidents, occurrences, facts, matters, acts and/or omissions which occurred prior to *cessation*.

5.7   Transfer to another approved regulator

Clause 5.3 above does not apply where the *insured firm* becomes an *authorised non-SRA firm* provided that the *approved regulator*, with which the *authorised non-SRA firm* is authorised, is a signatory to a protocol on terms agreed by the *SRA* which relates to switching between *approved regulators*.

6   Exclusions

The insurance must not exclude or limit the liability of the *insurer* except to the extent that any *claim* or related *defence costs* arise from the matters set out in this clause 6.

6.1   Prior cover

Any *claim* in respect of which the *insured* is entitled to be indemnified under a professional indemnity insurance contract for a period earlier than the *period of insurance*, whether by reason of notification of *circumstances* under the earlier contract or otherwise.

6.2   Death or bodily injury

Any liability of any *insured* for causing or contributing to death or bodily injury, except that the insurance must nonetheless cover liability for psychological injury or emotional distress which arises from a breach of duty in the performance of (or failure to perform) legal work.

6.3   Property damage

Any liability of any *insured* for causing or contributing to damage to, or destruction or physical loss of, any property (other than property in the care, custody or control of any *insured* in connection with the *insured firm's practice* and not occupied or used in the course of the *insured firm's practice*), except that the insurance must nonetheless cover liability for such damage, destruction or loss which arises from breach of duty in the performance of (or failure to perform) legal work.

6.4   Partnership disputes

Any actual or alleged breach of the *insured firm's partnership* or shareholder agreement or arrangements, including any equivalent agreement or arrangement where the *insured firm* is an *LLP* or a *company* without a share capital.

6.5 *Employment breaches, discrimination, etc.*

Wrongful dismissal, repudiation or breach of an employment contract or arrangement, termination of a training contract, harassment, discrimination or like conduct in relation to any *partnership* or shareholder agreement or arrangement or the equivalent where the *insured firm* is an *LLP* or a *company* without a share capital, or in relation to any employment or training agreement or arrangement.

6.6 *Debts, trading liabilities and funding arrangements*

Any:

(a) trading or personal debt of any *insured*; or

(b) legal liability assumed or accepted by an *insured* or an *insured firm* under any contract or agreement for the supply to, or use by, the *insured* or *insured firm* of goods or services in the course of the *insured firm's practice*, save that this exclusion 6.6(b) will not apply to any legal liability arising in the course of an *insured firm's practice* in connection with its or any *insured's* use of or access to the HM Land Registry network (including, without limitation, access under a Network Access Agreement made under the Land Registration (Network Access) Rules and the Land Registration (Electronic Communications) Order 2007) other than an obligation to pay search fees or other charges for searches or services provided by HM Land Registry to the *insured firm*; or

(c) guarantee indemnity or undertaking by any particular *insured* in connection with the provision of finance, property, assistance or other benefit or advantage directly or indirectly to that *insured*.

6.7 *Fines, penalties, etc*

Any:

(a) fine or penalty; or

(b) award of punitive, exemplary or like damages under the law of the United States of America or Canada, other than in respect of defamation; or

(c) order or agreement to pay the costs of a complainant, regulator, investigator or prosecutor of any professional conduct complaint against, or investigation into the professional conduct of, any *insured*.

6.8 *Fraud or dishonesty*

The insurance may exclude liability of the *insurer* to indemnify any particular *person* to the extent that any civil liability or related *defence costs* arise from dishonesty or a fraudulent act or omission committed or condoned by that *person*, except that:

(a) the insurance must nonetheless cover each other *insured*; and

(b) the insurance must provide that no dishonesty, act or omission will be imputed to a body corporate unless it was committed or condoned by, in the case of a *company*, all *directors* of that *company*, or in the case of an *LLP*, all *members* of that *LLP*.

6.9 *Directors' or officers' liability*

The insurance may exclude liability of the *insurer* to indemnify any natural person in their capacity as a *member* of an *LLP* or *director* or officer of a body corporate (other than a *recognised body*, *licensed body* (in relation to the activities regulated by the *SRA* in accordance with the terms of the body's licence) or a service, administration, trustee or nominee *company* referred to in clause 1.3(b) except that:

(a) the insurance must nonetheless cover any liability of that *person* which arises from a breach of duty in the performance of (or failure to perform) legal work; and

(b) the insurance must nonetheless cover each other *insured* against any vicarious or joint liability.

6.10 *War and terrorism, and asbestos*

The insurance may exclude, by way of an exclusion or endorsement, liability of the *insurer* to indemnify any *insured* in respect of, or in any way in connection with:

(a) terrorism, war or other hostilities; and/or

(b) asbestos, or any actual or alleged asbestos-related injury or damage involving the use, presence, existence, detection, removal, elimination or avoidance of asbestos or exposure to asbestos,

provided that any such exclusion or endorsement does not exclude or limit any liability of the *insurer* to indemnify any *insured* against civil liability or related *defence costs* arising from any actual or alleged breach of duty in the performance of (or failure to perform) legal work or failure to discharge or fulfil any duty incidental to the *insured firm's practice* or to the conduct of *private legal practice*.

6.11 *International trade sanctions*

The *insurer* shall be deemed not to provide cover and shall not be liable to pay any *claim* or provide any benefit under the insurance to the extent that the provision of such cover, payment of such *claim* or provision of such benefit would expose the *insurer* to any sanction, prohibition or restriction under United Nations resolutions or the trade or economic sanctions, laws or regulations of the European Union, United Kingdom, Australia or United States of America.

7 General conditions

7.1 *As agreed*

The insurance may contain such general conditions as are agreed between the *insurer* and the *insured firm*, but the insurance must provide that the special conditions required by clause 4 prevail to the extent of any inconsistency.

7.2   *Reimbursement*

The insurance may provide that each *insured* who:

> (a) committed or condoned (whether knowingly or recklessly):
>
>> (i) any breach of the duty to make a fair presentation of the risk, or misrepresentation; or
>>
>> (ii) any breach of the terms or conditions of the insurance; or
>>
>> (iii) dishonesty or any fraudulent act or omission; or
>
> (b) undertakes, either itself or by any of its *principals, employees,* consultants or agents or any *person* on its behalf, any activity during the *cessation period* in connection with *private legal practice* save to the extent that the activity is undertaken to discharge any of its obligations within the scope of its *existing instructions* or is necessary in connection with the discharge of any such obligation,

will reimburse the *insurer* to the extent that is just and equitable having regard to the prejudice caused to the *insurer's* interests by such failure to make a fair presentation of the risk, misrepresentation, breach, dishonesty, act or omission, provided that no *insured* shall be required to make any such reimbursement to the extent that any such breach of the terms or conditions of the insurance was in order to comply with any applicable *regulatory arrangements* of the *SRA*.

The insurance must provide that no failure to make a fair presentation of the risk, misrepresentation, breach, dishonesty, act or omission will be imputed to a body corporate unless it was committed or condoned by, in the case of a *company*, all *directors* of that *company*, or in the case of an *LLP*, all *members* of that *LLP*.

The insurance must provide further that any right of reimbursement contemplated by this clause 7.2 against any *person* referred to in clause 1.3(d) (or against the estate or legal personal representative of any such *person* if they die or become legally incapacitated) is limited to the extent that is just and equitable having regard to the prejudice caused to the *insurer's* interests by that *person* having committed or condoned (whether knowingly or recklessly) the failure to make a fair presentation of the risk, misrepresentation, breach, dishonesty, act or omission.

7.3   *Reimbursement of defence costs*

The insurance may provide that each *insured* will reimburse the *insurer* for *defence costs* advanced on that *insured's* behalf which the *insurer* is not ultimately liable to pay.

7.4   *Reimbursement of the excess*

The insurance may provide for those *persons* who are at any time during the *period of insurance principals* of the *insured firm*, together with, in relation to a *sole practitioner*, any *person* held out as a *partner* of that practitioner, to reimburse the *insurer* for any *excess* paid by the *insurer* on an *insured's* behalf. The *sum insured* must be reinstated to the extent of reimbursement of any amount which eroded it as contemplated by clause 3.4.

7.5 *Reimbursement of moneys paid pending dispute resolution*

The insurance may provide that each *insured* will reimburse the *insurer* following resolution of any coverage dispute for any amount paid by the *insurer* on that *insured's* behalf which, on the basis of the resolution of the dispute, the *insurer* is not ultimately liable to pay.

7.6 *Withholding assets or entitlements*

The insurance may require the *insured firm* to account to the *insurer* for any asset or entitlement of any *person* who committed or condoned any dishonesty or fraudulent act or omission, provided that the *insured firm* is legally entitled to withhold that asset or entitlement from that *person*.

7.7 *Premium*

The premium may be calculated on such basis as the *insurer* determines and the *insured firm* accepts including, without limitation, a basis which recognises *claims* history, categories of work performed by the *insured firm*, numbers of *principals* and *employees*, revenue derived from the *insured firm's practice* and other risk factors determined by the *insurer*.

8   Law and Jurisdiction

These *MTC* and any dispute or claim (including non-contractual disputes or claims) arising out of or in connection with them or their subject matter or formation shall be governed by and construed in accordance with the law of England and Wales and subject to the jurisdiction of the courts of England and Wales.

ANNEX 2
SPECIAL PROVISIONS FOR RELS

1.   If:

(a)   one or more of the *principals* of an *insured firm* are *RELs* who claim that professional indemnity insurance, or a professional indemnity fund, under their home professional rules provides the *insured firm's practice* with professional indemnity cover in all respects equivalent in its conditions and extent to that which would be provided under the *MTC* (Full Home State Cover);

(b)   no more than 25% of the *principals* of the *insured firm* are *solicitors*; and

(c)   the *SRA* is so satisfied, (including, without limitation, by reason of any provider of the Full Home State Cover entering into such agreement as the *SRA* may require from time to time),

the *insured firm* and its *principals* shall for so long as such cover continues (and, where the *SRA* has required such agreement, for so long as such agreement remains in force and its requirements are complied with by the provider(s) of the Full Home State Cover that are party to it) be exempted from the obligation to take out and maintain *qualifying insurance*.

2.   If on an application by one or more *RELs* who are *principals* in an *insured firm*, the *SRA* is satisfied that the *insured firm's practice* has professional indemnity cover under home professional rules but that the equivalence is only partial (Partial Home State Cover) (including, without limitation, by reason of the provider of the Partial Home State Cover entering into such agreement as the *SRA* may require from time to time), the *insured firm* and its *principals* shall for so long as such cover continues (and, where the *SRA* has required such agreement, for so long as such agreement remains in force and its requirements are complied with by the provider(s) of the Partial Home State Cover that are party to it) be exempted from the obligation to take out and maintain *qualifying insurance*, on condition that they take out and maintain a difference in conditions policy, which shall provide cover including the *MTC* as modified by the following changes (but not otherwise):

(a)   Clause 4.5 shall be deleted and replaced with the following:

4.5 No 'other insurance' provision

The insurance must not provide that the liability of the *insurer* is reduced or excluded by reason of the existence or availability of any other insurance other than as contemplated by clauses 6.1 or 6.12. For the avoidance of doubt, this requirement is not intended to affect any right of the *insurer* to claim contribution from any other *insurer* which is also liable to indemnify any *insured*.

(b)   Clause 4.8 shall be deleted and replaced with the following:

4.8 Resolution of disputes

The insurance must provide that, if there is a dispute as to whether a *practice* is a *successor practice* for the purposes of clauses 1.1, or 5.5, the *insured* and the *insurer* will take all reasonable steps to resolve the dispute in conjunction with any related dispute between any other party which has insurance complying with these *MTC* and that party's insurer, and in conjunction with the provider of the *Partial Home State Cover*.

(c)   Clause 4.12 shall be added:

4.12 Period of insurance

The period of insurance must not expire prior to the date with effect on which the *Partial Home State Cover* expires or is avoided.

(d)   The following clause shall be added:

6.12 Partial Home State Cover

The insurance may exclude any liability of the insurer to the extent that any such liability is covered under the terms of the *Partial Home State Cover* irrespective of whether recovery is actually made in respect of such liability.

3.   In the event of an *insured firm* which has the benefit of an exemption under paragraph 1 or paragraph 2 of this annex ceasing for whatever reason to enjoy that exemption but continuing to carry on a practice it shall be treated for all the

purposes of these rules as though it had commenced the practice on the date when such exemption ceased.

4. Rule 5 (Insolvency of Participating Insurer) shall apply to an *insured firm* which has the benefit of an exemption under paragraph 1 or paragraph 2 of this annex in like manner as though the insurance company or entity or fund providing professional indemnity cover under its home professional rules, on the basis of which exemption or partial exemption was granted, was a *participating insurer*.

5. In the case of an *insured firm* which has the benefit of an exemption under paragraph 2 of this annex all the provisions of these rules shall apply to the additional professional indemnity insurance required under that paragraph to be taken out with a *participating insurer*.

Supplemental notes

Made by the SRA Board on 5 December 2018.

Made under sections 31 and 37 of the Solicitors Act 1974, section 9 of the Administration of Justice Act 1985, and section 83 of, and paragraph 19 of Schedule 11 to the Legal Services Act 2007.

The SRA Indemnity Insurance Rules 2013 do not apply in respect of any *indemnity period* beginning on or after 24 November 2019 but they remain in force in respect of the *indemnity period* from 1 October 2013 to 24 November 2019 inclusive.

[Last updated: 25 November 2019]

The prescribed organisations and terms under which Solicitors, RELs and RFLs are allowed to hold client money in their own name

Status

This mandatory statement prescribes the types of organisations where solicitors, RELs and RFLs who work in them can hold client money in their own name, pursuant to paragraph 4.3 of the SRA Code of Conduct for Solicitors, RELs and RFLs.

It also prescribes the terms that the SRA has determined should apply to the holding of client money in their own name by any such solicitors, RELs and RFLs.

Introduction

Paragraph 4.3 of the SRA Code for Solicitors, RELs and RFLs permits solicitors, RELs and RFLs to hold client money in their own name in certain limited circumstances, including if they work in an organisation of the kind prescribed by the SRA under the rule.

This statement sets out:

● the type of organisations prescribed by the SRA;

● and the relevant terms.

This statement may be revised or updated from time to time.

Prescribed organisations

For the purposes of paragraph 4.3 of the SRA Code for Solicitors, RELs and RFLs, you are permitted to hold client money in your own name if you are a solicitor, REL or RFL working in a non-commercial body. A non-commercial body is defined in the SRA Glossary as body that falls within section 23(2) of the Legal Services act 2007 (a "Prescribed Organisation").

Prescribed terms that apply

If you work in a Prescribed Organisation and you wish to be able to hold client money, you must comply, and make sure that the Prescribed Organisation complies with, the following terms. Please note that all defined terms referred to below are set out in the SRA Glossary.

PRESCRIBED TERMS

1: Client money

1.1 *"Client money"* is money held or received by you:

(a) relating to *regulated services* delivered by you to a *client*;

(b) on behalf of a third party in relation to *regulated services* delivered by you (such as money held as agent, stakeholder or held to the sender's order);

(c) as a trustee or as the holder of a specified office or appointment, such as donee of a power of attorney, Court of Protection deputy or trustee of an occupational pension scheme;

(d) in respect of your *fees* and any unpaid *disbursements* if held or received prior to delivery of a bill for the same.

1.2 You ensure that *client money* is paid promptly into a *client account* unless:

(a) in relation to money falling within 1(c), to do so would conflict with your obligations under rules or regulations relating to your specified office or appointment;

(b) the *client money* represents payments received from the Legal Aid Agency for your *costs*; or

(c) you agree in the individual circumstances an alternative arrangement in writing with the *client*, or the third party, for whom the money is held.

1.3 You ensure that *client money* is available on demand unless you agree an alternative arrangement in writing with the *client* or the third party for whom the money is held.

1.4 You ensure that *client money* is returned promptly to the *client*, or the third party for whom the money is held, as soon as there is no longer any proper reason to hold those funds.

2: Client account

2.1 You only maintain a *client account* at a branch (or the head office) of a *bank* or a *building society* in England and Wales.

2.2 You ensure that the name of any *client account* includes:

(a) your name; and

(b) the word "client" to distinguish it from any other type of account held or operated by the Prescribed Organisation

2.3 You must not use a *client account* to provide banking facilities to *clients* or third parties. Payments into, and transfers or withdrawals from a *client account* must be in respect of the delivery by you of *regulated services*.

3: Client money must be kept separate

3.1   You keep *client money* separate from money belonging to you or the Prescribed Organisation.

3.2   You ensure that you allocate promptly any funds from *mixed payments* you receive to the correct client account or any other accounts operated by the Prescribed Organisation.

3.3   Where you are holding *client* money and some or all of that money will be used to pay your *costs*:

(a)   you must give a bill of *costs*, or other written notification of the *costs* incurred, to the client or the paying party;

(b)   this must be done before you transfer any *client money* from a *client account* to make the payment; and

(c)   any such payment must be for the specific sum identified in the bill of *costs*, or other written notification of the *costs* incurred, and covered by the amount held for the particular *client* or third party.

4: Withdrawals from client account

4.1   You only withdraw *client money* from a *client account*:

(a)   for the purpose for which it is being held;

(b)   following receipt of instructions from the *client*, or the third party for whom the money is held; or

(c)   on the *SRA*'s prior written authorisation or in *prescribed* circumstances.

4.2   You appropriately authorise and supervise all withdrawals made from a *client account*.

4.3   You only withdraw *client money* from a *client account* if sufficient funds are held on behalf of that specific client or third party to make the payment.

5: Duty to correct breaches after discovery

5.1   You correct any breaches of these rules promptly upon discovery. Any money improperly withheld or withdrawn from a *client account* must be immediately paid into the account or replaced as appropriate.

6: Payment of interest

6.1   You account to *clients* or third parties for a fair sum of *interest* on any *client money* held by you on their behalf.

6.2   You may by a written agreement come to a different arrangement with the *client* or the third party for whom the money is held as to the payment of *interest*, but you must provide sufficient information to enable them to give informed consent.

7: Client accounting systems and controls

7.1   You keep and maintain accurate, contemporaneous, and chronological records to:

(a)   record in client ledgers identified by the *client's* name and an appropriate description of the matter to which they relate:

(i)   all receipts and payments in your name which are *client money* on the client side of the client ledger account;

(ii)   all receipts and payments in your name which are not *client money* on the business side of the client ledger account;

(b)   maintain a list of all the balances shown by the client ledger accounts of the liabilities to *clients* (and third parties), with a running total of the balances; and

(c)   provide a cash book showing a running total of all transactions through *client accounts* held or operated by you.

7.2   You obtain, at least every five weeks, statements from *banks*, building societies and other financial institutions for all *client accounts* and business accounts held or operated by you.

7.3   You complete at least every five weeks, for all *client accounts* held or operated by you, a reconciliation of the *bank* or *building society* statement balance with the cash book balance and the client ledger total, a record of which must be signed by someone authorised to do so by the Prescribed Organisation. You should promptly investigate and resolve any differences shown by the reconciliation.

7.4   You keep readily accessible a central record of all bills or other written notifications of *costs* given by you.

8: Obtaining and delivery of accountants' reports

8.1   The *SRA* may require you to obtain or deliver an accountant's report to the *SRA* on reasonable notice if the SRA considers that it is in the public interest to do so. You must ensure that any such report is prepared and signed by an accountant who is a member of one of the *chartered accountancy bodies* and who is, or works for, a registered auditor.

8.2   The *SRA* may disqualify an accountant from preparing a report for the purposes of this rule if:

(a)   the accountant has been found guilty by their professional body of professional misconduct or equivalent; or

(b)   the *SRA* is satisfied that the accountant has failed to exercise due care and skill in the preparation of a report under these rules.

8.3   The *SRA* may specify from time to time matters that you must ensure are incorporated into the terms on which an accountant is engaged.

8.4   You must provide to an accountant preparing a report under these rules:

   (a)   details of all client accounts held or operated by you in your own name at any *bank*, *building society* or other financial institution at any time during the *accounting period* to which the report relates; and

   (b)   all other information and documentation that the accountant requires to enable completion of their report

8.5   You must store all accounting records in relation to client accounts held or operated in your name securely and retain these for at least six years.

[Supplemental notes]

[Last updated: 25 November 2019]

The prescribed circumstances in which you can withdraw client money from client account to pay to a charity of your choice

Rule 5.1 (c) of the SRA Accounts Rules

Status

Rule 5.1 (c) of the SRA Accounts Rules (Accounts Rules) provide that client money can only be withdrawn from a client account on the SRA's prior written authorisation or in prescribed circumstances.

This mandatory statement prescribes the circumstances in which such withdrawals can be made without our prior written authorisation. These circumstances are limited to withdrawals of residual client account balances of £500 or less on any one client matter provided the balance is paid to a charity of your choice and if you have met the conditions set out.

This statement must be complied with by all SRA authorised firms and their staff.

This statement may be revised or updated from time to time.

For amounts over £500 you will need our authority before removing this money from the client account. Please use our application form [**www.sra.org.uk/solicitors/ resources/withdrawal-of-residual-client-balances**].

Introduction

The SRA Accounts Rules (Accounts Rules) require you to return client money promptly to the client, or third party for whom the money is held, (including refunds received after the client has been accounted to) as soon as there is no longer a proper reason to hold those funds (Rule 2.5).

A residual client account balance is money that you have not returned to your client at the end of a retainer and it is now difficult for you to do so as you cannot identify or trace the client.

Firms should, therefore, very rarely be holding residual client account balances.

However, you may withdraw residual client balances of £500 or less on any one client matter in the prescribed circumstances set out below.

Prescribed circumstances under Rule 5.1 (c)

You may withdraw residual client balances of £500 or less on any one client matter from a client account provided:

1.   the balance is paid to a charity of your choice

2.   you have taken reasonable steps to return the money to the rightful owner. The reasonableness of such steps will depend on:

    i.   the age of the residual balance;

    ii.   the amount of the residual balance;

    iii.   if you have access to the client's most up to date contact details;

    iv.   if not, the costs associated with tracing your client.

We expect you to make more intensive efforts to locate the rightful owner for larger or more recent residual balances or for balances where more details are held about the client.

3.   you record the steps taken to return the money to the rightful owner and retain those records, together with all relevant documentation for at least six years;

4.   you keep appropriate accounting records, including:

    i.   a central register which records the name of the rightful owner on whose behalf the money was held, the amount, name of the recipient charity (and their charity number) and the date of the payment; and

    ii.   all receipts from the charity and confirmation of any indemnity provided against any legitimate claim subsequently made for the sum they have received.

5.   you do not deduct from the residual balance any costs incurred in attempting to trace or communicate with the rightful owner.

The records referred to in points 3 and 4 above may be requested by your reporting accountant who will look at whether you have followed these prescribed circumstances.

For amounts over £500 you will need our authority before removing this money from the client account. Please use our application form.

Additional guidance

You may choose to pay the money to a charity that does not offer you an indemnity but if it does not, you will be liable to pay the money to the client if they contact you later to claim it.

Some ways in which you may be able to trace your client include:

- making use of social media

- making a search of Companies House and/or the Probate Registry

- making use of the Department of Work and Pensions' letter forwarding service

- undertaking any free searches on the internet.

[Supplemental notes]

[Last updated: 25 November 2019]

SRA Glossary

The Standards and Regulations Glossary comprises a set of defined terms which are used in the Standards and Regulations. Terms being used in their defined sense appear as italicised text within the individual sets of provisions of the Standards and Regulations. The same terms in the Standards and Regulations may appear as italicised text in some cases but not in others. Where they are not italicised, for reasons relating to the specific context, they are not being used in their defined sense and take their natural meaning in that context.

academic stage of training means the undertaking by an individual of the following programmes of study which satisfy the requirements of the *Joint Statement*:

(a) a *Qualifying Law Degree*;

(b) a *CPE*;

(c) an *Exempting Law Degree*; or

(d) an *Integrated Course*;

at an *approved education provider*

accounting period means the period for which your accounts are made up, and that:

(a) begins at the end of the previous accounting period; and

(b) comprises a period of 12 months unless you change the period for which your accounts are ordinarily made up or the accounting period covers your first report or a report after a break from practice in which case the accounting period may be for a period of less than 12 months or for more than 12 months, up to a maximum period of 18 months

accounting records means all reconciliations, *bank* and *building society* statements (paper or electronic), original passbooks, signed letters of engagement with reporting accountants, the accountants' reports (whether qualified or not), any *client's* written instructions to hold *client money* other than in accordance with these rules, records and documents, including electronic records, relating to any *third party managed accounts* and any other records or documents necessary to show compliance with the SRA Accounts Rules

AJA means the Administration of Justice Act 1985

AJA (2012) means the Administration of Justice Act 1985.

ancillary insurance intermediary has the meaning given to "*IDD* ancillary insurance intermediary" in the *FCA* Handbook

applicant means for the purposes of the SRA Compensation Fund Rules a *person* applying for a grant out of the Compensation Fund.

approved education provider means a provider recognised by the *SRA* as providing a *Qualifying Law Degree, CPE, Exempting Law Degree,* or an *Integrated Course*

approved regulator means any body listed as an approved regulator in paragraph 1 of Schedule 4 to the *LSA* or designated as an approved regulator by an order under paragraph 17 of that Schedule

arrangement (2012) in relation to financial services, fee sharing and *referrals* in Chapters 1, 6 and 9 of the *SRA Code of Conduct*, means any express or tacit agreement between you and another *person*, whether contractually binding or not.

asset includes money, documents, wills, deeds, investments and other property

authorised body means:

(a) a body that has been authorised by the *SRA* to practise as a *licensed body* or a recognised body; or

(b) a *sole practitioner's* practice that has been authorised by the *SRA* as a *recognised sole practice*

authorised decision maker in relation to a decision, means a person authorised to make that decision by the *SRA* under a schedule of delegation

authorised education provider means a provider recognised by the *SRA* as providing the *Legal Practice Course* or the Professional Skills Course

authorised insurer has the meaning given in section 87(1A), (1B) and (1C) of the *SA*

authorised non-SRA firm means a firm which is authorised to carry on legal activities as defined in section 12 of the *LSA* by an *approved regulator* other than the *SRA*

authorised person

(a) subject to sub-paragraph (b) below, means a *person* who is authorised by the *SRA* or another *approved regulator* to carry on a legal activity as defined under s12 of the *LSA* and the term "non-authorised person" shall be construed accordingly; and

(b) in the SRA Financial Services (Scope) Rules, has the meaning given in section 31 of the *FSMA*

authorised training provider means a *person* authorised by the *SRA* under the SRA Education, Training and Assessment Provider Regulations to take on and train a *trainee*

bank has the meaning given in section 87(1) of the *SA*

barrister means a person called to the Bar by one of the Inns of Court and who has completed pupillage and is authorised by the General Council of the Bar to practise as a barrister

beneficiary means a *person* with a beneficial entitlement to funds held by the SRA on *statutory trust*

best list means a list of potential beneficial entitlements to *statutory trust* monies which, in cases where it is not possible to create a *reconciled list*, is, in the view of the *SRA*, the most reliable that can be achieved with a reasonable and proportionate level of work taking into account the circumstances of the *intervention* and the nature of the evidence available

building society means a building society within the meaning of the Building Societies Act 1986

CBTL credit agreement has the meaning given in the *FCA* Handbook

cessation means where the *insured firm's practice* ceases during the *period of insurance* or after the *period of insurance* in circumstances where the *insured firm* has not obtained insurance complying with the *MTC* and incepting on and with effect from the day immediately following the expiry of the *policy period*

cessation period means the period commencing on the expiry of the *extended policy period* where, during the *extended policy period* the relevant *authorised body* has not ceased *practice* or obtained a *policy* of *qualifying insurance* incepting with effect on and from the day immediately following expiration of the *policy period*, and ending on the date which is the earlier to occur of:

(a) the date, if any, on which the *authorised body* obtains a *policy* of *qualifying insurance* incepting with effect on and from the day immediately following expiration of the *policy period*;

(b) the date which is 90 days after the commencement of the *extended policy period*; or

(c) the date on which the *insured firm's practice* ceases

character and suitability includes fitness and propriety under rule 13.1 of the SRA Authorisation of Firms Rules

charity has the meaning given in section 1 of the Charities Act 2011

chartered accountancy bodies means the Institute of Chartered Accountants in England and Wales; the Institute of Chartered Accountants of Scotland; the Association of Chartered Certified Accountants; or the Institute of Chartered Accountants in Ireland

circumstances means an incident, occurrence, fact, matter, act or omission which may give rise to a *claim* in respect of civil liability.

circumstances (2012) means an incident, occurrence, fact, matter, act or omission which may give rise to a *claim* in respect of civil liability.

claim means a demand for, or an assertion of a right to, civil compensation or civil damages or an intimation of an intention to seek such compensation or damages. For these purposes, an obligation on an *insured firm* and/or any *insured* to remedy a breach of the SRA Accounts Rules, or any rules which replace them in whole or in part, shall be treated as a claim, and the obligation to remedy such breach shall be treated as a civil liability for the purposes of clause 1 of the *MTC*, whether or not any *person* makes a demand for, or an assertion of a right to, civil compensation or civil damages or an intimation of an intention to seek such compensation or damages as a result of such breach, except where any such obligation may arise as a result of the insolvency of a bank (as defined in section 87 of the *SA*) or a *building society* which holds client money in a client account of the *insured firm* or the failure of such bank or *building society* generally to repay monies on demand

claim (2012) means a demand for, or an assertion of a right to, civil compensation or civil damages or an intimation of an intention to seek such compensation or damages. For these purposes, an obligation on an *insured firm* and/or any *insured* to remedy a breach of the Solicitors' Accounts Rules 1998 (as amended from time to time), or any rules (including, without limitation, the *SRA Accounts Rules*) which replace the Solicitors' Accounts Rules 1998 in whole or in part, shall be treated as a claim, and the obligation to remedy such breach shall be treated as a civil liability for the purposes of clause 1 of the *MTC*, whether or not any *person* makes a demand for, or an assertion of a right to, civil compensation or civil damages or an intimation of an intention to seek such compensation or damages as a result of such breach, except where any such obligation may arise as a result of the insolvency of a bank (as defined in section 87 of the *SA*) or a *building society* which holds client money in a client account of the *insured firm* or the failure of such bank or *building society* generally to repay monies on demand.

claimant means:

(a)   a person making a *claim* to *statutory trust monies*; and

(b)   in the SRA Indemnity Insurance Rules and the *MTC,* a person or entity which has made or may make a claim including a claim for contribution or indemnity

client means the *person* for whom you act and, where the context permits, includes prospective and former clients

in the SRA Financial Services (Scope) Rules, in relation to any regulated *financial services activities* carried on by an *authorised body* for a trust or the estate of a deceased person (including a controlled trust), means the trustees or personal representatives in their capacity as such and not any person who is a *beneficiary* under the trust or interested in the estate

client account has the meaning given to it in the SRA Accounts Rules

client money has the meaning given in rule 2.1 of the SRA Accounts Rules

client money (overseas) means money held or received by your *overseas practice*:

    (a)   relating to services delivered by your *overseas practice* to a *client*;

    (b)   on behalf of a third party in relation to services delivered by your *overseas practice* (such as money held as agent, stakeholder or held to the sender's order);

    (c)   as a trustee or as the holder of a specified office or appointment;

    (d)   in respect of *fees* and any unpaid *disbursements* if held or received prior to delivery of a bill for the same

COFA means a compliance officer for finance and administration and in relation to a *licensable body* is a reference to its *HOFA*

COLP means compliance officer for legal practice and in relation to a *licensable body* is a reference to its *HOLP*

Companies Acts means the Companies Act 1985 and the Companies Act 2006

company means a company incorporated in a state to which the Establishment of Lawyers Directive 98/5/EC applies and registered under the *Companies Acts* or a *societas Europaea*

competing for the same objective means any situation in which two or more *clients* are competing for an "objective" which, if attained by one *client*, will make that "objective" unattainable to the other *client* or *clients*, and "objective" means an asset, contract or business opportunity which two or more *clients* are seeking to acquire or recover through a liquidation (or some other form of insolvency process) or by means of an auction or tender process or a bid or offer, but not a public takeover

compliance officer is a reference to a body's *COLP* or its *COFA*

conflict of interest means a situation where your separate duties to act in the best interests of two or more *clients* in relation to the same or a related matters conflict

connected practices means a body providing legal services, established outside England and Wales which is not an *overseas practice* or an excluded body but is otherwise connected to an *authorised body* in England and Wales, by virtue of:

    (a)   being a parent undertaking, within the meaning of section 1162 of the Companies Act 2006, of the *authorised body*;

    (b)   being jointly managed or owned, or having a *partner, member* or *owner* in common, or controlled by or, with the *authorised body*;

    (c)   participating in a joint enterprise or across its practice generally, sharing *costs*, revenue or profits related to the provision of legal services with the *authorised body*; or

(d) common branding,

and in this definition:

(i) a "body" means a natural person or *company, LLP* or *partnership* or other *body corporate* or unincorporated association or business entity; and

(ii) an "excluded body" means a body which is part of:

(A) a Verein or similar group structure involving more than one body providing legal services in respect of which the *authorised body* in England and Wales connected to it is not regarded as being the body which is the headquarters of that Verein or similar group structure or a significant part of it;

(B) a joint practice, alliance or association or association with the *authorised body* in England and Wales connected to it which is controlled by a body providing legal services outside England and Wales; or

(C) a group of affiliated bodies providing legal services which is not managed or controlled by an *authorised body* in England and Wales

(iii) A "joint enterprise" means any contractual arrangements between two or more independent bodies which provide legal services, for profit and/or other defined purpose or goal which apply generally between them, not just agreed on a matter by matter basis

(iv) "Common branding" means the use of a name, term, design, symbol, words or a combination of these that identifies two or more legal practices as distinct from other legal practices or an express statement that a legal practice is practising in association with one or more other named firms

continuous payment authority means consent given to a client for a firm to make one or more requests to a payment service provider for one or more payments from the client's payment account, but excluding:

(a) a direct debit to which the direct debit guarantee applies; and

(b) separate consent given by a client to a firm, following the making of the regulated credit agreement, for the firm to make a single request to a payment service provider for one payment of a specified amount from the client's payment account on the same day as the consent is given or on a specified day

contract of insurance means (in accordance with article 3(1) of the *Regulated Activities Order*) any contract of insurance which is a *long-term insurance contract* or a *general insurance contract*

contributions (2012) means contributions previously made to the *fund* in accordance with Part III of the Solicitors' Indemnity Rules 2007 (or any earlier corresponding provisions), and any additional sums paid in accordance with Rule 16 of the *SRA Indemnity Rules*.

costs means your *fees* and *disbursements*

Council (2012) has the meaning given in section 87 of the *SA*.

court means any court, tribunal or inquiry of England and Wales, or a British court martial, or any court of another jurisdiction

CPE means the Common Professional Examination, namely, a course, including assessments and examinations, approved by the *SRA* on behalf of the *SRA* and Bar Standards Board for the purposes of completing the *academic stage of training* for those who have not satisfactorily completed a *Qualifying Law Degree*

credit agreement has the meaning given by article 60B(3) of the *Regulated Activities Order*

credit broking means an activity of the kind specified in article 36A of the *Regulated Activities Order*.

credit tokens means a card, check, voucher, coupon, stamp, form, booklet or other document or thing given to a *client* by a *person* carrying on a *credit-related regulated financial services activity* ("the provider"), who undertakes that:

(a) on production of it (whether or not some other action is also required) the provider will supply cash, goods or services (or any of them) on credit; or

(b) where, on the production of it to a third party (whether or not any other action is also required), the third party supplies cash, goods and services (or any of them), the provider will pay the third party for them (whether or not deducting any discount or commission), in return for payment to the provider by the *client* and the provider shall, without prejudice to the definition of credit, be taken to provide credit drawn on whenever a third party supplies the *client* with cash, goods or services, and

the use of an object to operate a machine provided by the person giving the object or a third party shall be treated as the production of the object to that person or third party

credit-related regulated financial services activities means any of the following activities specified in Part 2 or 3A of the *Regulated Activities Order*:

(a) entering into a regulated credit agreement as lender (article 60B(1));

(b) exercising, or having the right to exercise, the lender's rights and duties under a regulated credit agreement (article 60B(2));

(c) credit broking (article 36A);

(d) debt adjusting (article 39D(1) and (2));

(e) debt counselling (article 39E(1) and (2));

(f) debt collecting (article 39F(1) and (2));

(g) debt administration (article 39G(1) and (2));

(h) entering into a regulated consumer hire agreement as owner (article 60N(1));

(i) exercising, or having the right to exercise, the owner's rights and duties under a regulated consumer hire agreement (article 60N(2));

(j) providing credit information services (article 89A);

(k) providing credit references (article 89B);

(l) operating an electronic system in relation to lending (article 36H);

(m) agreeing to carry on a regulated activity (article 64) so far as relevant to any of the activities (a) to (l),

which is carried on by way of business and relates to a specified investment applicable to that activity or, in the case of (j) and (k), relates to information about a person's financial standing

debt management plan means a non-statutory agreement between a *client* and one or more of the *client's* lenders the aim of which is to discharge or liquidate the *client's* debts, by making regular payments to a third party which administers the plan and distributes the money to the lenders

defaulting practitioner has the meaning given in rule 5 of the SRA Compensation Fund Rules

defence costs means legal costs and disbursements and investigative and related expenses reasonably and necessarily incurred with the consent of the *insurer* in:

(a) defending any proceedings relating to a *claim*; or

(b) conducting any proceedings for indemnity, contribution or recovery relating to a *claim*; or

(c) investigating, reducing, avoiding or compromising any actual or potential *claim*; or

(d) acting for any *insured* in connection with any investigation, inquiry or disciplinary proceeding (save in respect of any disciplinary proceeding under the authority of the *SRA* or the *Tribunal*),

and does not include any internal or overhead expenses of the *insured firm* or the *insurer* or the cost of any *insured's* time

degree means a *UK* degree, awarded at level 6 (or above) of the Framework for Higher Education Qualifications, by a recognised degree-awarding body

director means a director of a *company;* and in relation to a *societas Europaea* includes:

    (a) in a two-tier system, a *member* of the management organ and a *member* of the supervisory organ; and

    (b) in a one-tier system, a *member* of the administrative organ

disbursements means any costs or expenses paid or to be paid to a third party on behalf of the *client* or trust (including any VAT element) save for office expenses such as postage and courier fees

discrimination has the meaning given in the Equality Act 2010

durable medium means any instrument which:

    (a) enables the recipient to store information personally addressed to them in a way accessible for future reference and for a period of time adequate for the purposes of the information; and

    (b) allows the unchanged reproduction of the information stored

eligible former principal (2012) means a *principal* of a *previous practice* where:

    (i) that *previous practice* ceased on or before 31 August 2000; and

    (ii) a *relevant claim* is made in respect of any matter which would have given rise to an entitlement of the *principal* to indemnity out of the *fund* under the Solicitors' Indemnity Rules 1999 had the claim been notified to Solicitors Indemnity Fund Limited on 31 August 2000; and

    (iii) the *principal* has not at any time been a "principal" of the *relevant successor practice* ("principal" having the meaning applicable to the *SIIR*); and

    (iv) at the time that the *relevant claim* is made the *principal* is not a "principal" in "private practice" ("principal" and "private practice" having the meanings applicable to the *SIIR*).

employee means an individual who is:

    (a) engaged under a contract of service by a *person,* firm or organisation or its wholly owned service company;

    (b) engaged under a contract for services, made between a firm or organisation and:

        (i) that individual;

        (ii) an employment agency; or

        (iii) a *company* which is not held out to the public as providing legal services and is wholly owned and directed by that individual, or

    under which the *person,* firm or organisation has exclusive control over the individual's time for all or part of the individual's working week, save that:

(A) for the purposes of the SRA Financial Services (Scope) Rules, means an individual who is employed in connection with the firm's *regulated financial services activities* under a contract of service or under a contract for services such that he or she is held out as an employee or consultant of the firm

(B) for the purposes of the SRA Indemnity Insurance Rules and the *MTC*, means any *person* other than a *principal*:

    (a) employed or otherwise engaged in the *insured firm's practice* (including under a contract for services) including, without limitation, as a solicitor, lawyer, trainee solicitor or trainee lawyer, consultant, associate, locum tenens, agent, appointed *person*, office or clerical staff member or otherwise;

    (b) seconded to work in the *insured firm's practice*; or

    (c) seconded by the *insured firm* to work elsewhere,

but does not include any person who is engaged by the insured firm under a contract for services in respect of any work where that person is required, whether under the SRA Indemnity Insurance Rules or under the rules of any other professional body, to take out or to be insured under separate professional indemnity insurance in respect of that work

and the term "employer" is to be construed accordingly

Establishment Directive (2012) means the Establishment of Lawyers Directive 98/5/EC

European cross-border practice means:

(a) professional activity regulated by the *SRA* in a state whose legal profession is a full, an associate or an observer member of the Council of Bars and Law Societies of Europe (CCBE state) other than the *UK*, whether or not you are physically present in that CCBE state; and

(b) any professional contact regulated by the *SRA* with a *lawyer* of a CCBE state other than the *UK*,

excluding professional contacts and professional activities taking place within a firm or in-house legal department

excess means the first amount of a *claim* which is not covered by the *insurance*

execution-only means a transaction which is effected by an *authorised body* for a *client* where the *authorised body* assumes on reasonable grounds that the *client* is not relying on the *authorised body* as to the merits or suitability of that transaction

exempt person in the SRA Financial Services (Scope) Rules means a *person* who is exempt from the general prohibition as a result of an exemption order made under section 38(1) or as a result of section 39(1) or 285(2) or (3) of the *FSMA* and who, in engaging in the activity in question, is acting in the course of business in respect of which that *person* is exempt

Exempting Law Degree means a *Qualifying Law Degree* incorporating a *Legal Practice Course*, approved by the *SRA*

existing instructions means instructions to carry out legal activities as defined in section 12 of the *LSA* received by an *authorised body* from a client, which the body has accepted, on terms that have been agreed by the client, prior to the body becoming subject to cover under the *cessation period*

Exit day has the meaning given in section 20 of the European (Withdrawal) Act 2018

expired run-off claim (2012) means any claim made against the *fund* for indemnity under the *SRA Indemnity Rules* in respect of which no *preceding qualifying insurance* remains in force to cover such claim, by reason only of:

(i) the run-off cover provided or required to be provided under the policy having been activated; and

(ii) the sixth anniversary of the date on which cover under such *qualifying insurance* would have ended but for the activation of such run-off cover having passed; or

(iii) (in the case of a firm in default or a run-off firm) the period of run-off cover provided or required to be provided under arrangements made to cover such claim through the *ARP* having expired.

expired run-off cover (2012) means either:

(i) (unless (ii) below applies) the terms of the *preceding qualifying insurance*, excluding clause 5 (Run-off cover) of the *MTC*, as if it were a contract between Solicitors Indemnity Fund Limited and the firm or person making an *expired run-off claim*; or

(ii) where they are provided to Solicitors Indemnity Fund Limited prior to payment of the *claim*, the terms of the *preceding qualifying insurance*, provided that:

(A) references in the *preceding qualifying insurance* to the qualifying insurer that issued such insurance shall be read as references to Solicitors Indemnity Fund Limited;

(B) any obligation owed by any *insured* under the *preceding qualifying insurance* to the qualifying insurer which issued such insurance shall be deemed to be owed to Solicitors Indemnity Fund Limited in place of such qualifying insurer, unless and to the extent that Solicitors Indemnity Fund Limited in its absolute discretion otherwise agrees;

(C) the obligations of the *fund* and/or any *insured* in respect of an *expired run-off claim* shall neither exceed nor be less than the requirements of the *MTC* which, in accordance with the applicable *SIIR*, such *preceding qualifying insurance* included or was required to include.

Solicitors Indemnity Fund Limited shall be under no obligation to take any steps to obtain the terms of any such *preceding qualifying insurance*, which for these purposes includes the terms on which it was written in respect of the *insured firm* or person in question, and not merely a standard policy wording.

extended policy period means the period commencing at the end of the *policy period* and ending on the date which is the earlier to occur of:

(a) the date, if any, on which the firm obtains a *policy* of *qualifying insurance* incepting on and with effect from the day immediately following the expiration of the *policy period*;

(b) the date which is 30 days after the end of the *policy period*; or

(c) the date on which the *insured firm's practice* ceases

FCA means the Financial Conduct Authority

fees means your own charges or profit costs (including any VAT element)

financial benefit includes any commission, discount or rebate, but does not include your *fees* or *interest* earned on any *client account*

Financial Services Register means the record maintained by the *FCA* as required by section 347 of the *FSMA* and including those *persons* who carry on, or are proposing to carry on, *insurance distribution activities*

foreign lawyer has the meaning given in section 89(9) of the Courts and Legal Services Act 1990

foreign lawyer (2012) means an individual who is not a *solicitor* or barrister of England and Wales, but who is a member, and entitled to practise as such, of a legal profession regulated within a jurisdiction outside England and Wales.

FSMA means the Financial Services and Markets Act 2000

Fund means the fund established and maintained under rule 1.1 of the SRA Compensation Fund Rules

fund (2012) means the fund maintained in accordance with the *SRA Indemnity Rules*.

general insurance contract means any contract of insurance within Part I of Schedule 1 to the *Regulated Activities Order*

high-cost short-term credit means a *regulated credit agreement*:

(a) which is a borrower-lender agreement or a P2P agreement;

(b) in relation to which the APR is equal to or exceeds 100%;

(c) either:

    (i) in relation to which a financial promotion indicates (by express words or otherwise) that the credit is to be provided for any period up to a maximum of 12 months or otherwise indicates (by express words or otherwise) that the credit is to be provided for a short term; or

    (ii) under which the credit is due to be repaid or substantially repaid within a maximum of 12 months of the date on which the credit is advanced;

(d) which is not secured by a mortgage, charge or *pledge*; and

(e) which is not:

    (i) a *credit agreement* in relation to which the lender is a community finance organisation; or

    (ii) a home credit loan agreement, a bill of sale loan agreement or a borrower-lender agreement enabling a borrower to overdraw on a current account or arising where the holder of a current account overdraws on the account without a pre-arranged overdraft or exceeds a pre-arranged overdraft limit

higher courts means the Crown Court, High Court, Court of Appeal and Supreme Court in England and Wales

higher courts advocacy qualification means either:

(a) Higher Courts (Civil Advocacy) Qualification which entitles the *solicitor* or *REL* to exercise rights of audience in all civil proceedings in the *higher courts*, including judicial review proceedings in any *court* arising from any criminal cause; or

(b) Higher Courts (Criminal Advocacy) Qualification which entitles the *solicitor* or *REL* to exercise rights of audience in all criminal proceedings in the *higher courts* and judicial review proceedings in any *court* arising from any criminal cause

HOFA means a Head of Finance and Administration within the meaning of paragraph 13(2) of Schedule 11 to the *LSA*

HOLP means a Head of Legal Practice within the meaning of paragraph 11(2) of Schedule 11 to the *LSA*

home finance mediation activity has the meaning given in the *FCA* Handbook

IDD means Directive (EU) 2016/97 on insurance distribution

immigration work means the provision of immigration advice and immigration services, as defined in section 82 of the Immigration and Asylum Act 1999

indemnity period means in the SRA Indemnity Insurance Rules and the *MTC*, the period of one year starting on 1 September 2000, 2001 or 2002, the period of 13 calendar months starting on 1 September 2003, or the period of one year starting on 1 October in any subsequent calendar year

indemnity period (2012) means:

(i) in the *SRA Indemnity Insurance Rules*, the period of one year starting on 1 September 2000, 2001 or 2002, the period of 13 calendar months starting on 1 September 2003, or the period of one year starting on 1 October in any subsequent calendar year; and

(ii) in the *SRA Indemnity Rules*, the period of one year commencing on 1 September in any calendar year from 1987 to 2002 inclusive, the period of 13 calendar months commencing on 1 September 2003, and the period of one year commencing on 1 October in any subsequent calendar year.

insolvency event means in relation to a *participating insurer*:

(a) the appointment of a provisional liquidator, administrator, receiver or an administrative receiver;

(b) the approval of a voluntary arrangement under Part I of the Insolvency Act 1986 or the making of any other form of arrangement, composition or compounding with its creditors generally;

(c) the passing of a resolution for voluntary winding up where the winding up is or becomes a creditors' voluntary winding up under Part IV of the Insolvency Act 1986;

(d) the making of a winding up order by the court;

(e) the making of an order by the court reducing the value of one or more of the *participating insurer's* contracts under section 377 of *FSMA*; or

(f) the occurrence of any event analogous to any of the foregoing insolvency events in any jurisdiction outside England and Wales.

insurance distribution has the meaning given in the *FCA* Handbook

insurance distribution activity means any of the following regulated activities as specified in the *Regulated Activities Order* which are carried on in relation to a *contract of insurance* or rights to or interests in a *life policy*:

(a) dealing in investments as agent (article 21)

(b) arranging (bringing about) deals in investments (article 25(1))

(c) making arrangements with a view to transactions in investments (article 25(2))

(d) assisting in the administration and performance of a contract of insurance (article 39A)

(e) advising on investments (except peer to peer agreements) (article 53(1))

(f) agreeing to carry on a regulated activity in (a) to (e) above (article 64).

insurance distribution officer means the individual within the management structure of the firm who is responsible for *insurance distribution activity*

insurance intermediary has the meaning given to "IDD insurance intermediary" in the *FCA* Handbook

Insurance Product Information Document has the meaning given in the *FCA* Handbook

insurance undertaking has the meaning given to "IDD insurance undertaking" in the *FCA* Handbook

insurance-based investment product has the meaning given in the *FCA* Handbook

insured means each person and entity named or described as a person to whom the insurance extends and includes, without limitation, those referred to in clause 1.3 in the MTC

insured (2012) in the *SRA Indemnity Insurance Rules* means each person and entity named or described as a person to whom the insurance extends and includes, without limitation, those referred to in clause 1.3 in the *MTC* and, in relation to *prior practices* and *successor practices* respectively, those referred to in clauses 1.5 and 1.7 of the *MTC*.

insured firm means the *authorised body* which contracted with the *insurer* to provide the insurance

insured firm's practice means:

(a) the legal *practice* carried on by the *insured firm* as at the commencement of the *period of insurance*; and

(b) the continuous legal *practice* preceding and succeeding the *practice* referred to in paragraph (i) (irrespective of changes in ownership of the *practice*)

insurer means:

(a) for the purposes of the SRA Financial Services (Conduct of Business) Rules 2001 a firm with permission to effect or carry out *contracts of insurance* (other than a bank); and

(b) for the purposes of the *SRA Indemnity Insurance Rules* and the *MTC* the underwriter(s) of the insurance

Integrated Course means a course incorporating the foundations of legal knowledge as set out in the Academic Stage Handbook and the *Legal Practice Course*

interest includes a sum in lieu of interest

interest holder means a *person* who has an interest or an indirect interest, or holds a *material interest*, in a body (and "indirect interest" and "interest" have the same meaning as in the *LSA*), and references to "holds an interest" shall be construed accordingly

intervened practitioner means the *solicitor, recognised body, licensed body, REL* or *RFL* whose practice or practices are the subject of an *intervention*

intervention means the exercise of the powers specified in section 35 of and Schedule 1 to the *SA*, or section 9 of and paragraphs 32 to 35 of Schedule 2 to the *AJA*, or section 89 of and paragraph 5 of Schedule 14 to the Courts and Legal Services Act 1990, or section 102 of and Schedule 14 to the *LSA*

introducer means any person, business or organisation who or that introduces or refers *clients* to your business, or recommends your business to *clients* or otherwise puts you and *clients* in touch with each other

Joint Statement means the Joint Statement on *Qualifying Law Degrees*, prepared jointly by the *SRA* and the Bar Standards Board, setting out the conditions a law degree course must meet in order to be recognised by the *SRA* as a *Qualifying Law Degree*

lawyer means a member of one of the following professions, entitled to practise as such:

(a) the profession of *solicitor, barrister* or advocate of the *UK*;

(b) an *authorised person* other than one authorised by the *SRA*;

(c) any profession approved by the *SRA* for *RFL* status; and

(d) any other regulated legal profession specified by the *SRA* for the purpose of this definition

lawyer of England and Wales means:

(a) a *solicitor*; or

(b) an individual who is authorised to carry on legal activities in England and Wales by an *approved regulator* other than the *SRA*, but excludes an individual registered with the Bar Standards Board under the European Communities (Lawyer's Practice) Regulations 2000

lead insurer means the insurer named as such in the contract of insurance in accordance with clause 2.6 of the *MTC*

Legal Ombudsman means the scheme administered by the Office for Legal Complaints under Part 6 of the *LSA*

legal or equitable mortgage includes a legal or equitable charge and, in Scotland, a heritable security

Legal Practice Course means a course provided by an *authorised education provider* which meets the *prescribed* requirements

legal services body has the meaning given in section 9A of the *AJA*

legally qualified has the meaning given in section 9A(6) of the *AJA* save that, for a body to meet the management and control requirements enabling it to fall within section 9A(6)(h), it must be:

(a) a *recognised body;*

(b) a *licensed body* in which *lawyers* are entitled to exercise, or control the exercise of more than 90 percent of the *voting rights* of that *licensed body*;

(c) an *authorised non-SRA firm* in which lawyers are entitled to exercise, or control the exercise of more than 90 percent of the *voting rights* of that *authorised non-SRA firm*

licensable body has the meaning given in section 72 of the *LSA*

licensed body means a body licensed by the SRA under section 71(2) of the *LSA* in accordance with the SRA Authorisation of Firms Rules

licensed body (2012) means a body licensed by the *SRA* under Part 5 of the *LSA*.

life office means a *person* with permission to effect or carry out *long-term insurance contracts*

life policy means a *long-term insurance contract* other than a *pure protection contract* or a *reinsurance contract*, but including a *pension policy*

LLP means a limited liability partnership incorporated under the Limited Liability Partnerships Act 2000

long-term insurance contract has the meaning given in Part II of Schedule 1 to the *Regulated Activities Order*

LSA means the Legal Services Act 2007

manager means:

(a) the sole principal in a *recognised sole practice;*

(b) a *member* of a *LLP*;

(c) a *director* of a *company*;

(d) a *partner* in a *partnership*; or

(e) in relation to any other body, a member of its governing body

master insurer policy (2012) means an insurer under a master policy.

master policy (2012) means a policy referred to in Rule 5 of the *SRA Indemnity Rules*.

material interest has the meaning given to it in Schedule 13 to the *LSA*

MCD means the Mortgage Credit Directive 2014/17/EU on credit agreements for consumers relating to residential immovable property

MCD credit agreement has the meaning given in the *FCA* Handbook

member means:

- (a) in relation to a *company*, a person who has agreed to be a member of the *company* and whose name is entered in the *company's* register of members; and

- (b) in relation to an *LLP*, a member of that *LLP*

member (2012)

- (i) means:

    - (A) in relation to a *company*, a *person* who has agreed to be a member of the *company* and whose name is entered in the *company's* register of members; and

    - (B) in relation to an *LLP*, a member of that *LLP*; save that

- (ii) for the purposes of the *SRA Indemnity Rules*, means a member of a practice, being:

    - (A) any principal (including any *principal*) therein;

    - (B) any *director* or officer thereof, in the case of a *recognised body* or a *licensed body* which is a *company*;

    - (C) any member thereof in the case of a *recognised body* or a *licensed body* which is an *LLP*;

    - (D) any *recognised body* or a *licensed body* which is a *partner* or held out to be a *partner* therein and any officer of such *recognised body* or a *licensed body* which is a *company*, or any member of such *recognised body* or a *licensed body* which is an *LLP*;

    - (E) any person employed in connection therewith (including any *trainee solicitor*);

    - (F) any *solicitor* or *REL* who is a consultant to or associate in the practice;

    - (G) any *foreign lawyer* who is not an *REL* and who is a consultant or associate in the practice; and

    - (H) any *solicitor* or *foreign lawyer* who is working in the practice as an agent or locum tenens, whether he or she is so working under a contract of service or contract for services;

and includes the estate and/or personal representative(s) of any such persons.

mixed payments means a payment that includes both *client money* and non-*client money*

MTC means the minimum terms and conditions with which a policy of *qualifying insurance* is required by the SRA Indemnity Insurance Rules to comply, a copy of which is annexed as an annex 1 to those rules.

MTC (2012) means the minimum terms and conditions with which a *policy* of *qualifying insurance* is required by the *SRA Indemnity Insurance Rules* to comply, a copy of which is annexed as Appendix 1 to those Rules.

non-commercial body means a body that falls within section 23(2) of the *LSA*

non-mainstream regulated activities means a *regulated financial services activity* of an *authorised body* regulated by the *FCA* in relation to which the conditions in the Professional Firms' Sourcebook (5.2.1R) are satisfied

non-registered European lawyer (2012) means:

   (i) in the *SRA Indemnity Rules*, a member of a legal profession which is covered by the *Establishment Directive*, but who is not:

      (A) a *solicitor*, *REL* or *RFL*,

      (B) a barrister of England and Wales, Northern Ireland or the Irish Republic, or

      (C) a Scottish advocate; and

   (ii) in the *SRA Financial Services (Scope) Rules*, a member of a profession covered by the *Establishment Directive* who is based entirely at an office or offices outside England and Wales and who is not a *solicitor*, *REL* or *RFL*.

non-SRA firm means a sole practitioner, partnership, LLP or company which is not authorised to practise by the SRA, and which is either:

   (a) authorised or capable of being authorised to practise by another approved regulator; or

   (b) not capable of being authorised to practise by any approved regulator

occupational pension scheme means any scheme or arrangement which is comprised in one or more documents or agreements and which has, or is capable of having, effect in relation to one or more descriptions or categories of employment so as to provide benefits, in the form of pensions or otherwise, payable on termination of service, or on death or retirement, to or in respect of earners with qualifying service in an employment of any such description or category

overseas means outside England and Wales

overseas (2012) means outside England and Wales.

overseas client account means an account at a bank or similar institution, subject to supervision by a public authority, which is used only for the purpose of holding *client money* and the title, designation or account detail allow the account to be identified as belonging to the *client* or *clients* of a *solicitor* or *REL*, or that they are being held subject to a trust

overseas practice means:

(a) a branch office of an *authorised body*;

(b) a subsidiary company of an *authorised body*;

(c) a subsidiary undertaking, within the meaning of section 1162 of the Companies Act 2006, of an *authorised body*;

(d) an entity whose business, management or ownership are otherwise in fact or law controlled by an *authorised body*;

(e) an individual acting as a representative (whether as an *employee* or agent) of an *authorised body*; or

(f) a sole principal whose business, management or ownership are otherwise in fact or law controlled by an *authorised body*,

established outside England and Wales and providing legal services

overseas practice (2012)

(i) means:

(A) a branch office of an *authorised body*;

(B) a *subsidiary company* of an *authorised body*;

(C) a subsidiary undertaking, within the meaning of section 1162 of the Companies Act 2006, of an *authorised body*;

(D) an entity whose business, management or ownership are otherwise in fact or law controlled by an *authorised body*;

(E) an individual acting as a representative (whether as an employee or agent) of an *authorised body*; or

(F) a sole principal whose business, management or ownership are otherwise in fact or law controlled by an *authorised body*,

established outside England and Wales and providing legal services; and

(ii) in the *SRA Indemnity Rules* means a *practice* carried on wholly from an *overseas* office or offices, including a *practice* deemed to be a *separate practice* by virtue of paragraph (ii) of the definition of *separate practice*.

own interest conflict means any situation where your duty to act in the best interests of any *client* in relation to a matter conflicts, or there is a significant risk that it may conflict, with your own interests in relation to that or a related matter

owner means, in relation to a body, a *person* with any interest in the body, save that:

(a) in the SRA Authorisation of Firms Rules, and the SRA Authorisation of Individuals Regulations, owner means any person who holds a *material interest* in an *authorised body*, and in the case of a *partnership*, any partner regardless of whether they hold a *material interest* in the *partnership*; and

(b) for the purposes of the SRA Principles and the SRA Code of Conduct for Firms means a *person* who holds a *material interest* in the body; and

(c) for the purposes of the SRA Assessment of Character and Suitability Rules includes *owners* who have no active role in the running of the business as well as *owners* who do,

and "own" and "owned" shall be construed accordingly

panel solicitors (2012) means any solicitors appointed by the Solicitors Indemnity Fund in accordance with Rule 14.15 of the *SRA Indemnity Rules*.

Partial Home State Cover has the meaning given in annex 2 to the SRA Indemnity Insurance Rules

participating insurer means an *authorised insurer* which has entered into a *participating insurer's agreement* with the *SRA* which remains in force for the purposes of underwriting new business at the date on which the relevant contract of *qualifying insurance* is made

participating insurer's agreement means an agreement in such terms as the *SRA* may prescribe setting out the terms and conditions on which a *participating insurer* may provide professional indemnity insurance to *solicitors* and others in *private legal practice* in England and Wales

partner means a *person* who is or is held out as a partner in a *partnership*

partnership means a body that is not a *body corporate* in which persons are, or are held out as, *partners*

partnership (2012) means a body that is not a *body corporate* in which *persons* are, or are held out as, *partners*, save that in the *MTC* means an unincorporated *insured firm* in which *persons* are or are held out as *partners* and does not include an *insured firm* incorporated as an *LLP*.

pawn means any article subject to a *pledge*

pawnee means a *person* who takes any article in *pawn* and includes any *person* to whom the rights and duties of the original pawnee have passed by assignment or operation of law

payment includes any form of consideration whether any benefit is received by you or by a third party (but does not include the provision of hospitality that is reasonable in the circumstances) and "pay" and "paid" shall be construed accordingly

pension policy means a right to benefits obtained by the making of contributions to an *occupational pension scheme* or to a *personal pension* scheme, where the contributions are paid to a *life office*

period of insurance means the period for which the insurance operates

period of recognised training means training required under the SRA Authorisation of Individuals Regulations

person includes a body of persons (corporate or unincorporated)

person (2012) includes a body of persons (corporate or unincorporated)

personal pension scheme means any scheme or arrangement which is not an *occupational pension scheme* or a *stakeholder pension scheme* and which is comprised in one or more instruments or agreements, having or capable of having effect so as to provide benefits to or in respect of people on retirement, or on having reached a particular age, or on termination of service in an employment

personal recommendation means a recommendation that is presented as suitable for the person to whom it is made, or is based on a consideration of the circumstances of that person

pledge means a *pawnee*'s rights over an article taken in *pawn*

policy means:

    (a) for the purposes of the SRA Financial Services (Conduct of Business) Rules 2001 the meaning given in the *FCA* Handbook; and

    (b) for the purposes of the SRA Indemnity Insurance Rules and the *MTC* a contract of professional indemnity insurance made between one or more *persons*, each of which is a *participating insurer*, and an *authorised body*

policy period means the *period of insurance* in respect of which risks may attach under a *policy*, but excluding the *extended policy period* and the *cessation period*

practice means the whole or such part of the *private legal practice* of an *authorised body* as is carried on from one or more offices in England and Wales

practice (2012) means the activities, in that capacity, of:

(i)   a *solicitor*;

(ii) an *REL*, from an office or offices within the *UK*;

(iii) a member of an *Establishment Directive profession* registered with the *BSB* under the *Establishment Directive*, carried out from an office or offices in England and Wales;

(iv) an *RFL*, from an office or offices within England and Wales, as:

    (A) an *employee* of a *recognised sole practice*; or

    (B) a *manager, employee, member* or *interest holder* of an *authorised body* or a *manager, employee* or owner of an *authorised non-SRA firm*;

(v)   an *authorised body*;

(vi) a *manager* of an *authorised body*;

(vii) a person employed in England and Wales by an *authorised body*;

(viii) a *lawyer of England and Wales*; or

(ix) an *authorised non-SRA firm*;

and "practise" and "practising" should be construed accordingly; save for in:

(i)   the *SRA Indemnity Insurance Rules* where "practice" means the whole or such part of the *private practice* of a *firm* as is carried on from one or more offices in England and Wales;

(ii) the *SRA Indemnity Rules* where it means a practice to the extent that:

    (A) in relation to a *licensed body*, it carries on *regulated activities*; and

    (B) in all other cases, it carries on *private practice* providing professional services as a sole *solicitor* or *REL* or as a *partnership* of a type referred to in Rule 6.1(d) to 6.1(f) and consisting of or including one or more *solicitors* and/or *RELs*, and shall include the business or practice carried on by a *recognised body* in the providing of professional services such as are provided by individuals practising in *private practice* as *solicitors* and/or *RELs* or by such individuals in *partnership* with *RFLs*, whether such practice is carried on by the *recognised body* alone or in *partnership* with one or more *solicitors*, *RELs* and/or other *recognised bodies*; and

(iii) in the *SRA Overseas Rules* where it shall be given its natural meaning.

Practice Skills Standards means the standards published by the *SRA* which set out the practice skills *trainees* will develop during the *period of recognised training* and use when qualified

practising overseas means the conduct of a practice:

(a) of an *overseas practice*;

(b) of a *manager, member* or *owner* of an *overseas practice* in that capacity;

(c) of a *solicitor* established outside England and Wales for the purpose of providing legal services in an *overseas* jurisdiction; and

(d) of an *REL* established in Scotland or Northern Ireland for the purpose of providing legal services in those jurisdictions

preceding qualifying insurance (2012) means, in the case of any *firm* or person who makes an *expired run-off claim*, the policy of *qualifying insurance* which previously provided run-off cover in respect of that *firm* or person, or which was required to provide such cover, or (in the case of a firm in default or a run-off firm) arrangements to provide such run-off cover through the *ARP*.

prescribed means prescribed by the *SRA* from time to time

previous practice (2012) means any *practice* which shall have ceased to exist as such for whatever reason, including by reason of:

(i) any death, retirement or addition of *principals*; or

(ii) any split or cession of the whole or part of its practice to another without any change of *principals*.

principal means:

(a) where the *authorised body* is or was:

(i) a *recognised sole practice* – the *sole practitioner*;

(ii) a *partnership* – each *partner*;

(iii) a *company* with a share capital – each *director* of that *company* and any *person* who:

(A) is held out as a *director*; or

(B) beneficially owns the whole or any part of a share in the *company*; or

(C) is the ultimate beneficial owner of the whole or any part of a share in the *company*;

(iv) a *company* without a share capital – each *director* of that *company* and any person who:

(A) is held out as a *director*; or

(B) is a *member* of the *company*; or

(C) is the ultimate owner of the whole or any part of a body corporate or other legal *person* which is a *member* of the *company*;

(v) an *LLP* – each *member* of that *LLP*, and any *person* who is the ultimate owner of the whole or any part of a body corporate or other legal *person* which is a *member* of the *LLP*;

(b) where a body corporate or other legal *person* is a *partner* in the *authorised body*, any *person* who is within paragraph (a)(iii) of this definition (including sub-paragraphs (A) and (C)), paragraph (a)(iv) of this definition (including sub-paragraphs (A) and (C)), or paragraph (a)(v) of this definition

principal (2012)

(i) subject to paragraphs (ii) to (iv) means:

    (A) a *sole practitioner*;

    (B) a *partner* in a *partnership*;

    (C) in the case of a *recognised body* which is an *LLP* or *company*, the *recognised body* itself;

    (D) in the case of a *licensed body* which is an *LLP* or *company*, the *licensed body* itself;

    (E) the principal *solicitor* or *REL* (or any one of them) employed by a *non-solicitor employer* (for example, in a law centre or in commerce and industry); or

    (F) in relation to any other body, a member of its governing body;

(ii) in the *SRA Authorisation Rules*, *SRA Practice Framework Rules* and *SRA Practising Regulations*, means a *sole practitioner* or a *partner* in a *partnership*;

(iii) in the *SRA Indemnity Insurance Rules* means:

    (A) where the *firm* is or was:

        (I) a *sole practitioner* – that practitioner;

        (II) a *partnership* – each *partner*;

        (III) a *company* with a share capital – each *director* of that *company* and any *person* who:

            (01) is held out as a *director*; or

            (02) beneficially owns the whole or any part of a share in the *company*; or

            (03) is the ultimate beneficial owner of the whole or any part of a share in the *company*;

        (IV) a *company* without a share capital – each *director* of that *company* and any *person* who:

            (01) is held out as a *director*; or

            (02) is a *member* of the *company*; or

            (03) is the ultimate owner of the whole or any part of a *body corporate* or other legal person which is a *member* of the *company*;

(V)   an *LLP* – each *member* of that *LLP*, and any *person* who is the ultimate owner of the whole or any part of a *body corporate* or other legal person which is a *member* of the *LLP*;

(B)   where a *body corporate* or other legal person is a *partner* in the *firm*, any *person* who is within paragraph (A)(III) of this definition (including sub-paragraphs (01) and (03) thereof), paragraph (A)(IV) of this definition (including sub-paragraphs (01) and (03) thereof), or paragraph (A)(V) of this definition;

(iv)   in the *SRA Indemnity Rules*, means:

(A)   a *solicitor* who is a *partner* or a sole *solicitor* within the meaning of section 87 of the *SA*, or an *REL* who is a *partner*, or who is a sole practitioner, or an *RFL* or *non-registered European lawyer* who is a *partner*, and includes any *solicitor*, *REL*, *RFL* or *non-registered European lawyer* held out as a principal; and

(B)   additionally in relation to a *practice* carried on by a *recognised body* or a *licensed body* alone, or a *practice* in which a *recognised body* or a *licensed body* is or is held out to be a *partner*:

(I)   a *solicitor*, *REL*, *RFL* or *non-registered European lawyer* (and in the case of a *licensed body* any other person) who:

(01)   beneficially owns the whole or any part of a share in such *recognised body* or *licensed body* (in each case, where it is a *company* with a share capital); or

(02)   is a member of such *recognised body* or *licensed body* (in each case, where it is a *company* without a share capital or an *LLP* or a *partnership* with legal personality); or

(II)   a *solicitor*, *REL*, *RFL* or *non-registered European lawyer* (and in the case of a *licensed body* any other person) who is:

(01)   the ultimate beneficial owner of the whole or any part of a share in such *recognised body* or *licensed body* (in each case, where the *recognised* body or *licensed body* is a *company* with a share capital); or

(02)   the ultimate owner of a member or any part of a member of such *recognised body* or *licensed body* (in each case, where the *recognised body* or *licensed body* is a *company* without a share capital or an *LLP* or a *partnership* with legal personality).

prior practice means each *practice* to which the *insured firm's practice* is ultimately a *successor practice* by way of one or more mergers, acquisitions, absorptions or other transitions, but does not include any such *practice* which has elected to be insured under run-off cover in accordance with clause 5.5 of the MTC

private legal practice means the provision of services in private *practice* as a *solicitor* or *REL* in an *authorised body* including, without limitation:

(a) providing such services in England, Wales or anywhere in the world in a *recognised sole practice*, a *recognised body* or a *licensed body* (in respect of an activity regulated by the *SRA* in accordance with the terms of the body's licence);

(b) the provision of such services as a secondee of the *insured firm*;

(c) any insured acting as a personal representative, *trustee*, attorney, notary, insolvency practitioner or in any other role in conjunction with a *practice*;

(d) the provision of such services by any *employee*; and

(e) the provision of such services pro bono;

but does not include:

(f) discharging the functions of any of the following offices or appointments:

(i) judicial office;

(ii) Under Sheriffs;

(iii) members and clerks of such tribunals, committees, panels and boards as the Council may from time to time designate but including those subject to the Tribunals and Inquiries Act 1992, the Competition Commission, Legal Services Commission Review Panels, Legal Aid Agency Review Panels and Parole Boards;

(iv) Justices' Clerks; or

(v) Superintendent Registrars and Deputy Superintendent Registrars of Births, Marriages and Deaths and Registrars of Local Crematoria

private practice (2012)

(i) for the purposes of the *SRA Indemnity Insurance Rules*:

(A) in relation to a *firm* which is a *licensed body* means its *regulated activities*; and

(B) subject to paragraph (A) of this definition, in relation to all *firms* includes without limitation all the professional services provided by the *firm* including acting as a personal representative, trustee, attorney, notary, insolvency practitioner or in any other role in conjunction with a *practice*, and includes services provided pro bono publico,

but does not include:

(C) *solicitor* or *REL* in the course of employment with an employer other than a *firm*; or

(D) *non-SRA firm* or by an *REL* through an *Exempt European Practice*; or

(E) discharging the functions of any of the following offices or appointments:

   (I) judicial office;

   (II) Under Sheriffs;

   (III) members and clerks of such tribunals, committees, panels and boards as the *Council* may from time to time designate but including those subject to the Tribunals and Inquiries Act 1992, the Competition Commission, Legal Services Commission Review Panels, Legal Aid Agency Review Panels and Parole Boards;

   (IV) Justices' Clerks;

   (V) Superintendent Registrars and Deputy Superintendent Registrars of Births, Marriages and Deaths and Registrars of Local Crematoria; or

   (VI) such other offices as the *Council* may from time to time designate;

(F) *solicitor* or *REL's* family, or registered charities; or

(G) in respect of a sole *solicitor* or a sole *REL*, *practice* consisting only of:

   (I) providing professional services without remuneration for friends, relatives, or to companies wholly owned by the *solicitor* or *REL's* family, or registered charities; and/or

   (II) administering oaths and statutory declarations; and/or

   (III) activities which could constitute *practice* but are done in the course of discharging the functions of any of the offices or appointments listed in paragraphs (E)(I) to (VI) above.

(ii) for the purposes of the *SRA Indemnity Rules* "private practice" shall be deemed to include:

   (A) the acceptance and performance of obligations as trustees; and

   (B) notarial practice where a solicitor notary operates such notarial practice in conjunction with a solicitor's practice, whether or not the notarial fees accrue to the benefit of the solicitor's practice;

but does not include:

   (C) practice to the extent that any fees or other income accruing do not accrue to the benefit of the *practice* carrying on such practice (except as provided by paragraph (B) in this definition);

   (D) practice by a *solicitor* or *REL* in the course of his or her employment with an employer other than a *solicitor*, *REL*, *recognised body*, *licensed body* or *partnership* such as is referred to in Rule 6.1(d) to 6.1(f); in which connection and for the avoidance of doubt:

      (I) any such *solicitor* or *REL* does not carry on private practice when he or she acts in the course of his or her employment for persons other than his or her employer;

(II)   any such *solicitor* or *REL* does not carry on private practice merely because he or she uses in the course of his or her employment a style of stationery or description which appears to hold him or her out as a *principal* or *solicitor* or *foreign lawyer* in private practice; or

(III) any practice carried on by such a *solicitor* outside the course of his or her employment will constitute private practice;

(E)   discharging the functions of the following offices:

(I)   judicial office;

(II)   Under Sheriffs;

(III) members and clerks of such tribunals, committees, panels and boards as the *Council* may from time to time designate but including those subject to the Tribunals and Inquiries Act 1992, the Competition Commission, Legal Services Commission Review Panels and Parole Boards;

(IV) Justices' Clerks;

(V)   Superintendent Registrars and Deputy Superintendent Registrars of Births, Marriages and Deaths and Registrars of Local Crematoria;

(VI) such other offices as the *Council* may from time to time designate.

professional service means, for the purposes of the SRA Financial Services (Scope) Rules, services provided by an *authorised body* in the course of its practice and which do not constitute carrying on a *regulated financial services activity*

publicity includes all promotional material and activity, including the name or description of your firm, stationery, advertisements, brochures, websites, directory entries, media appearances, promotional press releases, and direct approaches to potential *clients* and other *persons*, whether conducted in person, in writing, or in electronic form, but does not include press releases prepared on behalf of a *client*

pure protection contract means:

(a) a *long-term insurance contract*:

(i)   under which the benefits are payable only in respect of death or of incapacity due to injury, sickness or infirmity;

(ii)   which has no surrender value or the consideration consists of a single premium and the surrender value does not exceed that premium; and

(iii) which makes no provision for its conversion or extension in a manner which would result in its ceasing to comply with (a) or (b); or

(b) a *reinsurance contract* covering all or part of a risk to which a *person* is exposed under a *long-term insurance contract*

qualifying insurance means a policy that provides professional indemnity insurance cover in accordance with the *MTC* but only to the extent required by the *MTC*

qualifying insurance (2012) means a *policy* that provides professional indemnity insurance cover in accordance with the *MTC* but only to the extent required by the *MTC*.

Qualifying Law Degree means a degree which meets the requirements of the *Joint Statement*

recognised body means a body recognised by the *SRA* under section 9 of the *AJA*

recognised body (2012) means a body recognised by the *SRA* under section 9 of the *AJA*.

recognised jurisdiction means a jurisdiction we have recognised against prescribed criteria

recognised sole practice means the practice of a sole *solicitor* or *REL* which is recognised by the *SRA* under section 9 of the *AJA*

reconciled accounts means that all elements of the accounting records of an *intervened practitioner's* practice are consistent with each other

reconciled list means a list of beneficial entitlements to *statutory trust monies* created from a set of *reconciled accounts*

record of training means a record created and maintained by a *trainee*, which contains details of the work they have performed as a *trainee*, how the *trainee* has acquired, applied and developed their skills by reference to the *Practice Skills Standards* and the *trainee's* reflections on their performance and development plans

referral fee means a referral fee as defined within section 57(7) of the Legal Aid, Sentencing and Punishment of Offenders Act 2012

register includes:

(a) the roll and the register of solicitors with practising certificates kept under Part I of the *SA*,

(b) the *register of European lawyers*;

(c) the *register of foreign lawyers*; and

(d) the register of *authorised bodies* kept under the *AJA* and the *LSA*

register of European lawyers means the register of European lawyers maintained by the *SRA* under regulation 15 of the European Communities (Lawyer's Practice) Regulations 2000 (SI 2000/1119)

register of foreign lawyers means the register of foreign lawyers maintained by the *SRA* under section 89 of the Courts and Legal Services Act 1990

Regulated Activities Order means the Financial Services and Markets Act 2000 (Regulated Activities) Order 2001

regulated activity (2012) means:

- (i) subject to sub-paragraph (ii) below:

  - (A) any *reserved legal activity*;

  - (B) any *non-reserved legal activity* except, in relation to an *MDP*, any such activity that is excluded on the terms of the licence;

  - (C) any other activity in respect of which a *licensed body* is regulated pursuant to Part 5 of the *LSA*; and

- (ii) in the *SRA Financial Services (Scope) Rules*, an activity which is specified in the *Regulated Activities Order*.

regulated claims management activities means activities which are regulated activities as specified under articles 89G to 89M of the *Regulated Activities Order*

regulated consumer hire agreement has the meaning given by article 60N(3) of the *Regulated Activities Order*

regulated credit agreement has the meaning given by article 60B(3) of the *Regulated Activities Order*

regulated financial services activities means an activity which is specified in the *Regulated Activities Order*

regulated individual means:

- (a) a *solicitor*;

- (b) an *REL*; and

- (c) a *manager*, *member* or *owner* of an *overseas practice*.

regulated person (2012)

- (i) in the *SRA Indemnity Rules* has the meaning given in section 21 of the *LSA*;

- (ii) means, in the *SRA Disciplinary Procedure Rules*:

  - (A) a *solicitor*;

  - (B) an *REL*;

(C)   an *RFL*;

(D)   a *sole practitioner* in a *recognised sole practice*;

(E)   a *recognised body*;

(F)   a *manager* of a *recognised body*;

(G)   a *licensed body*;

(H)   a *manager* of a *licensed body*;

(I)   an *employee* of, or in, an *authorised body*, a *solicitor*, or an *REL*; or

(J)   to the extent permitted by law, any person who has previously held a position or role described in (A) to (I) above;

(iii) for the purposes of the *SRA Cost of Investigations Regulations* means the persons at paragraph (ii) (A) to (J) above and also includes a *person who has an interest in a licensed body* and, to the extent permitted by law, any person who has previously held an interest in a *licensed body*.

regulated services means the legal and other professional services that you provide that are regulated by the *SRA* and includes, where appropriate, acting as a trustee or as the holder of a specified office or appointment

regulatory arrangements has the meaning given to it by section 21 of the *LSA*

regulatory objectives has the meaning given to it by section 1 of the *LSA*

reinsurance contract means a *contract of insurance* covering all or part of a risk to which a *person* is exposed under a *contract of insurance*

reinsurance distribution has the meaning given in the *FCA* Handbook

REL means a European lawyer registered in the *register of European lawyers*

REL (2012) means registered European lawyer, namely, an individual registered with the *SRA* under regulation 17 of the European Communities (Lawyer's Practice) Regulations 2000 (SI 2000/ no.1119).

relevant indemnity period (2012) in relation to *contributions* or indemnity means that *indemnity period* in respect of which such *contributions* are payable or such indemnity is to be provided in accordance with the *SRA Indemnity Rules*.

relevant insolvency event occurs in relation to a body if:

(a)   a resolution for a voluntary winding up of the body is passed without a declaration of solvency under section 89 of the Insolvency Act 1986;

(b)   the body enters administration within the meaning of paragraph 1(2)(b) of Schedule B1 to that Act;

(c) an administrative receiver within the meaning of section 251 of that Act is appointed;

(d) a meeting of creditors is held in relation to the body under section 95 of that Act (creditors' meeting which has the effect of converting a members' voluntary winding up into a creditors' voluntary winding up);

(e) an order for the winding up of the body is made;

(f) all of the *managers* in a body which is unincorporated have been adjudicated bankrupt; or

(g) the body is an *overseas company* or a *societas Europaea* registered outside England, Wales, Scotland and Northern Ireland and the body is subject to an event in its country of incorporation analogous to an event as set out in paragraphs (a) to (f) above

occurs in relation to an individual if:

(a) the individual is adjudged bankrupt;

(b) a debt relief order has been made under Part 7A of the Insolvency Act 1986 in respect of that individual; or

(c) the individual has entered into an individual voluntary arrangement or a partnership voluntary arrangement under the Insolvency Act 1986.

relevant licensed body means a *licensed body* other than:

(a) an unlimited company, or an *overseas* company whose members' liability for the company's debts is not limited by its constitution or by the law of its country of incorporation; or

(b) a nominee company only, holding *assets* for clients of another *practice*; and

   (i) it can act only as agent for the other *practice*; and

   (ii) all the individuals who are *principals* of the *licensed body* are also *principals* of the other *practice*; and

   (iii) any fee or other income arising out of the *licensed body* accrues to the benefit of the other *practice*; or

(c) a *partnership* in which none of the *partners* is a limited company, an *LLP* or a legal person whose *members* have limited liability

relevant recognised body means a *recognised body* other than:

(a) an unlimited company, or an *overseas* company whose members' liability for the company's debts is not limited by its constitution or by the law of its country of incorporation; or

(b) a nominee company only, holding *assets* for clients of another *practice*; and

   (i) it can act only as agent for the other *practice*; and

(ii) all the individuals who are *principals* of the *recognised body* are also *principals* of the other *practice*; and

(iii) any fee or other income arising out of the *recognised body* accrues to the benefit of the other *practice*; or

(c) a *partnership* in which none of the *partners* is a limited company, an *LLP* or a legal person whose *members* have limited liability; or

(d) a *sole practitioner* that is a *recognised body*

relevant successor practice (2012) means in respect of a *previous practice*, a *successor practice* or a "successor practice" (as defined in Appendix 1 to the *SIIR*) (as may be applicable) against which a *relevant claim* is made.

remuneration means any commission, fee, charge or other payment, including an economic benefit of any kind or any other financial or non-financial advantage or incentive offered or given in respect of *insurance distribution activities* and references to "remunerate" and "remunerated" shall be construed accordingly

reserved legal activities has the meaning given in section 12 of the LSA

responsible authorised body in respect of an *overseas practice* means the *authorised body* referred to in whichever of paragraph (a) to (f) of the definition of "*overseas practice*" is applicable to that practice

retail investment product has the meaning given in the *FCA* Handbook.

RFL means a foreign lawyer registered in the *register of foreign lawyers*

RFL (2012) means registered foreign lawyer, namely, an individual registered with the *SRA* under section 89 of the Courts and Legal Services Act 1990.

running account credit means a facility under a *credit agreement* under which the borrower or another *person* is enabled to receive from time to time from the lender, or a third party, cash, goods or services to an amount or value such that, taking into account payments made by or to the credit of the borrower, the credit limit (if any) is not at any time exceeded

SA means the Solicitors Act 1974

SA (2012) means the Solicitors Act 1974

security has the meaning given by article 3(1) of the *Regulated Activities Order* but does not include an investment which falls within the definition of a packaged product

separate business means, where you own, manage or are employed by an *authorised body*,

a separate business:

(a) which you own;

(b) which you are owned by;

(c) where you actively participate in the provision of its services, including where you have any direct control over the business or any indirect control over the business through another *person*, or

(d) which you are connected with,

and which is not an *authorised body*, an *authorised non-SRA firm*, or an *overseas practice*

separate practice (2012) means:

(i) a *practice* in which the number and identity of the *principals* is not the same as the number and identity of the *principals* in any other *practice*. When the same *principals* in number and identity carry on *practice* under more than one name or style, there is only one *practice*;

(ii) in the case of a *practice* of which more than 25% of the *principals* are *foreign lawyers*, any *overseas* offices shall be deemed to form a separate practice from the offices in England and Wales;

(iii) in the case of an *overseas* office of a *practice*, the fact that a *principal* or a limited number of *principals* represent all the *principals* in the *practice* on a local basis shall not of itself cause that *overseas* office to be a separate practice provided that any fee or other income arising out of that office accrues to the benefit of the *practice*; and

(iv) in the case of a *recognised body* or *licensed body* the fact that all of the shares in the *recognised body* or *licensed body* (as the case may be) are beneficially owned by only some of the *principals* in another *practice*, shall not, of itself, cause such a *recognised body* or *licensed body* (as the case may be) to be a separate practice provided that any fee or other income arising out of the *recognised body* or *licensed body* accrues to the benefit of that other *practice*.

SIF means the Solicitors Indemnity Fund

SIIR (2012) means the Solicitors' Indemnity Insurance Rules 2000 to 2010, the SRA Indemnity Insurance Rules 2011 to 2012 or the *SRA Indemnity Insurance Rules* or any rules subsequent thereto.

societas Europaea means a European public limited liability company within the meaning of Article 1 of Council Regulation 2157/2001/EC

Society (2012) means the Law Society, in accordance with section 87 of the *SA*.

sole practitioner means a *solicitor* or a *REL* who is the sole principal in a practice (other than an incorporated practice)

sole practitioner (2012) means a *solicitor* or an *REL practising* as a sole principal in a *practice* (other than an incorporated *practice*) and does not include a *solicitor* or an *REL practising in-house*, save for the purposes of:

(i) the *SRA Accounts Rules* and *SRA Indemnity Insurance Rules* where references to "practising" are to be given their natural meaning; and

(ii) the *SRA Authorisation Rules* where it includes (as the context may require) a *solicitor* or *REL* intending to *practise* as a sole principal in a *practice* (other than incorporated *practice*).

solicitor means a person who has been admitted as a solicitor of the Senior Courts of England and Wales and whose name is on the roll, save that in the SRA Indemnity Insurance Rules and the *MTC* this includes a person who practises as a solicitor whether or not the person has in force a practising certificate, and also includes practice under home title of a former *REL* who has become a solicitor

solicitor (2012) means a person who has been admitted as a solicitor of the Senior Courts of England and Wales and whose name is on the roll kept by the *Society* under section 6 of the *SA*, save that in the *SRA Indemnity Insurance Rules* includes a person who *practises* as a solicitor whether or not he or she has in force a practising certificate, and also includes *practice* under home title of a former *REL* who has become a solicitor.

SRA means the Solicitors Regulation Authority

SRA Code of Conduct for Individuals means SRA Code of Conduct for Solicitors, RELs and RFLs

SRA Codes of Conduct means the SRA Code of Conduct for Solicitors, RELs and RFLs and the SRA Code of Conduct for Firms

stakeholder pension scheme means a scheme established in accordance with Part I of the Welfare and Pensions Reform Act 1999 and the Stakeholder Pension Scheme Regulations 2000

statutory trust means the trust created by Schedule 1 of the *SA*, or Schedule 14 of the *LSA*, over monies vesting in the Society following an *intervention*

statutory trust account means an account in which *statutory trust monies* are held by the SRA following an *intervention*

statutory trust monies means the monies vested in the Society under the *statutory trust*.

substantially common interest means a situation where there is a clear common purpose between the *clients* and a strong consensus on how it is to be achieved

successor practice

(a) means a *practice* identified in this definition as 'B', where:

    (i)   'A' is the *practice* to which B succeeds; and

    (ii)   'A's owner' is the owner of A immediately prior to transition; and

    (iii) 'B's owner' is the owner of B immediately following transition; and

    (iv) 'transition' means merger, acquisition, absorption or other transition which results in A no longer being carried on as a discrete legal *practice*.

(b) B is a successor practice to A where:

    (i)   B is or was held out, expressly or by implication, by B's owner as being the successor of A or as incorporating A, whether such holding out is contained in notepaper, business cards, form of electronic communications, publications, promotional material or otherwise, or is contained in any statement or declaration by B's owner to any regulatory or taxation authority; and/or

    (ii)   (where A's owner was a *sole practitioner* and the transition occurred on or before 31 August 2000) – the *sole practitioner* is a *principal* of B's owner; and/or

    (iii) (where A's owner was a *sole practitioner* and the transition occurred on or after 1 September 2000) – the *sole practitioner* is a *principal* or *employee* of B's owner; and/or

    (iv) (where A's owner was a *recognised body* or a *licensed body* (in respect of an activity regulated by the SRA in accordance with the terms of the body's licence)) – that body is a *principal* of B's owner; and/or

    (v)   (where A's owner was a *partnership*) – the majority of the *principals* of A's owner have become *principals* of B's owner; and/or

    (vi) (where A's owner was a *partnership* and the majority of *principals* of A's owner did not become *principals* of the owner of another legal *practice* as a result of the transition) – one or more of the *principals* of A's owner have become *principals* of B's owner and:

        (A) B is carried on under the same name as A or a name which substantially incorporates the name of A (or a substantial part of the name of A); and/or

        (B) B is carried on from the same premises as A; and/or

        (C) the owner of B acquired the goodwill and/or *assets* of A; and/or

        (D) the owner of B assumed the liabilities of A; and/or

        (E) the majority of staff employed by A's owner became *employees* of B's owner.

(c) notwithstanding the foregoing, B is not a successor practice to A under paragraph (b) (ii), (iii), (iv), (v) or (vi) if another *practice* is or was held out by the owner of that other *practice* as the successor of A or as incorporating A, provided that there is insurance complying with the *MTC* in relation to that other *practice*

sum insured means the *insurer's* limit of liability under a *policy* in respect of any one *claim* (exclusive of *defence costs*)

supplementary run-off cover means run-off cover provided by the Solicitors Indemnity Fund following the expiry of run-off cover provided to an *authorised body* in accordance with the SRA Indemnity Insurance Rules or otherwise under a *policy* (but subject to compliance with the *MTC*)

third party managed account means an account held at a *bank* or *building society* in the name of a third party which is an authorised payment institution or small payment institution that has chosen to implement safeguarding arrangement in accordance with the Payment Services Regulations (as each defined in the Payment Services Regulations 2017) regulated by the *FCA*, in which monies are owned beneficially by the third party, and which is operated upon terms agreed between the third party, you and your *client* as an escrow payment service

trainee means any person undertaking a *period of recognised training*

training principal means a *solicitor* or *barrister* nominated by an *authorised training provider* to oversee a *period of recognised training* within that organisation

transaction means the purchase, sale, subscription or underwriting of a particular investment specified in Part III of the *Regulated Activities Order*

Tribunal means the Solicitors Disciplinary Tribunal which is an independent statutory tribunal constituted under section 46 of the *SA*

trustee includes a personal representative, and "trust" includes the duties of a personal representative

turnover means the amounts derived from the provision of goods and services in the most recent financial year, after deduction of:

(a) trade discounts;

(b) value added tax; and

(c) any other taxes based on the amounts so derived

UK means United Kingdom, made up of: England, Scotland, Wales, and Northern Ireland

undertaking means a statement, given orally or in writing, whether or not it includes the word "undertake" or "undertaking", to someone who reasonably places reliance on it, that you or a third party will do something or cause something to be done, or refrain from doing something

vocational stage of training means:

    (a) the *Legal Practice Course*;

    (b) a required *period of recognised training*; and

    (c) the Professional Skills Course

voting rights in a body includes the right to vote in a partners', members', directors' or shareholders' meeting, or otherwise in relation to the body, and "control the exercise of voting rights" shall be interpreted as including de facto as well as legal control over such rights

[Last updated: 31 December 2020]

[B]   Appendices

[B1] SRA enforcement strategy

Published 7 February 2019 | Updated 25 November 2019

1.1   Introduction

Our approach to enforcement is guided by our public interest purpose.

Our May 2014 policy statement (updated in November 2015) sets out our approach to regulation in order to meet the regulatory objectives and in particular, our public interest purpose.

It is important we regulate in a way that helps maintain and build public trust and confidence in solicitors. That means protecting consumers, setting and enforcing high professional standards, and supporting access to affordable legal services, the rule of law and the administration of justice.

As well as making sure solicitors are competent, we want to promote a culture where ethical values and behaviours are embedded.

Our SRA Principles and Codes of Conduct aim to drive high professional standards. Through them we seek to give a clear message to the public, regulated individuals and firms about what regulation stands for and what a competent and an ethical legal profession looks like.

We work in the public interest, protecting consumers, setting and enforcing high professional standards, and supporting access to affordable legal services, the rule of law and the administration of justice.

Our regulation therefore seeks to:

- ensure a strong, competitive, and highly effective legal market
- ensure a focus on quality and client care
- promote a culture in which ethical values and behaviours are embedded.

Our codes provide a benchmark which solicitors[1] and firms are expected to meet. In doing so, we will not second guess the approach they take or the way in which they choose to comply. We do, however, require all those we regulate to be familiar with our standards, explanatory guidance, and the law and regulation governing their work, and to be able to explain and justify their decisions and actions.

We have a number of regulatory tools at our disposal to support compliance. These include:

- conducting thematic reviews of areas of risk
- publishing a risk outlook highlighting our priority risks
- providing advice and support through our Professional Ethics helpline and a range of toolkits and guidance

- SRA Innovate, a service which helps legal services providers to develop their business in new ways.

However, the public and the profession have a right to expect that wrongdoing will be met by robust and proportionate sanctions, and that we as a regulator will enforce our standards or requirements evenly, consistently and fairly. We need to be accountable for our actions and to demonstrate that we will act fairly and proportionately.

This strategy explains how we use our enforcement powers, where there are concerns about failure to meet our standards or requirements. The strategy also provides clarity for the public, and for regulated individuals and firms, about what we expect of those we regulate.

All of our decision-makers are required to exercise their judgment on the facts of each case, on the basis of the guidance set out in this document and our suite of decision-making guidance [**www.sra.org.uk/sra/decision-making/guidance**], which also explains our approach to publishing our regulatory decisions.

1.2   Reporting concerns

We need others to alert us when things go wrong which may be the result of a breach of our rules by a solicitor or firm that we regulate. The public, clients and judiciary all play an important role and we provide resources to help them to make a report [**www.sra. org.uk/consumers/problems/report-solicitor**].

Solicitors and firms also play an important role: Our codes of conduct place obligations on those we regulate to report to us any facts or matters which they reasonably believe are capable of amounting to a serious breach of our standards or requirements. These include a duty to report, in similar circumstances, to another legal services regulator where a breach of their regulatory requirements is indicated.

Reporting behaviour that presents a risk to clients, the public or the wider public interest, goes to the core of the professional principles of trust and integrity. It is important that solicitors and firms let us know about serious concerns promptly, where this may result in us taking regulatory action. We do not want to receive reports or allegations that are without merit, frivolous or of breaches that are minor or technical in nature – that is not in anyone's interest. We do want to receive reports where it is possible that a serious breach of our standards or requirements has occurred and where we may wish to take regulatory action.

This strategy and supporting material [**www.sra.org.uk/sra/strategy-2017-2020/sub-strategies/enforcement-practice**] explain the factors which we take into account to determine what makes a breach serious and therefore should be referred to when deciding whether and what to report to us.

When to report

Prompt reporting is important. We may have additional information relating to the issues, and/or may need to use our powers to investigate or take urgent steps to protect the public. This may include imposing practice restrictions or in the most serious cases of all using our intervention powers to close a firm.

Firms may wish to investigate matters themselves – and indeed we want to encourage firms to resolve and remedy issues locally where they can. However, where a serious breach is indicated, we are keen for firms to engage with us at an early stage in their internal investigative process and to keep us updated on progress and outcomes. And, we may nonetheless wish to investigate the matter, or an aspect of a matter, ourselves – for example because our focus is different, or because we need to gather evidence from elsewhere.

Early engagement also allows us to make sure that we can understand any patterns or trends, using information we already hold. Sometimes we will want to gather information regarding particular types of risk to consumers, to understand patterns and trends. An example is cybercrime: we would expect a firm to inform us about attacks against it, even where this may raise no concerns about the conduct, behaviour or systems of the firm or any regulated person, where proportionate to do so: By way of example, some larger firms report that routine attacks are made against their computer systems every day but sophisticated IT systems are in place to counter these. In such circumstances it is likely to be disproportionate to report each attempt made but we would still wish to be notified of any novel or significant attacks, or near misses.

Whether or not a matter should be reported is a matter of judgment, which will depend on the individual facts and circumstances. If you are unsure about whether to make a report, you should err on the side of caution and do so.

Who should report

If you are an individual solicitor, or registered European or foreign lawyer, any obligation to make a report to us will be satisfied if you provide the information to your firm's compliance officer (as appropriate), on the understanding that they will do so.[2] This avoids multiple or duplicate reports being made and allows compliance officers to use their expertise to make professional judgments in light of the facts (and following investigation, where appropriate). We would not require or expect the individual to check whether a report has subsequently been made, in those circumstances. However, if you believe a report should be made under our standards or requirements, you should be prepared to make a report yourself if you are not satisfied that they will take the same view. As the compliance officer, you may wish to explain to the relevant individual why you do not consider that the threshold for reporting has been met. This will help them to understand if there are reasons they might not have been aware of why a report is not required, and can help the firm to develop good practice this area.

We understand that making such judgments can be difficult, and we are aware that internal pressures and influences may be at play. We want firms to give compliance officers, and others, support in discharging their duties and in exercising their judgment about what and when to report.

Further, our Codes of Conduct make it clear that those we regulate must not prevent any person from providing information to us[3] and that anyone making or proposing to make a report to the SRA, must not be victimised, or subject to detrimental treatment, for doing so.[4] This is irrespective of whether any regulatory action is taken as a result of the report. It will ultimately be for us to decide whether regulatory action is necessary in the public interest, and we may decide it is not – for example, once we have investigated further – for good reason.

Getting help

If you need any help in reaching a decision whether to make a report, you can:

- contact our Professional Ethics helpline [tel. 0370 606 2577, email professional. ethics@sra.org.uk]

- if you want to make a confidential report you can contact our Red Alert line.

We will always discuss with those who contact us any needs or concerns they may have about involvement in our process, as well as provide regular updates about how we are handling their concerns. In particular, we are able to provide advice on what information may be provided to us and our powers to receive and consider confidential and privileged information.

1.3   What is the purpose of enforcement?

Lawyers have a fiduciary relationship which brings obligations to clients. They also have obligations to the court and to members of the wider public who may be affected by their work (for example, as party to a dispute or in connection with the legal matter in hand) which are critical for the effective administration of justice and operation of the rule of law.[5]

Our role is to regulate in the public interest; to protect clients and consumers of legal services, and to uphold the rule of law and the administration of justice.

This means we focus on issues which present an underlying risk to the public interest, ensuring that any decision to investigate a complaint or report is a proportionate response to that risk.

Our actions are not designed to punish people for past misdemeanours. While the sanctions we impose may be punitive, they do not have that primary purpose. As Sir Thomas Bingham said in *Bolton v Law Society*:

> There is, in some of these orders, a punitive element: a penalty may be visited on a solicitor who has fallen below the standards required of his profession in order to punish him for what he has done and to deter any other solicitor tempted to behave in the same way. Those are traditional objects of punishment. But often the order is not punitive in intention ... In most cases the order of the Tribunal will be primarily directed to one or other or both of two other purposes. One is to be sure that the offender does not have the opportunity to repeat the offence ... The second purpose is the most fundamental of all: to maintain the reputation of the solicitors' profession as one in which every member, of whatever standing, may be trusted to the ends of the earth.[6]

The role of enforcement action can therefore be seen as:

- protecting clients and the public: controlling or limiting the risk of harm, and ensuring the individual or firm is not able to repeat the offending or similar behaviour or is, at least, deterred from doing so

- sending a signal to those we regulate more widely with the aim of preventing similar behaviour by others

- maintaining and upholding standards of competence and ethical behaviour

- upholding public confidence in the provision of legal services.

2.1 Our approach to enforcement

We recognise that both human and system error are unavoidable. And that to adopt a blanket response to non-compliance that does not take into account ethical behaviour, and the underlying purpose for the standard or requirement in question, can be counterproductive. Not only does it increase the regulatory burden, but risks inhibiting the development of shared values, the exercise of judgment and a culture of openness which allows for learning from mistakes.

Not every referral will lead us to open an investigation. Some cases fall outside of our regulatory remit. And we will not need to take action solely to address a breach that is minor in nature and where the evidence suggests that it is unlikely to be repeated and there is no ongoing risk.

Focus on serious issues

We focus our action on the most serious issues: our codes of conduct confirm that we will take action in relation to breaches which are serious, either in isolation or because they demonstrate a persistent failure to comply or a concerning pattern of behaviour. The concept of "serious breach" is described further below. However, this includes within it matters that can be described as serious "misconduct" – or conduct that is improper and falls short of ethical standards. It also includes other serious breaches of our standards or requirements – for example, those relating to failures of firms' systems and controls.

Taking account of aggravating and mitigating factors

Even where we have opened an investigation, we will not necessarily sanction all breaches, but will take into account the circumstances including any aggravating and mitigating factors, while ensuring that the wider public interest (including the protection of the public) is upheld. This means that if the circumstances indicate that there is no underlying concern in terms of the public interest, we will close the matter without (further) investigation. If appropriate, we can close the case with advice, which may include a warning that further breaches may result in a greater sanction being imposed in future.

The importance of constructive engagement

Our approach is to ensure that we only take those steps that are required in order to protect and promote the public interest. Therefore, when a case is subject to investigation, we will, if appropriate, seek to pursue methods of constructive engagement to support firms and individuals to achieve compliance.

Guidance, supervision and monitoring, coupled with an open, cooperative and constructive approach by firms and individuals, may lead us to decide against taking formal action. In those cases, we will expect the firm or individual to take prompt remedial action, agreed with us where necessary. In these circumstances, we will ask firms and individuals voluntarily to provide us with information and evidence of the steps taken to resolve matters.

For example, if a compliance officer for finance and administration (COFA) identifies a failure to pay to clients their residual balances and puts in place an action plan to remedy the breach, we may agree specific measures and targets in a compliance plan to which all the managers sign up. The plan would include regular updates to us so that we can monitor progress and escalate the matter if we have concerns about continuing risk.

Cooperation with an investigation by a firm or individual will be relevant throughout the life of a case at key decision making stages and may in some cases inform the progress of the investigation – for example whether formal steps need to be taken to compel evidence, or whether we are able to agree disposal by way of a regulatory settlement agreement (see our guidance on the use of our investigation powers and on regulatory settlement agreements) – or indeed the ultimate outcome that is appropriate in the public interest (see further below and in the table at Annex A).

2.2   Factors which affect our view of seriousness

Where a formal response is required, we will take action that is proportionate to the risk, weighing the interests of the public against those of the individual or firm involved. We will consider the available sanctions and controls in turn, starting with the least restrictive. The full range of regulatory and disciplinary outcomes available to us (both sanctions and controls), their purpose and indicative criteria for their use, is in Annex A.

As we have said, our response will reflect the seriousness of any breach. Our assessment of seriousness will necessarily involve looking at past conduct and behaviour.

However, our assessment of any future risk will look forward as well as back. Mitigating features of a case which might be indicative of reduced or low future risk include:

- expressions of apology

- regret

- remorse

- no evidence of repetition of the misconduct, or a pattern of misconduct.

Further, we can take into account the systems in place and environment in which the events took place; and the responsibility or control the individual had over the matters in question. This allows us to respond robustly, but appropriately, to concerns raised in relation to solicitors working in diverse range of practice settings, including outside of an authorised body.

In taking into account mitigation, we will distinguish between "contextual" mitigation –which relates to the events giving rise to the alleged breach and has a bearing on the nature and seriousness of the breach – and personal mitigation – which relates to the background, character and circumstances of the individual or firm and which is usually more relevant to sanction.

Contextual mitigation might include features of the environment in which the solicitor was working and which affected their judgment or any action they were able to take. Personal mitigation might include:

- testimonials or evidence of insight

- cooperation with any investigation or audit processes or
- remedial action taken since the events.

Sometimes information will be relevant to both: for example past misconduct or findings demonstrating a pattern of behaviour or a propensity to behave (for example) dishonestly.

We recognise the stressful circumstances in which many solicitors and firms are working and are aware that the health of the individual at the time of the events may have a significant bearing on the nature and seriousness of the alleged breach.

Further, we are aware of the impact that being complained about and going through an investigation can have on people – and that this can exacerbate or trigger health issues. We have procedures in place to support those going through our processes, to make sure that we are fair and take into account their health needs and make reasonable adjustments to enable them to participate fully.

The nature of the allegation

We see certain types of allegations as inherently more serious than others: for example, we will always take seriously allegations of abuse of trust, taking unfair advantage of clients or others, and the misuse of client money; as we will sexual and violent misconduct, dishonesty and criminal behaviour (described further below).

Information security is also of high importance to the public and protection of confidential information is a core professional principle in the Legal Services Act 2007.[7]

However, there are some common factors that affect the view we take of how serious an allegation is as set out below.

Intent/Motivation

The seriousness of a breach may be dependent on the intention behind it. We will distinguish between people who are trying to do the right thing and those who are not.

Human and system error is inevitable and we will generally take no action where a poor outcome is solely the result of a genuine mistake. However, we may take action where a failure to meet our standards or requirements arises from a lack of knowledge which the individual should or could reasonably be expected to have acquired, or which demonstrates a lack of judgment which is of concern. We would take into account matters such as the experience and seniority of the individual involved (in other words, whether they knew, or should have known, better).

Where a firm or an individual has been a victim, for example, of cybercrime, our primary focus would not be to penalise them for any adverse outcomes arising. However, we are likely to review, for example, whether their systems and procedures were robust enough and reasonable protective measures were in place.

In relation to errors of law or professional judgment, generally we will not penalise a single negligent act or an omission without evidence of seriously or persistently poor levels of competence which demonstrate behaviour falling well below expected standards. We are likely to consider such matters as more serious where a firm or an individual has knowingly acted outside their competence or has failed to take reasonable steps to update their knowledge and skills, or those of their employees.

We will view more seriously events which demonstrate that the individual or firm has a deliberate or reckless disregard for their obligations. Recklessness is serious because it demonstrates inappropriate risk taking, and a lack of regard for the consequences of one's actions.

Conduct or behaviour which demonstrates a lack of honesty or integrity are at the highest end of the spectrum, in a "profession whose reputation depends on trust". The Courts have stated that any solicitor who is shown to have discharged his professional duties with anything less than complete integrity, probity and trustworthiness must expect severe sanctions to be imposed upon them by the Solicitors Disciplinary Tribunal. The most serious involves proven dishonesty.[8]

This is important because of the uneven relationship, which requires clients to place their trust in their lawyers, for example, because of the information asymmetry between them, or the access the lawyer has to the client's funds and often to sensitive personal information. Trust in the legal profession is also important to support the rule of law, because of the influence and impact the profession has upon the court process and the administration of justice.

When considering intent and motivation, we will consider factors such as whether the conduct was planned and premeditated, persistent or repeated. We will look at any benefit or advantage gained from the conduct and any response to the events including demonstrable insight and remedial action, or whether there has been an attempt to conceal a problem which can act as an aggravating factor, as well as being seen as an episode of dishonest misconduct in itself.

Harm and impact

We take into account the harm caused by the individual or firm's actions and the impact this has had on the victim. This will be fact sensitive and depend on individual circumstances. We will look at the numbers of victims, the level of any financial loss or any physical or mental harm. We will also consider behaviour which harms an individual's personal autonomy and dignity, and treat fundamental rights to privacy and non-discriminatory treatment as at the higher end of seriousness, irrespective of any financial or other harm.

We also take into account harm that could reasonably have been anticipated to arise from the conduct or behaviour in question. This directs our focus onto behaviour that represents a risk, even if harm may not have materialised. For example, a solicitor may seek to mislead the court by creating a false document, which, in the event, is not relied upon in court and does not result in a different outcome for the parties.

For this reason, the question of whether harm materialised is not determinative of whether we will take action: we may take action where no harm has arisen where the behaviour gave rise to a real risk of harm, or other aggravating features are present; and we may decide not to take action where harm arose from a genuine mistake or where other mitigating features are present.

However, in some cases, the actual harm suffered will increase the seriousness of the conduct, and either lead to a more serious outcome (for example, if a solicitor misuses client funds and this leads to a large number of clients suffering hardship and distress as a result) or will lead us to the decision that the case requires us to take action to maintain public confidence.

Vulnerability

As described above, solicitors and clients have an uneven relationship, but not all clients are the same.

Some clients will be more susceptible to harm, for example, as a result of:

- barriers preventing access to legal services, or the lack of choice of legal provider, for example due to cost or geographical location
- the situation giving rise to the need for advice, for example, involvement in a sensitive family matter
- the effect of a poor outcome leading to a greater impact, such as loss of personal liberty, or deportation in an asylum case
- their personal attributes or circumstances, such as a health issue or learning disability.

Vulnerability is not static: it may be short term, or permanent; and may result from the structure of the market, the nature of the legal services, the client's personal circumstances, or a combination of factors.[9] Corporate clients may have large in-house teams and be sophisticated purchasers of legal services – but may also be vulnerable in some transactions or circumstances.

We consider it an important part of our role to protect those who are less able to protect themselves and will consider an allegation to be particularly serious where the client's – or a third party's – vulnerability is relevant to the culpable behaviour. This may be because:

- the solicitor took advantage of the person's vulnerability to, for example, provide misleading information
- of the raised awareness the solicitor should have had about the need, for example, to communicate effectively or ensure that the client is in a position to protect their own rights or
- of any enhanced impact on the client as a result of their vulnerability which the solicitor could and should have anticipated.

Role, experience and seniority

We recognise that certain stages in an individual's career can present a steep learning curve – such as becoming a trainee, a newly qualified solicitor, or a partner for the first time. We would expect solicitors to gain a deeper understanding of appropriate behaviour and of the law and regulation governing their work, as their career progresses. And for those with more seniority and experience to have higher levels of insight, foresight, more knowledge and better judgment.

Part of being fair and proportionate is ensuring that those within an organisation, with real control and influence over the situation, are held accountable. The context in which professionals work, the culture of an organisation and pressure from peers and managers, is likely to have significant impact on their actions and decisions.[10] Therefore, we recognise that a person's inexperience or relatively junior role within an organisation may impact on their ability to take appropriate action, although will not be an answer to serious misconduct such as dishonesty.

Regulatory history and patterns of behaviour

Once we have identified a breach of our standards or requirements, a key factor when deciding what to do next will be whether the behaviour forms part of a pattern of repeated misconduct or regulatory breaches. This can indicate a propensity to commit certain breaches of our standards or requirements, or a failure in systems and controls, or an unwillingness or inability to learn lessons. This may result in our taking action even if such breaches on their own might be regarded as less serious.

For this reason, we will review our records for previous complaints and findings against the individual or firm. This will include information about any findings made by other courts, tribunals and regulatory bodies as well as previous SRA matters resulting in, for example, a financial penalty or closure of a case with an advice or a warning, and previous disciplinary matters before the Tribunal where allegations were found proved, together with any sanction imposed.

Remediation

When assessing the risk of future harm, factors such as the length of time since the events, insight into the conduct or behaviour, and any remedial action taken, are relevant to our decision whether to investigate an allegation and, if so, what action to take. For example, a firm with weak systems may have been a victim of a cyber-attack, and promptly taken action to ensure that this could not happen again. A timely self-report and early engagement provides us with evidence of that insight and gives us confidence that the firm has an ethical culture and the ability to manage risk.

However, there are some kinds of conduct for which such considerations have less relevance. For example, where the misconduct indicates a lack of honesty or integrity, we may consider that the matter cannot be remediated or that in any event, action is necessary in order to uphold public confidence in the legal profession. As stated in *Bolton v The Law Society*:

> Because orders made by the Tribunal are not primarily punitive, it follows that considerations which would ordinarily weigh in mitigation of punishment have less effect on the exercise of this jurisdiction than on the ordinary run of sentences imposed in criminal cases. ... All these matters are relevant and should be considered. But none of them touches the essential issue, which is the need to maintain among members of the public a well-founded confidence that any solicitor whom they instruct will be a person of unquestionable integrity, probity and trustworthiness ... The reputation of the profession is more important than the fortunes of any individual member. Membership of a profession brings many benefits, but that is a part of the price.

Relationship with legal practice and our core regulatory jurisdiction – other regulators

We operate within a wider framework of bodies that are currently providing oversight and redress in this sector. We are aware that our regulation will overlap with others where individuals regulated by other regulators such as, for example, barristers or members of the Chartered Institute of Legal Executives (CILEx) are working alongside solicitors in a firm we regulate. Further, the Legal Ombudsman (LeO) deals with service complaints about regulated lawyers and legal service providers. We have arrangements with LeO to make sure that there is a clear understanding about the type of complaints that should be handled by LeO in the first instance, and which by us.

Individuals and firms we regulate will also commonly be subject to other, non-legal, regulatory jurisdictions. They will be subject to the Information Commissioner's Office (ICO) in relation to their handling of personal data, or, for example, the Institute of Chartered Accountants in England and Wales (ICAEW) where working in or as an accountancy multi-disciplinary practice.

We will not investigate an issue which is the jurisdiction of another regulator or prosecuting authority, unless it also raises an issue which is core to our regulatory role and public interest purpose. The closer the matter is to our role and purpose, the more likely it is that we will take action. For example, enforcement of data protection legislation is a matter for the ICO, but if a data protection breach also involves the disclosure of confidential client information, then we will investigate that as a regulatory offence. *More guidance on our approach to taking forward an investigation where there are parallel proceedings* [**www.sra.org.uk/sra/decision-making/guidance/ investigations-parallel**].

Private life

Our key role is to act on wrongdoing which relates to an individual or a firm's legal practice. We will not get involved in complaints against a solicitor which relate solely to, for example, their competence as a school governor or their involvement in a neighbour dispute. However, our Principles set out the core ethical values we require of all those we regulate and apply at all times and in all contexts – and apply both in and outside of practice (as the context permits).

We are concerned with the impact of conduct outside of legal practice including in the private lives of those we regulate if this touches on risk to the delivery of safe legal services in future.[11] The closer any behaviour is to professional activities, or a reflection of how a solicitor might behave in a professional context, the more seriously we are likely to view it. For example, an allegation of financial impropriety against a solicitor when acting as a Member of Parliament, will raise a question as to their fitness to manage client funds. However, we will also be interested in matters that are so serious that they are capable of damaging public confidence, such as dishonest or discriminatory conduct in any context.

As stated above, the Principles apply outside of practice but only insofar as the context permits: So for example, the obligation to act in a client's best interests relates to their best legal interests in any matter in which you act for them; and would not extend to how you behave towards them in a personal or social matter.

In addition, whilst the Principles apply outside of practice to individuals who are not themselves authorised (such as employees or non-lawyers holding roles that are approved by us – such as managers of firms), we will take their role into consideration. Our interest in employees relates to their role as an employee and any behaviour that touches on their suitability as such, which will generally derive from their conduct in practise. When it comes to other role holders, we will also consider their wider fitness or suitability to be approved in that role; and, for example, to have management or control over a legal business. So conduct such as mishandling funds relating to a non-legal business or appointment, will potentially bring our regulation into play.

In both cases, in addition to a breach of the Principles, we have separate powers to restrict their ability to engage in legal practice where the behaviour of a non-authorised person outside of practice has resulted in a criminal offence.

Criminal convictions

We will always investigate criminal convictions or cautions whether or not these relate to the individual's practice, given the importance of rule-abiding behaviour and public confidence in those involved in the overall effectiveness of our criminal justice system.

However, we continue to take a proportionate approach to our regulation and are less likely to be concerned about behaviour which is at a low-level in terms of seriousness (for example, actions that result in fixed penalty notices, or minor motoring offences). We will take more seriously convictions for drink driving, assault and other offences against the person, and property offences. At the most serious end of the spectrum are convictions resulting in custodial sentences, particularly those relating to dishonesty, fraud, bribery and extortion; those associated with terrorism, money laundering or obstructing the course of justice (such as perjury or witness tampering) or facilitating or concealing serious or organised criminality by others; or those involving violence, sexual misconduct or child sexual abuse images.

2.3   Inter-relationship between factors

The factors set out in section 2.2 are not the only factors which may affect our view of seriousness, and do not all have to be present.

For example, when a matter raises serious integrity issues, judgments about harm have less impact: a case involving dishonest behaviour which does not directly harm another party, such as providing false details in a CV or reference, will still be viewed by us as behaviour which is fundamentally incompatible with the practice of law.

There are also some types of misconduct which are actionable without evidence of intent or harm, such as the use of a client account as a banking facility or involvement in a transaction which bears the hallmark of fraud, because of the significant link between those behaviours and the risk of the solicitors and law firms being used willingly or unwillingly to facilitate crime.

In many cases the factors will be interlinked. For example, a client or third party's vulnerability might provide an opportunity to take unfair advantage, indicating intentional misconduct, or exacerbating the impact of their behaviour.

3   Who is enforcement action taken against?

During an investigation, we will consider the position of both the firm and the individuals working within that firm in order to reach an informed decision as to whom we should be seeking to enforce against.

Our principles set out the values we expect all those we regulate to uphold; however, we have separate codes of conduct and authorisation requirements for solicitors and for firms we regulate. And we have certain standards and requirements (such as those relating to the operation of client accounts) that apply solely to firms.

Where obligations apply equally to firms and individuals, we are able to take enforcement action, in the public interest, against both or either, where there has been a serious breach.

We would take action against an individual where they were personally responsible. This addresses the risk they, as an individual, present to clients or to the wider public interest. It also ensures that specific action can be taken (such as striking off the Roll or imposing conditions on their practising certificate), to ensure that they cannot avoid accountability and/or repeat similar behaviour simply by moving firms. Further, firms may cease to exist, deliberately or otherwise, and therefore where an individual is directly culpable, we will generally proceed against them in order to mitigate that risk. This is more likely where the practice is small and may, in effect, have no separation from its principal or partners.

However, we will usually take action against a firm alone, or in addition to taking action against an individual, where there is a breach of the code of conduct for firms or of our other requirements. For example:

- to mark the firm's responsibility and to hold it to account for the breach, especially where it is not possible or proportionate to establish individual responsibility.

- when the events demonstrate a failure which relates to the culture, systems, supervision arrangements or processes for which the firm, as a whole, should be held accountable.

- to encourage a culture of compliance and management of future risk.

- when firm-specific action is appropriate. This might include a fine to remove the benefit obtained from the wrongdoing, suspension or revocation of the firm's authorisation, or firm-based conditions or compliance plans. Examples of the latter might include: requirements relating to the firm's governance or oversight arrangements, mandatory remedial action such as establishing compliance systems or reporting to us of accounting records, or restrictions to prevent certain work being carried out or funds being held.

This ensures that the firm as a whole is responsible for future compliance and the management of risk.

As indicated above, we are able to take action in relation to systemic failure and this function is likely to become increasingly relevant as reliance upon information technology and artificial intelligence increases.

Employees and role-holders – managers, owners and compliance officers

A finding against a firm is not a finding of personal misconduct against the partners or other managers. We can, however, take disciplinary action against employees and managers responsible for a breach by their firm and can impose control orders preventing them from working in a law firm without our approval. And we have specific powers in relation to approved role-holders (which include managers and compliance officers within a firm), which include withdrawing or imposing conditions on their approval, as well as disqualifying people from taking up those roles. *Read more guidance on our powers against non-authorised persons* [**www.sra.org.uk/sra/decision-making/guidance/general-regulation-non-authorised-persons**].

Generally, we will only hold managers to account for the actions of the firm (as opposed to their own conduct or behaviour) where they had a responsibility for – or should have known about and should have intervened into – the relevant events.

Appendix A: Sanctions and Controls

Introduction

This table sets out the powers available to us when we take enforcement action against a regulated individual or firm for a breach of our regulatory requirements or for conduct which falls below the standards set out in our Principles and Codes of Conduct.

These include both sanctions and controls. The former are broadly intended to discipline the person to prevent similar behaviour by them or others, maintain standards and uphold public confidence in the profession. The latter are broadly intended to protect clients or the public by controlling or limiting the risk of harm.

Whilst not covered by the table below, our powers include interim or immediate protective measures as well as those which follow a finding. For example, we will take immediate action to suspend a person's practising certificate following certain events, such as a conviction for certain serious offences. We can also impose conditions on an interim basis where these are necessary and proportionate to address an identified risk pending a final outcome in the case. We are also able to intervene into a firm to protect clients' money or files in certain circumstances (see our guidance on intervening to protect clients [**www.sra.org.uk/sra/decision-making/guidance/consumer-intervening-protect-clients**]).

We also have the power to take certain action against people who, although not authorised by us directly as individuals, are involved in a firm that we regulate. These include the power to restrict their future employment or to prevent them holding certain roles in a firm. These powers are set out in our guidance on the regulation of non-authorised persons and approved role holders [**www.sra.org.uk/sra/decision-making/guidance/general-regulation-non-authorised-persons**].

The powers set out in the table below and guidance highlighted in the paragraphs above can in some cases effectively act as both a sanction and a control (for example, a decision to impose a warning, restrict a non-authorised person from employment in a law firm, or suspend a person's practising certificate). And they can be used in combination, where appropriate. For example, it may be appropriate to rebuke or fine a firm's employee for misleading a client, and also to restrict their future employment (as above).

The factors set out in the table below indicate some of the features which may lead us towards or away from imposing a particular sanction or control in any given circumstance. They do not comprise an exhaustive list and not all of the factors set out need to be present for us to consider that the relevant sanction or control is appropriate.

Some of the powers set out in the table below can only be exercised by the Solicitors Disciplinary Tribunal (SDT), such as the power to strike a solicitor off the roll or to impose greater than a specified level of fine on a solicitor or traditional law firm. The SDT has set out its approach to sanctions. However, the factors in the table below will help us to decide whether such a sanction is appropriate and to refer the matter to the SDT accordingly. Further information about the circumstances in which we will refer a matter for adjudication by the SDT is set out in our guidance [**www.sra.org.uk/ sra/decision-making/guidance/disciplinary-issuing-solicitors-disciplinary-tribunal-proceedings**].

[Table]

Letters which contain advice and warning

Purpose	Factors in favour	Factors against
To respond to a minor regulatory breach which is not sufficiently serious to require action to protect the public/public interest, to restrict the regulated person's ability to practise or to rebuke or impose a fine.	• Isolated incident • No actual or lasting harm to consumers or third parties, or harm that could easily have been anticipated to result from the conduct • Breach minor or no more than moderate in nature	Where closure with no action is appropriate, eg: • Issues relate solely to an inadvertent breach, or for some other reason there is no underlying concern about the individual or firm's conduct or behaviour that needs to be addressed or recorded – and therefore no regulatory action is required.
To advise the regulated person that they have breached our requirements/ standards and to explain how these apply to the situation in question.	• A degree of insight and understanding of the purpose of the regulatory standard/requirement • Apology/acknowledgment of breach/situation rectified as soon as possible	Where a more serious outcome is warranted to protect the public/public interest, eg: • Dishonesty/lack of integrity/abuse of trust
To warn the regulated person that should the conduct/behaviour be repeated or the situation continue, more serious action is likely to be taken. The warning may be taken into account in any future proceedings.	• Negligible or low risk of repetition • Evidence of insight and remediation, such as apology; self report; acknowledgement of breach, situation rectified; cooperation with the SRA	• Evidence of repetition of conduct/behaviour in question, particularly if previously warned/advised to stop • Evidence of a history of previous warnings suggesting a pattern of wilful disregard or recklessness of regulatory obligations
To promote understanding of our regulatory arrangements, and to raise standards by encouraging positive behaviour.		• Conduct/behaviour would tend to damage public confidence in the delivery of legal services • Intentional failure to comply/cooperate with regulatory obligations

Rebuke[12]		
Purpose	**Factors in favour**	**Factors against**
To sanction the regulated person for a breach of standards/requirements, but where the issues are only of moderate seriousness and do not require a higher level of response to maintain standards/uphold public confidence. To deter the individual and others from similar behaviour in future.	• No lasting significant harm to consumers or third parties • Conduct or behaviour reckless as to risk of harm/regulatory obligations • Breach rectified/remedial action taken, but persisted longer than reasonable/ only when prompted • Low risk of repetition • Some public sanction required to uphold public confidence in the delivery of legal services	• Any less serious sanction/outcome would be appropriate to protect the public/public interest Where a more serious outcome is warranted to protect the public/public interest; eg: • Dishonesty/lack of integrity/abuse of trust • Evidence of repetition of conduct/behaviour in question, particularly if previously warned/advised to stop • Intentional failure to comply/cooperate with regulatory obligations

Conditions[13] – Individual
(The factors to be taken into consideration, below, relate to conditions imposed as a final sanction and not interim conditions)

Purpose	Factors in favour	Factors against
To control the risk of harm arising from a repetition of a breach of our regulatory standards/ requirements. To restrict or prevent the involvement of an individual in certain activities or engaging in certain business agreements/associations or practising arrangements. To require an individual to take certain steps. To facilitate closer monitoring of an individual through regular reporting.	• Risk of serious harm or breach in the absence of conditions being imposed • Sufficient insight to enable compliance with conditions • Conduct/behaviour is likely to be repeated in the absence of control/support • Conditions available which address the risk of repetition/harm, and which are reasonable and proportionate, realistic and measurable • Evidence demonstrates person unsuitable for a particular role or activity which should be restricted	• Risk can be managed/matters remediated or rectified without formal regulatory intervention Where a more serious outcome is warranted to protect the public/public interest; eg: • Dishonesty/lack of integrity/abuse of trust • No conditions available which can manage the underlying conduct or behaviour • Previous history of failure to comply with regulatory obligations/evidence unable or willing to comply with conditions • Evidence unable/not competent to continue in legal practice at all • Continued practice, albeit restricted, would tend to damage public confidence in the delivery of legal services • Intentional failure to comply/cooperate with regulatory obligations

Conditions – Firm (The factors to be taken into consideration, below, relate to conditions imposed as a final sanction and not interim conditions)

Purpose	Factors in favour	Factors against
To control the risk of harm arising from a repetition of a breach of our regulatory standards/requirements. To restrict or prevent a firm, or one of its managers, employees, or interest holders from undertaking certain activities. To limit or prevent risks arising from a business agreement or an association which the firm has or is likely to enter into, or a business practice which the firm has or is likely to adopt. To require the firm to take certain steps. To facilitate effective monitoring of the firm through regular reporting	• Nature of breach relates to systemic/procedural issues • No lasting significant harm to consumers or third parties • Risk of serious harm or breach in the absence of conditions being imposed • Sufficient insight to enable compliance with conditions • Conduct/behaviour is likely to be repeated in the absence of control/support • Conditions available which address the risk of repetition/harm, and which are reasonable and proportionate, realistic and measurable • Evidence demonstrates firm, or person in firm, unsuitable for a particular activity which should be restricted	• Risk can be managed/matters remediated or rectified without formal regulatory intervention Where a more serious outcome is warranted to protect the public/public interest; eg: • Dishonesty/lack of integrity/abuse of trust • No conditions available which can manage the underlying conduct or behaviour • Previous history of failure to comply with regulatory obligations/evidence unable or willing to comply with conditions • No individual in firm who is willing and capable of implementing and monitoring compliance with conditions • Evidence that firm is unable to continue to operate or it would damage public confidence if it was to do so • Intentional failure to comply/cooperate with regulatory obligations

Financial penalty		
Purpose	Factors in favour	Factors against
To sanction the regulated firm or individual for a serious breach of standards/ requirements, but where protection of the public/public interest does not require suspension or a striking off. To deter the firm or individual and others from similar behaviour in future. For the level of fine, see the indicative fining guidance published by the SRA from time to time.	• Conduct/behaviour caused/had potential to cause significant harm • Direct control/responsibility for conduct/behaviour • Conduct planned/pre-meditated • Wilful or reckless disregard of risk of harm/regulatory obligations • Breach rectified/remedial action taken, but persisted longer than reasonable/ only when prompted • Fine appropriate to remove financial gain or other benefit as a consequence of the breach	• Any less serious sanction/outcome would be appropriate to protect the public/public interest • Evidence of insufficient means of the person directed to pay to pay Where a more serious outcome is warranted to protect the public/public interest; eg: • Continued practice would tend to damage public confidence in the delivery of legal services

Suspension of a solicitor from practice by the SDT		
Purpose	Factors in favour	Factors against
To protect the public/public interest by preventing an individual from practising as a solicitor, in circumstances which do not justify striking them off the roll.

Suspension can be for a fixed term or for an indefinite period. The length of the suspension reflects the seriousness of the findings and the length of time needed for the solicitor to remediate. An indefinite suspension marks conduct falling just short of striking off the roll.

To sanction the regulated person for a serious breach of standards/requirements.

To deter the individual and others from similar behaviour in future.

To show the public the consequences for a solicitor who commits serious misconduct. | • Conduct/behaviour caused/had potential to cause significant harm to consumers or third parties
• Dishonesty/lack of integrity
• Abuse of trust or exploitation of vulnerability
• Misconduct involving the commission of a criminal offence
• Direct control/responsibility for conduct/behaviour
• Conduct planned/pre-meditated
• Wilful or reckless disregard of risk of harm/regulatory obligations
• Breach not rectified/no remedial action taken
• Misconduct which continued over a period of time or was repeated | • Any less serious sanction/outcome would be appropriate to protect the public/public interest

Where a more serious outcome is warranted to protect the public/public interest; eg:
• Protection of the public/public interest requires a striking off
• Remaining on the roll would tend to damage public confidence in the delivery of legal services |

Striking off the roll by the SDT		
Purpose	Factors in favour	Factors against
To protect the public/public interest by preventing an individual from practising as a solicitor. To sanction the regulated person for a serious breach of standards/requirements. To deter the individual and others from similar behaviour in future. To signpost conduct or behaviour which is fundamentally incompatible with continued practice in the profession and to show the public the consequences for a solicitor who commits the most serious misconduct.	• The seriousness of the misconduct is at the highest level, such that a lesser sanction is inappropriate • Conduct/behaviour caused/had potential to cause significant harm to consumers or third parties • Dishonesty/lack of integrity • Abuse of trust or exploitation of vulnerability • Misconduct involving the commission of a criminal offence • Direct control/responsibility for conduct/behaviour • Conduct planned/pre-meditated • Wilful or reckless disregard of risk of harm/regulatory obligations • Breach not rectified/no remedial action taken • Misconduct which continued over a period of time or was repeated	• Any less serious sanction/outcome would be appropriate to protect the public/public interest

Suspension or revocation of firm's authorisation

Purpose	Factors in favour	Factors against
To protect the public/public interest by removing a firm's authorisation either permanently or temporarily. To sanction the firm for a serious breach of standards/ requirements. To act as a deterrent to the firm and others. To show the public the consequences for a firm that commits the most serious misconduct.	• The body has failed to demonstrate or maintain the requirements for (ongoing) authorisation, including the provision of information or payment of fees required under the standards and regulations • Conduct/behaviour caused/had potential to cause significant harm to consumers or third parties • Direct control/responsibility for conduct/behaviour • Conduct planned/pre-meditated • Wilful or reckless disregard of risk of harm/regulatory obligations • Breach not rectified/no remedial action taken and there is in effect no viable alternative to safeguard public protection	• Any less serious sanction/outcome would be appropriate to protect the public/public interest

Notes

1. Solicitor includes RELs and RFLs where the context permits.

2. 7.12 of the SRA Code of Conduct for Solicitors, RELs and RFLs.

3. 7.5 of the SRA Code of Conduct for Solicitors, RELs and RFLs; and 3.11 of the SRA Code of Conduct for Firms.

4. 7.9 of the SRA Code of Conduct for Solicitors, RELs and RFLs; and 3.12 of the SRA Code of Conduct for Firms.

5. "Lawyers … have a duty to their clients, but they may not win by whatever means". Lord Hoffman, *Arthur J S Hall v Simons* [2002] 1 AC.

6. *Bolton v The Law Society* [1993] EWCA Civ 32, para 15.

7. Section 1(3)(e) Legal Services Act 2007.

8. *Bolton v The Law Society* [1993] EWCA Civ 32, para 13.

9. See Recognising and Responding to consumer vulnerability, Legal Services Consumer Panel, October 2014.

10. See Designing Ethics Indicators for Legal Services Provision, Richard Moorhead et al, UCL Centre for Ethics and Law.

11. In the case of *Pitt and Tyas v GPhC* [April 2017] the court held that a Regulator could regulate the behaviour of a professional in to both their professional and private life.

12. SDT refers to this as a reprimand.

13. SDT refers to this as a Restriction Order.

See **www.sra.org.uk/solicitors/guidance/guidance** for recently published or updated guidance relevant to the SRA Standards and Regulations. At the time of printing, this includes the list below.

- Access to and disclosure of an incapacitated person's will (13 March 2017; updated 25 November 2019)

- Accountant's report and the exemption to obtain one (1 August 2017; updated 25 November 2019)

- Acting with honesty (8 August 2016; updated 25 November 2019)

- Acting with integrity (23 July 2019; updated 25 November 2019)

- Adequate and appropriate indemnity insurance (12 September 2019; updated 25 November 2019)

- Admission as a solicitor (8 August 2016; updated 25 November 2019)

- Agreeing regulatory and disciplinary outcomes (8 August 2016; updated 25 November 2019)

- Approval of employment under s.41 and s.43 of the Solicitors Act 1974 (25 November 2019)

- Approval of role holders (8 August 2016; updated 12 March 2021)

- Bogus law firms and identity theft (26 March 2012; updated 25 November 2019)

- Bringing criminal proceedings (8 August 2016; updated 25 November 2019)

- Can my business be authorised? (4 July 2019; updated 12 March 2021)

- Client care letters (23 July 2019; updated 25 November 2019)

- Closing down your practice (10 May 2013; updated 25 November 2019)

- Compliance with the money laundering regulations – firm risk assessment: warning notice (7 May 2019; updated 25 November 2019)

- Confidentiality of client information (25 November 2019)

- Conflicts of interest (29 October 2019; updated 2 March 2020)

- Dealing with claims for mis-sold payment protection insurance (PPI) (4 January 2012; updated 25 November 2019)

- Decision-making, reviews and attendance procedures (25 November 2019)

- Do I need to operate a client account? (4 July 2019; updated 25 November 2019)

- Does my business need to be authorised? (4 July 2019; updated 25 November 2019)

- Does my employer need to be authorised by an approved regulator? (12 September 2017; updated 25 November 2019)

- Does your interest in a licensed body require SRA approval? (7 March 2014; updated 8 March 2021)

- Drafting and preparation of wills (6 May 2014; updated 25 November 2019)

- Employers' duties (3 December 2012; updated 25 November 2019)

- European Lawyers practising in the UK (22 April 2016; updated 25 March 2021)

- Firm authorisation (4 July 2019; updated 25 November 2019)

- Firm closure due to financial difficulties (5 August 2020)

- Firm risk assessments (29 October 2019; updated 25 November 2019)

- Government's Technical Notice on the impact of a 'no deal' EU exit scenario on EU lawyers practising in the UK (12 October 2018; updated 6 May 2020)

- Granting authority to withdraw residual client balances (8 August 2016; updated 8 October 2020)

- Guidance note on the impact on exempt European lawyers of the Government's Statutory Instrument on the basis of a 'no deal' EU exit scenario (10 December 2018; updated 25 November 2019)

- Helping you keep accurate client accounting records (4 July 2019; updated 25 November 2019)

- Holiday sickness claims (6 September 2017; updated 25 November 2019)

- How we approach decisions to intervene (8 August 2016; 25 November 2019)

- How we deal with money when we intervene (Statutory Trusts) (8 August 2016; updated 5 July 2021)

- How we gather evidence in our regulatory and disciplinary investigations (25 November 2019)

- How we make decisions and the criteria we apply (5 November 2019)

- How we make our decision to authorise a firm (8 August 2016; updated 25 November 2019)

- How we recover our costs (8 August 2016; 25 November 2019)

- How we regulate non-authorised persons (8 August 2016; updated 25 November 2019)

- Identifying your client (issued 25 November 2019)

- If we are investigating you (issued 25 November 2019)

- Improper use of client account as a banking facility: warning notice (16 December 2014; updated 25 November 2019)

- Investment schemes including conveyancing (23 June 2017; updated 17 August 2020)

- Joint accounts and record keeping (4 July 2019; updated 25 November 2019)
- Law firms carrying on insurance distribution activities (27 September 2018; updated 25 November 2019)
- Legal Disciplinary Practices (25 November 2019)
- Making decisions to investigate concerns (8 August 2016; updated 25 November 2019)
- Making payments from the SRA Compensation Fund (Archived) (8 August 2016; updated 25 November 2019)
- Meeting our standards for good qualifying work experience (10 December 2020)
- Money laundering and terrorist financing (8 December 2014; updated 25 November 2019)
- Multi-disciplinary practices: Regulation of non-reserved legal activity (issued 14 September 2019; updated 5 March 2021)
- Not for profit sector – summary (23 July 2019; updated 25 November 2019)
- Offensive communications (24 August 2017; updated 25 November 2019)
- Offering inducements to potential clients or clients (25 June 2013; updated 25 November 2019)
- On-site investigations (inspections) (8 August 2016; updated 25 November 2019)
- Parallel investigations (8 August 2016; updated 25 November 2019)
- Payment Protection Insurance claims (29 August 2017; updated 25 November 2019)
- Planning for and completing an accountant's report (1 August 2017; updated 14 September 2020)
- Preparing to become a sole practitioner or an SRA-regulated freelance solicitor (4 July 2019; updated 25 November 2019)
- Public trust and confidence (25 November 2019)
- Publishing complaints procedure (5 November 2018; updated 25 November 2019)
- Publishing regulatory and disciplinary decisions (1 September 2016; updated 25 November 2019)
- Putting matters right when things go wrong, and own interest conflicts (25 November 2019)
- Q&A on the ban of personal injury referral fees (1 April 2013; updated 3 December 2019)
- Recovering costs and payments from third parties (8 August 2016; updated 25 November 2019)
- Referral fees LASPO and SRA Principles (11 October 2013; updated 25 November 2019)

- Registered Foreign Lawyers (23 July 2019; updated 25 November 2019)
- Reporting and notification obligations (25 November 2019)
- Reporting duties under the SRA Overseas Rules (25 November 2019)
- Responsibilities of COLPs and COFAs (25 November 2019)
- Risk factors in immigration work (7 December 2016; updated 25 November 2019)
- Risk factors in personal injury claims: warning notice (21 March 2016; updated 25 November 2019)
- Risk Outlook 2020/2021 (23 November 2021)
- Sole practitioners and small firms regulatory starter pack (8 January 2016; updated 25 November 2019)
- Solicitors and Compliance Officers for Legal Practice (COLPs) confirming qualifying work experience (10 December 2020)
- SRA consumer credit (22 December 2015; updated 11 November 2020)
- SRA investigations: Health issues and medical evidence (7 August 2020)
- Statement of our position regarding firms operating a client's own account (30 September 2019; updated 25 November 2019)
- Taking money for your firm's costs (14 September 2020)
- Tax avoidance your duties: warning notice (21 September 2017; updated 25 November 2019)
- The Insurance Act 2015 (6 July 2016; updated 25 November 2019)
- The Money Laundering, Terrorist Financing and Transfer of Funds (Information on the Payer) Regulations 2017 (2 March 2018; updated 25 November 2019)
- The prohibition of referral fees in LASPO 56-60 (25 March 2013; updated 25 November 2019)
- The SRA's approach to equality, diversity and inclusion (17 July 2019; updated 25 November 2019)
- The SRA's approach to financial penalties (13 August 2013; updated 25 November 2019)
- Third-party managed accounts (6 December 2017; updated 25 November 2019)
- Transparency in price and service (2 October 2018; updated 25 November 2019)
- UK's Exit from EU – Possible non-negotiated outcome at end of transition period (31 December 2020; updated 12 March 2020)
- UK's Exit from EU – the end of the implementation period and beyond (21 December 2020; updated 14 January 2021)
- Unregulated organisations – Conflict and confidentiality (23 July 2019; updated 25 November 2019)

- Unregulated organisations – for employers of SRA-regulated lawyers (23 July 2019; updated 25 November 2019)
- Unregulated organisations – giving information to clients (23 July 2019; updated 25 November 2019)
- Unsolicited approaches (advertising) to members of the public (16 December 2019)
- Use of non disclosure agreements (NDAs) (12 March 2018; updated 12 November 2020)
- Vocational training for trainee solicitors (25 November 2019)
- When do I need a practising certificate? (4 July 2019; updated 25 November 2019)

[Last updated: 5 July 2021]